THE TEUTONIC MYTHOLOGY
OF
RICHARD WAGNER'S
THE RING OF THE NIBELUNG

Volume II
The Family of Gods

William O. Cord

Studies in the History and Interpretation of Music
Volume 17

The Edwin Mellen Press
Lewiston●Queenston
Lampeter

Library of Congress Cataloging-in-Publication Data

(Revised for vol. 2 & 3)
Cord, William O.
    The Teutonic mythology of Richard Wagner's
"The Ring of the Nibelung."

    (Studies in the history and interpretation of
music ; v. 16-18)
    Contents: v. 1. Nine properties -- v. 2. The
family of gods -- v. 3. The natural and supernatural
worlds.
    1. Wagner, Richard, 1813-1883. Ring des Nibelungen.
2. Mythology, Germanic. 3. Legends--Germany.
I. Title. II. Series: Studies in the history and
interpretation of music ; vo. 16. etc.
ML410.W15C7 1989   782.1   89-12612
ISBN 0-88946-441-3 (v. 1)

This is volume 17 in the continuing series
Studies in History & Interpretation of Music
Volume 17 ISBN 0-88946-442-1
SHIM Series ISBN 0-88946-426—X

A CIP catalog record for this book
is available from the British Library.

The Edwin Mellen Press
Box 450   Box 67
Lewiston, New York   Queenston, Ontario
U.S.A. 14092   CANADA L0S 1L0

The Edwin Mellen Press, Ltd.
Lampeter, Dyfed, Wales
UNITED KINGDOM SA48 7DY

Printed in the United States of America

To Marge

Finally, . . . !

TABLE OF CONTENTS

THE TEUTONIC MYTHOLOGY OF RICHARD WAGNER'S
THE RING OF THE NIBELUNG

Volume I: Nine Dramatic Properties
Volume II: The Family of Gods
Volume III: The Natural and Supernatural Worlds

Other books by William O. Cord

José Rubén Romero: Cuentos y poemas inéditos
The Futile Life of Pito Perez (Translation)
La vida inútil de Pito Pérez (Editor)
*An Introduction to Richard Wagner's Der Ring des
    Nibelungen. A Handbook*
*Richard Wagner's The Ring of the Nibelung and
    Its Teutonic Mythology*
        Volume I - Nine Dramatic Properties
        Volume II - The Family of Gods
        Volume III - The Natural and Supernatural Worlds

Abbreviations

ME	-	Middle English
MHG	-	Middle High German
Mod. E	-	Modern English
Mod. G	-	Modern German
OE	-	Old English
OLG	-	Old Low German
OHG	-	Old High German
ON	-	Old Norse
OS	-	Old Saxon

NOTE:

The sources that Wagner used to develop the argument of his drama are also those that served as the basis for the studies of this volume. In the preparation of these essays, it became obvious early on that certain aspects of ancient Teutonic thought, as depicted in these sources, were common to more than one of the individual subject matters under investigation. Whenever that situation arises, that is, whenever one mythological matter is of import in more than one chapter, only the necessary data will be presented in the respective chapters, followed by an asterisk (*). For each item so indicated, a broader, more complete depiction will be found in Volume I, *Supplement C*. There are two additional supplements that are a part of that first volume, each of which may be of some informational value to readers. One such supplement discusses in summary form the ancient Teutonic world and its mythology. A second supplement focuses on the sources that Wagner consulted as he prepared the text of his *Ring* drama.

PREFACE

The essays in this volume represent studies of those Teutonic gods that Richard Wagner included in the *dramatis personae* of his monumental music drama, *Der Ring des Nibelungen*. These studies are complete in and of themselves, but they can be viewed as complements to those that are contained in that earlier companion volume that bore the title of *Nine Dramatic Properties*, and which studied certain major items of Wagner's Volsung story in much the same manner and format as found in the present work.

These studies present the Germanic deities as they are depicted in the numerous Eddas, sagas, legends, songs, stories, and tales that have come down through the ages, many of which were available to Wagner as source material. Interspersed with each presentation of mythical matters singular and pertinent to the respective subject is a presentation of the subject god or goddess as the composer developed that divine figure, and his or her respective role, in the *Ring* drama.

The purpose in such a format is really multifaceted. First, there will be placed side by side the two views of the gods of the Germanic world, that is, the gods and goddesses as they are in myth and legend, and as Wagner envisioned them in order that he might tell his story of the Nibelung gold, Wotan, and the destruction of the universe. Such an exposition will offer vivid pictures of the two depictions, and therefore the extent to which Wagner drew on his culture's mythology and to what extent, if any, he found cause to differ with the mythological picture that he found in his sources. Secondly, each of the individual presentations has its own validity, but such validity is especially welcome in the matter of the mythical picture of each god, a depiction which has not heretofore been available in the same scope and in the same breadth, or in the same consummate detail that is to be found in these essays. Thirdly, the serious follower of the *Ring* will leave these studies with a unique and distinct understanding of Wagner's drama, a fuller comprehension of the extensive and profound mythical content that serves as the drama's sound structural framework. Finally, as a kind of added gain, a new benefit if you will, the reader of these essays will be afforded a different and potentially new pathway to a fresher comprehension of the subtle but genius talent that guided Wagner in his composition, an appreciation of that special creative gift that allowed the composer from Saxony to prepare what is in the eyes of the world one of the most universal of all artworks.

There is no question that Wagner patterned the gods of his *Ring* after respective counterparts who had existed in the heathen Teutonic thought of an era long past. He understood most thoroughly how those early beliefs had affected and influenced not only the culture of its day, but also that which had come down to the modern Germanic peoples. Yet, if the aura of authentic mythicalness is ever-present throughout the *Ring*, there can be no doubt that Wagner occasionally turned the mythicalness of the past to his own favor. On occasion, he drew unrelated matters together and gave them a chronology and a seamless unity that satisfied his own personal dramatic or thematic convenience. Indeed, Wagner is also known to have made numerous modifications or alterations to his culture's mythical past. And it will come as a great surprise to many to learn that what often passes for mythicality in the *Ring* is really substance created by the master himself.

Make no mistake, however. There is ever-present in the *Ring* ample evidence of Wagner's belief that myth was the most appropriate vehicle with which to offer a dramatic expression of the human condition. His drama will also offer ample evidence of his intense belief that myth was the true clarion of the heart of all mankind.

And so, as the fascination for Wagner's *Ring* continues at its fever pitch, even after more than one hundred years of performances, the urge to study the work also continues. The studies of this volume, and those of its companion tome, meet that urge and fill the void that has existed for so long, that void that disallowed a complete and total presentation and discussion of the mythological thought that lay behind certain salient matters that Wagner chose to incorporate into his work.

There are two individual matters that should be explained here. It is immediately noted that Loge is included in this study of the gods. In a purely mythological sense, this shrewd and cunning character is not a god; he is not one of the divine figures that is to be found within the hierarchy of supreme beings that populated ancient Teutonic religious thought. Yet, Loge's role in the *Ring* is of such importance, and his involvement with divine matters is of such significance, that it seemed only proper to include him in these studies and to look at him much as we have viewed the others. Then, too, it can always be said that Wagner called his Loge a god, and in that light alone perhaps this spirit of another world merits inclusion in our discussions.

Finally, as was done in Volume I, so too here are all references to the gods of the *Ring* made with the German version of their names. This practice conforms to Wagner's method of naming his characters, and it also avoids what would only be utter linguistic confusion if any or all of the many other language versions of these names were to be used. Likewise, the only diacritical markings that are used in these studies are the umlauts that are necessary on certain German words.

W.O.C.
Rohnert Park, California

I
FREIA

All of the major figures that populate *Der Ring des Nibelungen* have their source as well as their inspiration in the colorful myths and legends that have become the treasure of the Germanic peoples. Wagner's Freia, his Goddess of Youth and Love, is no exception. Yet, of all the beings that the composer brought over into his drama, none is less a single character and more a composite being than this deity who is the focus of much of the activity of the first segment of the monumental tetralogy, *Das Rheingold*. In the simplest of terms, the Freia of Wagner's *Ring* is not entirely the goddess Freia that moved so delicately and so attractively through the minds and hearts of the ancient Teutonic believers. Rather, Wagner's goddess is a composite of several figures that are to be found in ancient Teutonic religious and folkloric thought. It is true that Wagner developed his Freia after the renowned goddess of Teutondom whom the Eddic literature presents in what can only be classified as rather definitive mythical terms. Yet, it is also true that the author of the Nibelung poem incorporated into his Freia some of the character and indeed some of the function of a second deity of the Germanic divine hierarchy, the goddess Idun, and further, he also wove into his goddess some aspects of a figure who is prominent in popular Germanic folklore, the specious Holda.

Freia, who is known in Nordic literature as *Freyja*, is without question one of the most important and one of the most significant goddesses of Teutondom. This divine being, after Fricka (*Frigge* in the North), is the most honored of the Teutonic goddesses, and there are regions of the Teutonic world in which the two shared what might be termed an equal divine rank as well as similar divine attributes and functions. Snorri Sturluson, in *The Prose Edda*, gives the pair an almost identical divine rank and further describes the two goddesses as "the holy ones." These somewhat similar divine figures and their rather extensive religious equality has given rise to a certain confusion regarding the mythical identification of these goddesses, and it has been on more than one occasion that each often has been mistaken for the other.

An element of the historic confusion that marks the relationship of Freia and Fricka has extended down into the modern day. A prime example is evidenced by the debate that still is common among some mythologists, the debate that argues as to which of the names of the two goddesses serves as the source for the name of the fifth day of the week, *Friday*. Those who support Freia as the figure for whom the day was named cite the Old Norse word *Friadagr*, which in Middle High German became *Fritac*, and *Freitag* in modern German. Those who support Fricka in this matter resort to the Anglo-Saxon name for the day, *Frige Daeg*. In terms of simple numbers, however, it would seem that those who award the honor to Freia are in the majority.

Freia's religious celebrity as a goddess to be invoked existed despite an anomaly in her divine relationship to the other gods and goddesses of Teutondom. This deity, her father Njord, and her brother Frey (*Froh* in Wagner's *Ring*) were *not*, originally at least, members of the race of gods that dominated the religious thought and worship of the earliest of Teutonic peoples. The principal race of gods, divine figures such as Wotan, Fricka, and Donner, and the numerous other gods who exercised divine control over heathen Teutondom, belonged to a group or clan that was known as *Aesir*. (The word *Aesir* is derived from the singular form *ass* or *aes*, which was a term that was synonymous with the word "god" in the early language of the people of the North.) At some time, however, and in a manner not clearly understood by mythologists, another race of gods came into existence in the region of the Baltic Sea. If at first these beings were essentially more water-spirits than gods, as some students believe, the stature of the race ultimately achieved that of divine beings, and the clan, known as Vanir (Wanes), became a second race of powerful Teutonic deities. Worship of members of this race of gods began slowly, but eventually religious homage, supplication, and invocation spread into what is today Norway where beliefs in these gods began to overlap the established religious beliefs in the Aesir. Apparently it was accepted that the two races coexisted, dwelling together so to speak, but it was also believed that there was not total accord between the clans.

The potential for religious disharmony because of this divine relationship was quite evident. However, to accommodate the two distinct races of gods into the overall religious pattern, and perhaps as a means to make for a more homogeneous religious thought, a belief arose that a war had erupted between the two groups. The Aesir hated a sorcerer named Gulveig who had practiced "the black art." Finally, the gods of Wotan's race killed the evil being, after which serious times set in. The Vanir tried to intervene in the matter and ultimately Wotan, angered and frustrated at the entire situation, threw his celebrated spear into a group of the gods that was discussing the matter.

Thus began what is known as *The First War* sometimes called *The Great War*. This war was, however, a struggle that neither of the divine races could win. Ultimately, an accord was reached, a treaty that ended the hostility and which called for an exchange of hostages. The Aesir gave up Mimir, the wise guardian of a well that lay under a root of the World Ash Tree, and Honir, a god who figures in the heathen Teutonic version of the creation of the first humans. To meet their part of the agreement, the Vanir handed over Njord, a god of the sea who had been born in Vanaheim ("Home of the Vanir") and on whom mariners and fishermen called when they sailed into deep waters. After Njord came over to the Aesir, he married Skadi, the daughter of a giant.

Two additional figures are considered to have been hostages who were delivered over to the Aesir by the Vanir. This pair was the children of Njord, the brother and sister Freia and Froh. These children were fathered by Njord in a union with his unnamed sister. *The Poetic Edda* as well as *The Ynlinga Saga* infer that this union, and hence the birth of the pair, occurred *before* Njord had been delivered into the hands of the Aesir and therefore, the children, like their father, were Vanir gods. *The Prose Edda* also speaks of Freia as a Vanir goddess, and there seems to be no serious doubt that these two figures -- who would go on to become two of the most important of gods in the Teutonic world -- were originally of the Vanir clan. However, there is a statement in *The Prose Edda* that the union between Njord and his sister took place *after* his marriage to Skadi, that is after the sea god had begun to dwell among the Aesir gods. If that chronology is accepted, Freia and Froh were not Vanir gods, but rather beings who had been born among the Aesir. Mythologists tend to disregard Snorri Sturluson's rather singular remark, both because the myths that are included in his *Edda* are often at variance with the same tales as found in *The Poetic Edda* -- myths that are accepted as the original and authoritative beliefs of the Teutonic peoples -- and also because it is known that Sturluson was a Christian and that much of the thought of Christianity found its way into the Icelander's writings thereby weakening, diluting, or even negating the essence and substance of his versions of the Teutonic myths. In addition, Sturluson once had referred to Freia as a Vanir and thus, his previous isolated remark concerning her possible Aesir origin is entirely discounted. Freia and her brother, like their father, are thus viewed as true Vanir gods who were handed over to the Aesir in accordance with the terms of the peace treaty that concluded The First War. (Curiously, the question of whether Freia and Froh are Vanir or Aesir gods is never really a matter of serious concern in the myths, and it is only in passing that the matter of their birthplaces comes into view. The two simply are accepted without question as part of the divine hierarchy of the Aesir gods.)

Wagner was aware of the war between the Aesir and the Vanir, and he knew of the treaty that ended that conflict. He considered the entire matter to be of no consequence to the argument of his drama. Neither did he give attention to the mythical possibility that Freia and her brother Froh had not been born into the dominant race of Teutonic gods. He saw this pair only as they carried out their divine activities and their divine functions in the religious world of the early Germanic peoples; he saw this pair as they were worshipped in the culture, as they were invoked by the people, revered and glorified with the same intensity as were the other gods.

In a word, Wagner viewed the gods of his *Ring* as members of a single divine race. (Wagner refrained from giving his race of gods a specific name, as he had done for his dwarves and his giants.) He reinforced that view with the mythical fact that Freia and Froh were indeed sister and brother, and he further strengthened that concept by means of the mythical confusion that enveloped Fricka and Freia, a divine similarity which, as has been indicated, frequently depicted the two goddesses as almost identical in divine attributes, stature, and function.

Wagner braced this mythical divine structure of his race of gods by creating for them a singular as well as unique familial relationship. Such ties obviously projected a more unified picture of divine solidarity and, as some will contend, the familial relationship of his gods enhanced the thematic unity of his own story. It was, without question however, a relationship that went beyond that found in the myths. For his *Ring*, Wagner retained the brother-sisterhood of his Froh and Freia, but he extended that relationship to include both Donner and Fricka. Thus, the four gods became brothers and sisters and, further, through the mythical relationship of Fricka as wife to Wotan -- which he retained -- Donner, Freia, and Froh become brothers and sister-in-law to the supreme god, Wotan. It would seem that Wagner considered these blood ties of significance as well as of importance because they seemed to allow for more intense emotional attachments among the five gods of his story, specifically in the matter of the gods' concern for Freia when she is about to be delivered over to the giants.

As with all the figures that are found in the Teutonic myths, Freia had a Nordic or northern name and a variation of that name in other Germanic regions. In the Scandinavian area the name for this goddess was *Freyja*, a name that does not appear in other Germanic languages. This word meant, literally, "lady," and was the companion word to that of her brother *Frey*, which meant "lord." (Frey was the mythical figure that served as inspiration to Wagner for his character Froh.) The name *Freyja* does not appear elsewhere as a proper name, but the word did become a part of other languages as a noun meaning "mistress" or "chief-lady." (Gothic - *frauja*; OHG - *fruwa* and *frowa*; MHG - *frouwe* and *frou*.) In time, the word *Fru* developed out of these variations and this word became a term that designated the wife of a man of high or noble rank. The native speaker of German converted *Fru* into *Frau*, the modern day correlative term of Herr, and used the word not only to indicate "wife" or "married woman" (*Mrs*), but also in reference to the Blessed Virgin of Christian belief, and in numerous compounds that refer to womanhood, women's clothes, and similar matters.

Although each god of the Teutonic world had a specific name by which he or she was known, it was common practice for the peoples of the day to address their gods and to refer to these deities by any of several secondary or bynames. Most of the words used as names were not in themselves true names, but rather terms that were descriptive of certain attributes or functions that were readily associated with the respective deity. Freia was no exception to this cultural practice and some of the more frequently used names for this goddess were *Menglod*, *Mardoll*, *Horn*, *Gefn*, *Syr*, and *Vanadis*. Wagner showed no dramatic interest in any of Freia's bynames, and in his *Ring* he used only her principal mythical name, which he Germanized, a procedure that he followed throughout his drama.

The overall depiction that the Teutonic myths present of the goddess Freia is not unlike that of most of the other Germanic gods. It is only in detail that there is a distinction. Freia resided in a large and beautiful hall whose name was *Sessrumnir* ("Rich in Seats") and which was located in *Folkvangar* ("Field of the Folk" or "Plain of the People"). The goddess had a fondness for jewelry, as did Fricka, and she was the owner of a famed necklace called *Brisingamen* ("Brising's Necklace") which, like most of the other treasures of the gods, had been fashioned by dwarves. (This necklace is called by name in the celebrated English epic *Beowulf*.) Again like most of the other gods, Freia possessed items that held a special magic. The most prominent of the items that the goddess owned was a *feather-dress* or *falcon-coat*, a kind of cloak that was made of silver and which, when worn, allowed the wearer to assume the form of a bird and to fly throughout the worlds* of the universe. This feather-dress and its unique magic was comparable to Wotan's great spear, Gungnir, which always granted victory in battle, to Donner's hammer Mjollnir, the weapon that created thunder and lightning, and to Froh's sword that fought by itself when held by a worthy warrior. A second item possessed by Freia was a bridal veil which apparently allowed the wearer to assume the form of a bride. This item becomes of interest in only one Eddic poem, and therefore it is not nearly so important or significant as the falcon-coat, but its association with Freia and with weddings created some of that confusion that related Freia with Fricka, the Germanic Goddess of Marriage. The goddess also possessed a chariot that was drawn by two cats, and -- like her brother -- Freia rode a boar that was capable of great speed. It is Freia's association with a boar that gave rise to one of her second names, *Syr*, which meant "Sow."

Freia was the wife of Od. Little is known about Od, although *The Poetic Edda* relates that he loved the goddess very much, and apparently that love was returned by the goddess. Sturluson writes in *The Prose Edda* that Od frequently went on long journeys and during his absences Freia wept for him, always crying tears of red gold. The couple had a daughter, *Hnoss* ("Gem"), who was so beautiful that her name became the word for 'treasure.' (An old Icelandic word for precious gems was *hnoss*.)

Sturluson also writes in his *Edda* that Freia was most faithful to her husband. The matter of Freia's fidelity to Od is put to question, however, by means of the contents of two of the poems in *The Poetic Edda*. In one poem, "Lokasenna" ("Loge's Wrangling"), Aegir, the sea god, hosts a great feast which most of the gods attend. During the festivities, Loge accuses Freia of having slept with all the gods and elves who are present at the party, and he specifically says that she has slept with her brother. Mythologists tend to give little serious attention to Loge's words, citing as their reasons no less than four mythical and cultural facts as their support. In the first regard, at the time that the demigod utters his remarks he is in a fit of rage. His anger had been raised because the gods had ordered him to leave Aegir's feast, at which he became quite furious, and he obviously sought to avenge what he considered to be an insult. Yet, if Loge's accusation is correct, Freia was not the only deity guilty of such conduct because the angered spirit spares the wrath of his verbal onslaught on few of those present, making -- as he does -- similar remarks about several of the other gods. Students of the myths are also aware that heathen Teutonic thought did not condemn such sexual activity outside marriage with the same intensity as did the later followers of Christian beliefs. These scholars usually interpret Sturluson's statement about Freia's fidelity more as a result of the Christian influence that was being felt in the northern regions in his time than as a true mythical belief. These same scholars also consider Loge's attack on Freia for having slept with her brother to be of little mythical consequence. Such relationships were not unusual among the gods, and in the case at hand, they recall the accepted belief that Freia and her brother were the products of such a union, that is the children of Njord and his sister, and that this mythical fact is always stated without any shade of moral judgment. (Readers of the *Ring* will immediately note Wagner's awareness of these mythical matters by means of Fricka's strong resentment of her husband's sexual wanderings, and through the relationship of the drama's Siegmund and Sieglinde as brother and sister.) However, it is true that Loge's words concerning Freia's supposed promiscuity receive a certain emphasis when they are echoed in a second Eddic poem, "Hyndluljod ("The Poem of Hyndla")". In the verses of this work, Hyndla, a giantess, makes reference to the goddess' sexual activity when she tells that many lovers have come to the goddess and have crawled up her skirts!

It is obvious that Wagner showed little concern for Freia's mythical husband. He sensed that the created relationship of the brother-sister ties of four of the gods, including Freia, and the retention of the mythical husband-wife bond of Fricka and Wotan were sufficient familial relationships for the gods of his drama. To favor Freia with a husband would only have complicated unnecessarily his argument, with no compensating thematic gain. Such an arrangement would also have detracted from the centrality of the goddess' role as he had so carefully envisioned it.

It is equally obvious that Wagner had no intent to depict his Freia as sexually promiscuous. He was very much aware that he had made his Freia "Goddess of Youth and Love," and his cultural sensibilities told him that such a depiction must be supported by a dramatic as well as a theatrical aura of purity and virtue. Any portrayal to the contrary would have detracted seriously from the character of his divine figure, and would have flawed the thematic aspects of his drama. At the same time, it would seem certain that anything less than a virtuous depiction of the goddess would have stimulated critical debate because of the scant mythical evidence to support such a picture. Wagner thus ignored those mythical activities of the goddess and those references to her character that were extraneous to the principal actions of his drama, and he concentrated solely on the more positive facets of Freia's divine being.

There was yet another aspect of the mythical concept of the goddess that Wagner chose to disregard as he developed the Freia of his *Ring*. This matter was the goddess' association with death, more specifically with the death of warriors. This was also a concern that was uppermost in the heathen Teutonic mind. According to early Germanic belief, the greatest honor that could befall a warrior was to be selected to join the elite army that Wotan maintained in celestial Valhalla. To be chosen for such service, one must have fought valiantly in battle and died a champion's death in the field. Wotan was the Lord of Valhalla and the supreme commander of this select group of heroes (*einjerar*) that was destined to fight on the side of the gods in "The Final Battle."* Wotan was also one of only two divine figures who could select those who, after death on the battlefield, would be brought to the heavenly abode. The second being to have such authority was Freia, and that authority allowed her to chose one half of all the warriors who were to be so honored in their death.

Students of the Teutonic myths have pondered at length the mythical statements that refer to Freia's divine power to select warriors for an afterlife in Valhalla. These scholars point out that the statements that depict such power, and which are to be found in both *Eddas*, are relatively short and unelaborated, and that there is not to be found in any of the myths an indication that Freia actually executed such power and carried out the activity of choosing those who would be raised to fight again. These scholars hold that the remarks that refer to such powers do not represent a belief that was completely accepted in the totality of early Teutonic religious thought. Freia, they argue further, was never known to have an association of any kind with the Allfather. These students maintain that if any goddess were empowered to select heroes to reside in Valhalla, that goddess would not be Freia, but rather Fricka. The latter was, after all, Wotan's wife, and in that capacity she was looked upon as the Supreme Goddess of Teutondom. Other students of the Teutonic past convert the last statement to their position by stating that there was an association between Freia and Wotan, and that this association came about through Freia's husband, Od. They argue that the name of the goddess' husband, *Od*, was a doublet of *Odin*, the name by which Wotan was known in the northern regions of ancient Teutondom. In this manner, Freia was a wife to Odin (Wotan), and therefore a deity of equal rank. Freia, then, as a goddess of equal rank to the Allfather, could have had the power and could have exercised the power of selecting one half of Teutondom's heroes.

The statements in the Eddic literature that accorded Freia the powers to determine who were to be the champions of Teutondom's celestial army infer that the goddess was essentially a *Valkyrie*. Indeed, those scholars who accept the statements as authentic mythical belief also maintain that Freia was, in fact, a Valkyrie. (In Teutonic thought, a Valkyrie was a supernatural being whose principal duty was to transport to Valhalla those chosen heroes who had died in battle, and there to accord them the appropriate services.) These students find support for their idea in at least two of the mythical tales, stories in which Freia or one of her possessions figures prominently. In one of these tales, the evidence comes in the form of a single word. Freia is speaking; the goddess believes it urgent that she *ride* to Valhalla. The verb used in the original Eddic poetry meant "to ride on horseback," and was reserved to indicate the manner in which Valkyries journeyed between the battlefield and Valhalla on their swift horses. Freia's destination in this instance is Valhalla, and some scholars contend that the use of this special word confirms that the goddess is truly functioning as a Valkyrie. (Wagner retained the semantics of this word in his "*Ride* of the Valkyries" that opens Act III of *Die Walküre*.) The Old Norse word survives in German as *reiten*, with the meaning of 'to ride on horseback.' The second bit of mythical information that seems to sustain the idea that Freia was a Valkyrie focuses on the *falcon* or *featherdress*, an item that belonged to the goddess and which appears frequently in the Eddic literature. The magic of this article of clothing allowed the wearer to assume the form of a bird, and scholars have likened that magic to that of the "featherdress" that changed young maidens into swans. There was an early belief that Valkyries possessed the magic to change themselves into swan-maidens who then haunted the pools and lakes that lay deep in the forest. It was believed that the beauty of these swan-maidens often tempted young men to their deaths in the waters. Some students maintain that the similarity of form of these two items, and the added matter of almost identical magic, plus the mythical fact that Valkyries could change themselves into swan-maidens, is irrefutable evidence that Freia was a Valkyrie.

These separate matters of mythical lore that seem to support the concept that Freia, the goddess, was also a Valkyrie receive added support from no less a scholar than Jakob Grimm. Grimm, whose many studies greatly influenced later scholarship on German antiquity and who along with his brother produced numerous works including what is popularly known in English as *The Grimm Brothers' Fairy Tales*, was convinced that Freia was indeed a Valkyrie. In his monumental four-volume study of Teutonic mythology, this foremost of mythologists called the goddess *Valfreyja* ("Mistress of the Slain"). Such a name obviously places Freia on a divine level equal in rank to Wotan, one of whose most important and significant names was *Valfader* ("Valfather"), which can be translated as "Father of the Slain."

The concept that Freia was directly associated, in one way or another, with Valhalla and the champions who resided there has never gained acceptance as a fundamental facet of early Teutonic mythological belief. The possibility of such an association, however, has intrigued numerous students. At times, this intrigue has been so insistent that these individuals often have proceeded to fuse the sparse mythological information about Freia and the champions of Valhalla with a known folkloric belief, and then to extract from that unique blend a singular theory regarding one of the goddess' functions. Into the substance of the Eddic statements that reveal that Freia chose some of the heroes for the army of the gods, these persons blended the popular northern belief that women, after they had died, would join the goddess Freia. By means of this mixture of Germanic mythology and folklore, they then concluded that Freia was mistress of her own Valhalla-like paradise, a celestial place in which only women were accepted! Needless to say, such an idea is wholly academic and has received no serious scholarly attention or consideration.

There was another association of Freia and death that Wagner also chose to disregard, but this death was no longer the death of mortals, but rather that of animals, and more specifically, the death of certain animals by sacrifice. Wagner introduced the element of animal sacrifice into his *Ring* drama in a somewhat passive manner. He obviously had reasoned that the matter of sacrifice would reflect certain ancient religious practice, and therefore would contribute in its own way to that mythical veil in which he sought to envelope his drama. He also sensed that the matter of animal sacrifice would enhance the characterization of the specific god or gods so honored. Wagner understood most clearly that there was no dramatic or thematic need for an actual scenic enactment of these sacrifices; his story made no such demand. He also realized that the ambience and the characterization that would result from such an act could be achieved by the proper dialogue, delivered, of course, at the appropriate time.

It is in the second act of *Götterdämmerung* that Wagner made animal sacrifice part and parcel of his drama. The scene is that in which Hagen summons the vassals in order that they may pay homage to their leader Gunther and his bride Brünnhilde, who are about to arrive. Hagen tells the gathered crowd that the gods must be honored if they are to look with favor on this marriage, and that honor will be expressed in sacrifice, one animal each for Wotan, Froh, Fricka, and Donner. Of the five gods that appear in the *Ring*, Wagner allowed four to receive the honor of sacrifice and he was to withhold that highest of cultural tributes from his Goddess of Youth and Love, Freia!

It is by means of Hagen's words that Wagner was able to realize a dramatic representation of the societal-religious practice of sacrifice which in its own way subtly increased the mythical sense he hoped to impart. It was also by means of Hagen's words regarding the intended animal sacrifices that Wagner was able to include yet another element that conveys even more the ancient ambience and which, at the same time, demonstrates further the composer's astute awareness of heathen Teutonic thought. As Hagen continues his address to the vassals, he designates specifically the kinds of animals that are to be sacrificed. He directs that the best of steers is to be slaughtered for Wotan, after which their blood is to be poured on Wotan's altar stone. He orders that Froh be honored by the sacrifice of a boar, and Fricka's blessing will be sought by the sacrifice of a sheep. To gain Donner's favor, a goat will be slain in the god's honor. Freia was not named as one of the gods to be invoked, and neither does Hagen call out the name of an animal that is to be sacrificed in her honor.

Wagner's venture into the mythical matter of animal sacrifice to honor the gods, as least as he realized it in the *Ring*, was, to say the least, enthusiastic. If it was his desire to depict this rite -- if only by reference -- as a means to achieve dramatic impact, he realized that it would be difficult to gain that end in any effective way by means of a single speech of relatively few words. Hagen's words, then, must have prominence, their own emphasis so to speak, and that emphasis could only be achieved by exaggeration. Thus it is that Hagen's utterance, brief as it is, nevertheless speaks of *four* gods, names *four* kinds of animals to be sacrificed, and in each case makes reference to *two* related mythical matters that were basic to early heathen Teutonic practices: invocation and sacrifice! There is no doubt that Hagen's words, thus conceived, reflected basic beliefs and practices of the past, but if Wagner blended and fused his details to create the idea that the occasion necessitated a grandiose, unified ritual (an exaggeration in itself), some of those details were extracted from the myths of his culture, while others were really of his own creation.

It is, of course, the anticipated marriage of Gunther and Brünnhilde that serves as the stimulus for Hagen's declarations. Such an occasion was, in fact, the kind that could evoke the ancient cultural practice that sought the blessing of Fricka, the Goddess of Marriage. However, Hagen's words honor not only Fricka, but also Wotan, Donner, and Froh and the inference in his words is that all of these gods can work their magic for the good of the marriage. This inference is of Wagner's own design because at no time in the myths of Teutondom does any god other than Fricka show divine concern for matters of this aspect of moral domestic life. The divine interests of the other three deities lie in other realms, in matters that are more extensive within the parameters of early Teutonic thought. Wotan, for example, focused his thoughts on the acquisition of knowledge and wisdom, and on matters of war and the prophesied destruction of the gods. Donner on the other hand was interested mainly in his confrontations with the enemies of the gods, the giants, and Froh concerned himself with matters of fertility and fruitfulness in agriculture.

One must understand, however, that in this matter of animal sacrifices Wagner resorted to his own self-granted dramatic license. It is historical fact that the early Teutonic peoples practiced the rite of animal sacrifice, but such sacrifices were not carried out in honor of each and every god of the Teutonic divine order. These people honored only certain deities, and the myths reveal that of Wagner's quartet of gods only Donner and Froh were regularly worshipped by means of animal sacrifice. Wotan was too supreme a god, too mighty in his powers, too divine to be reached by ordinary practices that also sought out lesser deities. It is true that sacrifice was offered Wotan, but such occasions were infrequent, then only in the direst of circumstances, and then as a single ritual devoted only to the Supreme God himself. It is also historical fact that there was no ritual of any kind that was offered to Fricka, indeed there was not even a cult that invoked this goddess, who mythically was a lesser deity than each of the gods of this present trio of colleagues. Thus it is that as part of this extended mythology, that is the mythology of the Teutonic past fused with mythological-like details that originate in the mind of Richard Wagner, the composer included the matter of animal sacrifice for two of Teutondom's deities for whom sacrifice was either seldom or never carried out! And, in contriving this ritual of worship and religious adoration, he omitted a sacrifice to one of the most loved and respected of the Teutonic goddesses, an act that was regularly if infrequently practiced by the ancient peoples.

Wagner, however, had not yet concluded with his own version of the ritual of animal sacrifice. As he had done with the calls for sacrifice in honor of the gods, so too did Wagner again resort to his own thoughts regarding the association of certain animals with specific gods. As noted earlier, Hagen specifies that a goat be slaughtered to honor Donner and that a boar be sacrificed to Froh. Such sacrifices offered no mythological problems because the references to these animals mirror mythological fact and cultural practices. It is Donner who is known as Lord of the Goats because of the two goats that draw his chariot through the heavens, animals which also serve him as food during his journeys. And the myths also tell of the boar that belonged to Froh, the animal that could run through the air faster than a horse, the animal that the gods prized as one of their great treasures. It was the mythology itself that gave Wagner the basis for Hagen' words. (The association of Froh with the boar and that of the goat with Donner remained prominent in societal thought well into the Christian era and remnants of those associations can still be discerned from time to time in the present day.) However, Wagner did not find in the myths any associations for Wotan and Fricka, that is, specific kinds of animals that could serve as sacrificial animals for these gods and which he could cause Hagen to name. Thus he was forced to create his own associations in order to complete the concept of the sacrificial ritual that he wished to depict in his drama.

The determinations of those species of animals that could serve as suitable sacrifices for Wotan and for Fricka were ultimately come by, but only after Wagner had given the matter considerable attention. In the case of Wotan, Wagner well understood that this god was the *Allfather*, the god of the universe and of all that existed in the World. As such, Wotan, essentially, was the god of *all* animals. The composer was also aware that in the myths this King of the Gods could readily be associated with certain specific animals. Wotan possessed the great horse Sleipnir, and he was also the master of two ravens (Hugin and Munin) that he sent out daily to gather news of the world. The composer also knew that Wotan had two wolves (Geri and Freki) that the god fed each day in Valhalla. (Wagner inferred this latter association when, in *Die Walküre* he caused Siegmund's father -- really Wotan -- to be called *Wolf*, while Siegmund himself was *Wolfing* or *Wolf Cub*.) Wagner also was aware that none of the animals that was associated with the Supreme God of Teutondom could be made the animal of sacrifice, not only because each had a special role in the existence of the gods, but also because none of these animals was a creature *whose flesh was regularly consumed*. At the same time, he understood that there never had been a sacrifice to Fricka, which in turn would force him to select the animal that would be slaughtered in her honor. Armed with these mythical facts and the cultural criteria that could be applied in matters of animal sacrifice, Wagner turned to the customs of the daily life of the Teutonic people to seek out the associations that he was to make in his drama. He confirmed that the people of that early life ate the flesh of several kinds of animals, in addition to that of goats and pigs. He learned that two other such animals whose flesh was regularly consumed were cattle and sheep, with the former being somewhat of a favorite meat. Wagner was satisfied with this cultural information which allowed him the two animals that would become the sacrificial beasts for the two gods. And, of course, the fact that cattle were looked upon as a favorite food dictated that such animals become the sacrifices for Wotan. Thus it was that *oxen* (steers) became the sacrificial animal for Wotan, and *sheep* would be sacrificed to Fricka, and each selection exhibited a total compatibility with heathen Teutonic beliefs and practices. (Wagner was consistent in his created association of Fricka and sheep. Later, as he wrote the poem of *Die Walküre*, he caused the goddess to make her appearance in the second act in a chariot that is drawn by rams!) Wagner had thus called for sacrifice in his drama. He had named the gods to be honored and he also had specified the animals that were to be slaughtered for these deities. Yet, of the five gods that are part of this drama, the five most significant and important gods in heathen Teutonic thought, only four are to be saluted through sacrifice, and it is Freia alone who is to be denied one of Teutondom's most sacred rituals, and one to which the goddess was mythically entitled. What was Wagner's reason for his exclusion of Freia from Hagen's call to the vassals?

It is mythical fact that on occasion sacrifices were made to Freia. It would seem logical to assume, then, that if Wagner had included invocation as well as sacrifice to Fricka, a goddess for whom neither invocation nor sacrifice was ever a part of her godhood, he certainly would have allowed Freia the same honor. Then, too, to honor *all* of the deities in his work would also have enhanced in a most unified way the primordial ambience that he desired his drama to project.

Wagner never explained why he excluded Freia from the group of gods whose blessings on the wedding of Brünnhilde and Gunther were to be sought by means of animal sacrifice. It would seem, however, that the composer's actions in this matter were the result of one of two factors, possibly the result of both. The first of these considerations is mythological in nature. Freia, like Donner and Froh, is closely associated with an animal, and this animal was an appropriate creature for sacrifice. This animal was a boar. (Obviously, Freia's association with cats, the animals that drew her chariot, could not be a consideration in the matter at hand.) A sacrifice to Freia would have been a simple matter, a minimal expansion of Hagen's words. However, it is possible that Wagner reasoned that if he were to include Freia among the gods to be honored by sacrifice, the animal to be sacrificed would have to be a boar, and such a situation might have occasioned some dramatic confusion because a boar was the same kind of animal that had been offered to Froh. Such duplicity was to be avoided because it suggested divine equality, and in the Teutonic mind Froh was by far the more important of the two gods! The second of the two factors that may have weighed on Wagner's mind becomes evident in the *Ring* story. In the drama Wagner develops a unique character in his goddess Freia. As was suggested earlier and which will be discussed shortly, Wagner's Freia is at once a goddess who is a dramatic blend of the mythical goddess herself and at least one figure of the mythological world and one taken from the field of German folklore. In addition, her role as Goddess of the Golden Apples has been created for her, an adaptation of the function of that second mythological figure that is part of her godhood. As the goddess who cultivates the apples that permit the gods to enjoy eternal youth, at least in Wagner's version, the goddess *serves* the other deities. At the same time, her fruit is not available to mortals, and in that sense Freia's divine powers are neither related with nor pertinent to Brünnhilde and Gunther in their marriage. To that consideration, Wagner may have added the dramatic fact that Freia alone among the gods is to serve as a pawn, as the reward to the giants for their labors on Valhalla, and in that capacity the goddess becomes the focal point in the conflict between the giants and the gods, a conflict that arises because she is so greatly desired by both parties, but for different reasons. In the eventual resolution of this conflict, Freia even becomes the medium of measurement for the amount of gold that is to replace her. Viewed in this manner, and aside from all else in the *Ring* story, Wagner's Freia is very much a special goddess, a supernatural figure with a singular significance that sets her apart from all others. Wagner must have been aware of this significance and therefore believed that any additional participation of the goddess in the sacrificial aspect of his tale would detract from that importance, and, therefore, become a cause of diminution of her character.

It seems certain that Wagner's reasons for his exclusion of Freia from the scene at hand can never be known. It cannot be ascertained that he wished to avoid a duplication of the kinds of animals that were to be slain in sacrifice, or that he desired to preserve in an isolated manner the special functions that he had given this goddess, or that he considered both of these matters. It remains, however, that Freia is the only deity for whom Hagen makes no call of sacrifice.

It may be only coincidence, yet it is also possible that Wagner anticipated that Hagen's call to the vassals for animal sacrifices to the gods could be interpreted as a religious slight to Freia. The composer seems to ward off such an interpretation and attempts to give the goddess her religious due by allowing Gutrune a few words to be delivered immediately after Siegfried returns from his errand on Gunther's behalf, but shortly before Hagen's call. Gutrune asks that Freia *smile* on the Volsung, on behalf of all women. Wagner's Goddess of Youth and Love has her singular moment of dramatic primacy!

There were, however, other attributes of the goddess that garnered Wagner's attention. Foremost among those several qualities was that of her beauty. Freia was viewed as the most beautiful of the Germanic goddesses, and -- of course -- lovely to look upon. Her beauty was celebrated throughout all of Teutondom, and it was complemented by a joyful and cheerful manner that made her even more attractive to all the people. Wagner considered this aspect of the goddess to be of primary significance to his thematic ideas and he resorted to several means to incorporate such a concept into his *Ring* drama. The most obvious of these means was dialogue, and Freia's beauty is disclosed by no less than three of the drama's principal figures. It is her brother Froh who first speaks of her beauty when he calls her "die Schöne," that is, "the beautiful one." Later, Fasolt is captivated by the goddess, and he refers to her as "die Holde," or "the lovely one." Finally, it is no less a god than Wotan who praises Freia's beauty when he speaks of her as "die liebliche Göttin, licht and leicht," words that tell of a lovely or charming goddess who is pleasant, sweet, and gentle.

These mythical attributes of loveliness and beauty, enhanced as they were by those of graciousness and charm, were naturally related to Freia's activities in matters of love. The myths tell that Freia was fond of love poetry, and although she was sensitive to the needs of people, she was especially disposed to lovers. Mythical concepts held that only good could come to a love affair upon which this goddess had bestowed her blessing.

Thus, lovers often invoked Freia's name to secure her favor for their personal union. (This belief regarding Freia's powers in matters of love, a belief that prevailed throughout the Teutonic regions, obviously contradicted the concept that Freia was a Valkyrie!) Wagner was attracted to this aspect of Freia's nature and, in his own manner, he introduced it into his drama, into the relationship between Siegfried and Gutrune. In the second act of *Götterdämmerung*, the Volsung returns to the Hall of the Gibichungs after he has won Brünnhilde for Gunther. At this point, Gutrune -- who has plotted with Hagen to win the hero for herself - welcomes Siegfried by invoking the goddess Freia and then she implores that the goddess bring joy to him and thus look favorably upon the two of them.

Freia's personal qualities and her intimate involvements in matters of love combine to give her an even greater presence in the amorous matters of the mythical world. It is only Freia, of all the goddesses, who becomes a kind of love-prize that is continuously sought by the supernaturals who inhabit the Germanic mythical universe. Such a representation, which Wagner was to adapt to his *Ring* story, is a prominent feature in Eddic literature. It appears in two different forms in no less than two tales, one told in a poem that is found in *The Poetic Edda* and the other recounted by Sturluson in *The Prose Edda*. In the poem "Thrymskvida" ("The Lay of Thrym"), a work that is considered by many to contain some of the finest verses in the Eddic collection, the King of the Giants, Thrym, steals Donner's magic hammer. The giant hides it deep in the earth and then announces that he will return it only if he is given Freia as wife. The goddess rejects the giant's demand and refuses to go to him. The gods are upset at the loss of the treasured hammer, and so they meet in counsel to determine a way in which the hammer can be retrieved. The gods finally decide that Donner himself should be the one who rescues the hammer although their plan is not one that meets with the approval of the God of Thunder. The gods have deigned that Donner should go to the giant, but in the disguise of Freia. He is to don her bridal veil, which will make him appear as a bride, and he is to wear Freia's famed necklace. After some coaxing, Donner at last agrees to go through with the plan, and then, disguised as Freia, and with Loge as his maid servant, he travels to the Land of the Giants, where the two present themselves to Thrym. The giant has doubts about what he sees, but ultimately the wily Loge convinces him that the disguised god is indeed the goddess Freia who has come to be his bride. At the appropriate time, the hammer is brought out to hallow the marriage of Freia and the giant. Donner seizes his celebrated weapon, slays Thrym with it, and "all the folk of the giants."

Wagner was obviously influenced by the adventure in which Freia is a much-desired prize, but it was in the second tale that he found thematic details that he felt he could use successfully in his dramatic argument. In the myth that Sturluson includes in his work, a giant has offered to build a stronghold for the gods. (Some mythologists believe that this stronghold is really Asgard, the Land of the Gods, which was destroyed, or at least heavily damaged, in the great war between the Aesir gods and the Vanir.) As payment for his work, the giant demands the goddess Freia, the sun, and the moon. The gods agree to this payment, but add the condition that the work must be finished by the first day of summer or the giant will forfeit any payment for his labors. The giant retorts that he will agree to that condition if he is allowed the use of his horse, Svadilfari, to haul the rocks. The gods agree, the pact is concluded, and the giant begins to work with the huge boulders that his horse carries to the site.

The giant makes rapid progress on the stronghold. Three days before the beginning of summer the gods realize that the giant is going to meet the deadline and thus fulfill his part of the agreement. The deities are concerned that they may have to give up Freia, the sun, and the moon. They believe that this situation is the kind of crisis that Loge usually causes and so they threaten to do him great harm if he does not resolve the matter for them. Loge understands the seriousness of his predicament and immediately prepares to come to the aid of the gods. He changes himself into a mare, cautiously approaches Svadilfari, and then entices the stallion away from the giant and into a forest. The giant was helpless and, without his horse, he has no stones with which to continue his work. He realizes that he cannot now meet the deadline and thus will not have Freia as a wife. The giant is greatly angered by the deception that the gods have played upon him and flies into a fury. The gods quickly call on Donner who steps forward and slays the giant with his trusty hammer. Freia is saved! (The union of Loge and Svadilfari results in the birth of Sleipnir, the eight-legged grey horse that was considered to be the best horse in the universe and which became the property of Wotan and which, according to some myths, sired another famed mythical horse, Grane!)

The reader of the *Ring* quickly discerns that Wagner became very much attracted to the story of the gods and their pact with the giant. If he felt that this tale strengthened the concept of Freia as a goddess of great beauty and loveliness, he also sensed that it could serve him as a thematic vehicle by means of which he could create the serious dilemma that would become the cause of his drama's complex intrigues. Thus, with only slight modifications, Wagner wove the essentials of the myth into *Das Rheingold*: Wagner's pact is between Wotan and the last two giants of the universe, the brothers Fasolt and Fafner; the stronghold that they construct is to be Valhalla, the home of the gods; the reward to Fafner and Fasolt for their labors is to be the goddess Freia. When the giants complete their work and it is time for Wotan to honor his part of the agreement, the other gods implore the Allfather to find some means whereby their beloved Freia will not go into the hands of Fasolt and his brother.

The situation quickly evolves into a serious psychological crisis. Wotan, the Supreme God, must honor the pledge, which is one of the most sacred obligations in all of Teutonic culture as well as mythical thought. Yet, if he honors his oath, he will forfeit one of the most honored goddesses of his divine kingdom. On the other hand, he can disregard the word he has given and somehow undo the oath in order to keep the Goddess of Love and Youth from the giants, but in so doing risk the evils of the curse that befalls one when he breaks with his word. This entanglement, this quandary, this dilemma, then, becomes the dramatic highpoint of the first part of the tetralogy, and the incident that sets the stage for all that is to follow in the remaining three parts of the drama.

Freia's several mythical qualities, activities, and functions -- all of an attractive and gentle nature -- were reason enough in Wagner's mind for him to create for this goddess a divine function for which there is no basis of any kind in Teutonic beliefs. In the *Ring* it is Freia who becomes the cultivator and the guardian of the Apples of Eternal Youth. This is the fruit whose magic allowed the gods to be ever-youthful. Wagner was aware that in the myths of the Germanic peoples it was not Freia who watched over these treasured apples, but rather *Idun*, the wife of Bragi, the God of Poetry. Idun guarded these valued fruits in a small chest.

Idun is not one of the more prominent deities of the Teutonic hierarchy. Her name, which means "One who renews," is found in only one poem of *The Poetic Edda*. In *The Prose Edda* she is called a goddess although she is not one of those deities who meets in council daily at the World Ash Tree, there to make judgments and decisions for the world. In this latter work, Idun figures in one tale in which she and the apples that she guards are abducted by the giant Thjazi. Deprived of their source of youth, the gods are greatly concerned. They approach Loge, who ultimately rescues the goddess and returns her and the apples to the worried gods.

Wagner never explained, or did he offer his reasons for investing the guardianship of Teutondom's magic apples with his Freia. Some students of the *Ring* have proposed that such an arrangement allowed the composer a convenient means by which he could achieve a greater dramatic and thematic unity within his poem without the need to introduce yet another figure in an already large *dramatis personae*. Others advance the idea that the apples of Teutondom and their magic represent a kind of fruitfulness, a mythical attribute that is much more easily associated with Freia than with Idun. It is also possible that Wagner sensed that such a guardianship as that which he had created enhanced the aura of divine significance that surrounded his goddess, a dramatic veil which, in turn, increased the import of her role in his story. Whatever the reasons, the Freia of the *Ring*, if not the Freia of Teutonic mythology, is the Goddess of the Golden Apples, and together the pair functions as a fundamental aspect of Wagner's tale of the gods and the giants. Wagner's created mythology is seldom noted, and then only by scholars of the myths. Indeed, the Wagner touch is not the least out of place.

Wagner was not, however, to restrict himself to Idun as the only figure from whom he would draw for the development of his goddess Freia. It would seem that Wagner apparently felt that the Freia of his *Ring*, even with the added guardianship of the magic fruit of Teutondom that he had given her, still lacked the divine presence that she obviously had in mythical thought. The composer wished to intensify that presence, and to that end he turned to yet another figure prominent as well as popular in the beliefs of the people. This second figure was not, like Idun, a Teutonic goddess, and it was not her function or principal activity that garnered his attention. In the main, it was the figure's attributes that attracted him. This second figure was *Holda*.

Wagner introduces the Freia-Holda association in the second scene of *Das Rheingold*. Fasolt, the giant, is speaking about Freia, and at one point he says:

> "Freia, die Holde,
> Holda, die Freie."
> ("Freia, the lovely one,
> Holda, the gracious one.")

(In these two lines Wagner, of course, is making a subtle play on the words *Holde* and *Holda* He uses the former, which is an adjective, as a substantive to equate with the figure's name. This linguistic identification of Freia and Holda as one and the same being is stated in other terms in the story, when Fafner remarks about the sheen of Holda's (Freia's) hair, and later in the drama when Freia calls herself by this second name, Holda.)

Holda is the German name for a figure that is frequently found in the numerous traditional tales and stories that circulated throughout Teutondom by means of the oral tradition. In other Germanic tongues this figure was known as *Hulda*, *Halle*, and *Hulle*, and there are extant a few tales in which she appears as *Frau Holl*. In the Nordic regions, where she is called *Hulle*, this being's activity was essentially singular in that she presided over cattle, and it was believed that she often visited the pastures in which herdsmen watched over their animals. This activity as well as the name stemmed directly from the Gothic word *haldan*, which meant to oversee cattle and to guard them as they grazed in the fields, and the Old Icelandic *halda*, which meant "to graze" in the sense of leading cattle to pasture. A derivation of these root words, with related meanings, was also used in both Old English and Middle English. Modern English retains the word in the form of "to hold," with one of its several meanings --"to restrain," that is, "to keep back" or "to stay" -- only faintly suggestive of the original meaning of "to guard." (Neither the word *Hulle* nor the figure she represents appears in Eddic literature although there is reference made in *The Prose Edda* to a *Huldr* who is a "wise-woman" or "prophetess".)

The popularity of the figure Holda was much greater and indeed more extensive in the southern region of Teutondom. In this area, of which Germany is the largest section, Holda participated in several distinct activities. In some sections of the region she was viewed as a wife who presided over the cultivation of flax, and who then used that flax in her spinning. In other areas, it was believed that Holda was a fair, white lady who could be observed at noon as she bathed in the waters of lakes and waterfalls. It was also believed that mortals could reach her dwelling only by passing through the waters. Viewed in this manner, Holda occasionally was called "Goddess of the Water-Springs," although the term *goddess* did not infer "divinity" as with the deities of Teutondom. In still other parts of the southern region Holda rode about in a wagon from which she caused the snow to fall, much as Donner brought on the rain. Despite her widespread popularity, Holda played no part in the folklore of Saxony, Bavaria, Austria or Switzerland.

Notwithstanding the several linguistic variations on her name, and the individual but distinct functions that she performed in separate geographic regions, Holda manifested certain attributes that were common to her wherever she was part of the culture. First, and above all else, Holda was a young creature, and very lovely to look upon. Her attractiveness was enhanced by the attractive blue garment and the delicate white veil that she always wore. Holda was kindly disposed to people, which apparently made her more attractive in the people's minds. According to the beliefs, Holda also boasted a merciful spirit and she was of a joyful nature, joyful at all times that is except when she was witness to some disorder or disturbance in household affairs. At such times, this quaint figure from folklore could be most insistent. Finally, Holda loved music and she was given to song.

The folkloric depiction of the northern *Hulle* and the Southern *Holda* are quite distinct despite the historical fact that in the earliest of times they were really one and the same figure, and the variations of their names are really developments from a single original root word. It is obvious that the northern figure came to embody, in one or another way, the Gothic or the Old Icelandic meanings of the name, as evidenced through association with cattle. On the other hand, the Southern figure -- with the same root word as the basis for her name -- held no importance for a single or special kind of activity. In the south of Teutondom, Holda's functions were less specialized and tended to vary from one area to another. It is apparent that the culture that was a part of southern Teutondom not only gave more emphasis to the Holda character, but it also showed more concern for the figure itself. If the northern peoples seemed to dwell on Hulle's activities, the southern peoples directed their attention more to Holda's physical nature, to the loveliness of her figure, to the sweetness of her character. This southern attitude reflected much more than simply a superficial concept; it bespoke what was really an ingrained pattern of societal thought. Holda's attractiveness, in time, became synonymous with her name, and the word that had given that name then took on the meanings of 'beauty' and 'charm' and 'graciousness,' attributes that could be applied in situations in which the figure herself did not appear as well as in situations that were unrelated to her. Thus it was that the Old German words *holt* and the Middle High German *holt* and *hold* came to mean "lovely" or "gracious" or "true" in the sense of *faithful*. The modern German *hold* (feminine *holde*) retains these meanings, and the ancient concept continues to manifest itself in contemporary times.

Wagner was quick to sense that the German concepts of the ancient Holda could help him to enhance the nature of his goddess Freia. He understood the matter of Holda's beauty, and he recognized the admiration and respect that this German figure held among the people. He also saw in the Holda figure a cordiality, a gentility, and a tenderness that most naturally complemented the nature of his Freia. These two figures, the folkloric Holda and the mythical Freia, became for Wagner essentially one and the same, and thus, Holda, if only in a secondary manner, became a part of his monumental drama.

There is a question that almost naturally comes to mind regarding Wagner's use of the Holda figure as an enhancement of the characterization of the goddess Freia. In view of his tale of gods and Valkyries, of giants and dwarves and Norns, that is, a tale of and about the powerful supernaturals of the Teutonic mythical world, why did Wagner choose to include a popular figure as a part of his story? Certainly, Holda makes no contribution to the thematic progress of the *Ring*. Her name is mentioned, without any form of dramatic buildup, and then, just as quickly as she appeared, she vanishes from the story. Holda is not a divine figure, and neither does she have any association with deities, with their activities, or --for that matter -- with any of the other supernatural figures that populate the heathen Germanic universe. Holda has no divine function. Neither does she have any role in the rituals and practices of the people. Holda has no place at all in the heathen Teutonic religious thought. Holda is nothing more or nothing less than a figure of folklore, a popular being who takes form and substance only in cultural manners and conduct, never in the essence of religious belief and concept. In that light, Holda is hardly the type to mix with the gods, hardly the type to have anything to do with their activities, or to be involved in the serious ways of Wotan and his cohorts. There is, then, no dramatic cause, nor is there a thematic reason for the existence of the figure Holda in the *Ring*!

In view of all that has been discussed regarding the existence of Holda in German folklore and the total absence of such a figure in Germanic mythology, and in light of the thoroughly mythical nature of the *Ring*, the question remains: Why did Richard Wagner bring Holda into his drama? The answer to such a question becomes quite readily available when the numerous analyses of Wagner's allegorical or philosophical intentions in the work are put to one side and a different approach to the *Ring* is taken, a search into the ideas and views that Wagner had about language and linguistic style, or perhaps linguistic technique. As in most matters that related to music-drama, Wagner had definite, indeed fixed ideas about language and its use in the dramatic composition of that art. Among other things, Wagner steadfastly maintained that alliteration, either external or internal, was an especially effective language when a more immediate or possibly a more intense reaction to a given speech, statement, or special dialogue was desired. He argued that alliteration caused attention to become more focused, that the emphasis desired was achieved automatically and therefore additional dialogue was not necessary.

Wagner resorted to alliterative language quite frequently throughout his drama. The short speech that he gave to Fasolt, that dialogue that introduces Holda into the *Ring*, is one such example. Wagner wrote:

"Freia, die Holde,
Holda, die Freie."

Although Fasolt's words are not an alliteration in the strictest semantic sense, they adequately represent the technique that Wagner deemed so important. In the example at hand, Wagner had found that the German language offered him several appropriate words that he could manipulate and with which, at the same time, he could develop the alliterative sounds that he sought. Obviously, in the composition of this dialogue, he realized that there was a certain compatibility in the Freia-Holda relationship that allowed his language to have meaning as well as effect. He understood that the nature of each figure complemented that of the other, and that these natures meshed sufficiently to allow an acceptable fusion of the two beings, hence the subtle play with words could be readily accepted. It was, then, not so much a matter of mythology or legend, or even folklore, that stirred Wagner to associate these two beings from distinct Germanic pasts. Rather, it was simply an inviting convenience that his language allowed him. He did not hesitate to make use of that language, even though he was aware that with his words he was actually creating his own mytho-folkloric depiction.

In the full form that Freia is found in Wagner's *Ring*, she is really something more than the cherished deity of Teutondom. She is, of course, the lovely goddess so coveted by the foremost enemies of the gods, the giants. She is also, however, Idun, the guardian of the magic apples of the gods. She is also the delicate creature who was Holda in German folklore. Wagner's Freia is, then, a trio of beings, a dramatic blend of three separate and distinct figures that the composer drew from German cultural and mythical history. There are those who would severely fault Wagner for his dramatic treatment of these beings, for what they consider to be his disregard for mythological and folkloric fact. These persons maintain that Wagner's actions produce an impure view of the Teutonic past. There are, however, those who vigorously support the composer's actions and defend his concept. These persons view the Freia of the *Ring* not so much as an altered view of Teutonic mythology but rather as a true representation of the creative genius mind of Richard Wagner.

II

FRICKA

The word *Fricka*, as a name, is the modern German word that developed out of the Old Norse *Frigg* (AS -*Fricq*; OHG - *Fricc, Frikk, Frikka, Frikkia*). It is by the Nordic name that the goddess is known in the Teutonic mythical literature which includes both the verse and the prose *Eddas*. Although there seems to be some confusion in the matter, numerous scholars maintain that it is the *Frigg/Fricka* name that early on became attached to the day of the week that in Teutonic languages honors this goddess: *Friday* in modern English, and *Freitag* in modern German. In ON the day was known as *Friadagr*, in AS it was *Frigedaeq*, and in MHG the day was called *Fritac*. It was, in turn, this same word -- *Frigg* -- that was linguistically related to the name of a supernatural being of greater antiquity, *Fjorgynn*, which means literally "Earth-Mother." This latter name was applied, if infrequently, to Fricka, who was thus looked upon as 'earth mother' in that she was the mother of the gods through her relationship with Wotan, who in turn was without question "Father of the Gods," and who, on occasion, was called *Fjorgyn*.

Linguistic matters aside, there is a rather curious paradox that emerges from the ancient Teutonic religious thought regarding the celebrated goddess Fricka. This figure is the ranking goddess of all Teutondom, a deity who is called the "foremost of goddesses" in *The Prose Edda*. This being is the principal goddess of all the goddesses throughout all of a vast geographical area, and yet, incredible as it may seem, mythical beliefs clearly show that Fricka actually had no cult of her own, and further, she was a goddess who was neither worshipped nor invoked!

It is true that the intensity of worship of some of the Germanic gods varied from region to region. It is also mythical fact that certain of the Teutonic deities were worshipped and invoked in certain specific regions, and those same deities, in the extreme, could be all but ignored in other Teutonic areas. These mythical facts are equally applicable even to the three major gods, the supreme *Triad* of Teutonic divinities, Wotan, Donner, and Froh. But, in the matter of Fricka, none of the above can be directly applied to her and her divine position simply because Fricka was more a goddess in name than a true divine being in the early heathen Germanic index of religious beliefs and practices.

It is important as well as necessary to note that Fricka was a constituent member of the early Germanic divine hierarchy. It should also be noted that her godhood was universal throughout all of the ancient Teutonic territory. Her divine appearances were acknowledged, and her godly functions were clearly understood and accepted. There was no question as to the existence, the position, and the functions of this primary goddess of Teutondom. Yet, despite her status as the preeminent goddess of the Teutonic world, as the ranking goddess of Teutondom, despite her divine presence among all the tribes and clans of Teutondom, despite her sharply defined divine activities, and despite her apparent exclusive recognition as "Mother of the Gods," the Germanic peoples never developed a ritual cult for Fricka as they had for other goddesses, all of whom were of an acknowledged lesser divine rank and status. Neither did these ancient peoples develop specific religious practices or rituals by means of which they demonstrated their beliefs in her powers, and neither did these people seek the blessings and benefits of those powers. In short, Fricka was at once the most powerful of goddesses, but she was a goddess without the necessary following that allowed her to act and to function as a true deity.

This unique paradox, that is, the situation of an esteemed and revered goddess who does not truly function as a goddess, is clearly evidenced throughout all of the Teutonic mythical literature. Such a picture is especially evident in the primary source for all study of Teutonic mythology, *The Poetic Edda*. In this major work Fricka wanders at length through the stanzas and poems about the gods, she speaks and she acts and reacts, and she is called frequently by name. Her attributes, her qualities, and her divine functions are amply delineated in this literature. Yet, in the final word, it must be said that the role that Fricka plays in the divine matters of the universe can easily be termed not only as a minor one, but really as an insignificant one.

Although it can be readily acknowledge that Fricka suffered a lack of fundamental import within early Teutonic religious beliefs, the mythical literature presents a rather extensive picture of this goddess, including her relationships within the divine hierarchy as well as her divine functions as perceived in the early Germanic views of the universe. First, and perhaps foremost of all else regarding the godhood of this interesting deity, was her relationship to the supreme god, Wotan, that is her relationship to him as *wife*. As could be expected, this relationship quite naturally facilitated and even fomented the previously mentioned concept of Fricka as 'earth mother,' a concept that suggested that she was a kind of female counterpart to the *Allfather*, but a concept that never became truly manifest.

The relationship of Fricka as wife to Wotan did not grant the goddess powers equal to those of her husband. This relationship, however, did create for her a status or rank that placed her in the forefront of all other goddesses. Rather than divine powers that would seem necessary to complement such rank, the heathen Germanic culture invested Fricka with capacities and functions that were singular and unique to her elevated godhood. While it is true, for example, that several of the other gods were gifted with the capacity to know the fate of this or that individual or group of individuals, the fate of this or that item in nature, it was Fricka alone who knew the fate of *all* living things. Possessed of this capability, it was then of no wonder that even the great god Wotan constantly sought out his wife and her knowledge as he persistently and actively attempted to garner the wisdom of the universe. (It should be noted here that despite this gift of special knowledge, Fricka did not prophesy, and further, at such times as Wotan consulted with his wife, it was not unusual for a heated argument to develop between the two.) It was because of Fricka's knowledge of the fate of all living things that *The Prose Edda* designates her as a *goddess-judge*, one of the twelve divine beings who regularly met at the World Ash Tree, there to make the decisions regarding the universe and to determine the destiny of all things in that universe.

Fricka was like all the other major gods of the early Germanic religious thought in that she resided in her own personal residence. The name of Fricka's dwelling was *Fensalir*, which Snorri Sturluson describes as "most magnificent." The word *Fensalir* translates as "sea halls," and such a meaning has caused some scholars to conclude that the name of Fricka's abode symbolized the setting of the sun each day on the ocean horizon. This mythical idea, in turn, has prompted some students to consider the possibility that Fricka was a sea-goddess. Although there may be some linguistic foundation regarding the concept of the word Fensalir and its relation to the seas and oceans, there is nothing in Fricka's character, in her nature, or in her numerous and varied activities that suggest or even infer that she was a goddess who had a relationship with water in any of its forms, or who was taken up by matters of the oceans.

There are other mythical factors, in addition to a special knowledge and a magnificent mansion, that signal the elevated divine rank that was accorded Fricka. A principal matter in this regard is the mythical fact that Fricka was served by handmaidens. Among all the goddesses of Teutondom, Fricka is the only deity who enjoys this attention, and such singularity unequivocally points to the very special godhood of this divine being. The first of the servants to attend Fricka is *Fulla*, a handmaiden recognized as such in both of the *Eddas*. In *The Prose Edda*, Sturluson writes that Fulla is, herself, a goddess, and -- in addition -- that she, like her mistress, is a goddess-judge. Sturluson elaborates on Fulla by describing her as a virgin who wore her hair loose and had a golden band around her head. (These latter aspects regarding Fulla have little mythical significance, and are mentioned here only as a means of presenting what is the most extensive description of any of the divine beings that is to be found in all of the Teutonic mythical literature.) Fulla's duties, at least according to *The Prose Edda*, were to care for Fricka's shoes and to carry her "little box." Presumably, the latter held the jewelry for which Fricka is known to have been quite fond.

There is one additional aspect about Fulla that merits inclusion here. The matter contributes to some mythical speculation because, unforunately, the statement found in the literature is not only brief and succinct, but also there is no further mythical depiction or elaboration. The statement that is so enigmatic yet so provocative is that which reveals that Fulla, a handmaiden to the ranking goddess of Teutondom, *knew and was well acquainted with all the secrets of her mistress*!

A second handmaiden to Fricka is *Gna*. Sturluson writes that Gna, like Fulla, was a goddess, although this being -- if indeed she existed in mythical beliefs -- is not mentioned or referred to in any of the tales that are part of *The Poetic Edda*. In view of Sturluson's persuasion by the Christian thought that was then overcoming northern Teutondom, and his resultant hesitant, but nevertheless somewhat indifferent, view and presentation of the Teutonic gods and other related heathen religious matters, some scholars have advanced the idea that Gna is really not a servant to Fricka, but rather another name of the goddess herself. In any event, Gna's only charge -- at least according to *The Prose Edda* -- was to go on errands for Fricka, a task that she accommplished by means of a horse that ran through the air and over the sea.

Sturluson mentions yet another servant to Fricka. This third handmaiden is called *Hlin*, a name that is found in each of the two Eddic writings. *The Prose Edda* refers to Hlin, as it had with Gna, as a goddess, although *The Poetic Edda* speaks of Hlin not as a goddess, and not even as a handmaiden to the first goddess of Teutondom, but rather as yet another name for Fricka herself. The question of Hlin's status in ancient Teutonic mythology, that is, as a handmaiden to the most important of the Germanic goddesses, as a goddess in her own right, or simply as another name for Fricka, is relatively unimportant when one takes note of the duty or charge that mythical beliefs gave her to carry out. It was Hlin's divine obligation to offer protection to those select men whom Fricka wished to save from danger! (As will be noted later, this divine function will lend substantial support to the idea that the name of Hlin is really more of a second name for Fricka than that of a separate divine being.)

The matter of the number of Fricka's handmaidens is, by any rationale, of little significance. There is nothing of mythical importance to be noted or even to be gained from an attempt to determine if Fricka had one, two, or perhaps three handmaidens. What bears recognition and merits consideration is the mythical fact that there is associated with the goddess the *concept* of personal servants, a concept and a belief that is unique and singular to Fricka alone, a belief that is never associated with any of the other goddesses of Teutondom! If nothing more, such a mythical fact will strengthen the view and give added credulity to the view of Fricka as the supreme goddess of the early Teutonic peoples.

Among other early Teutonic beliefs attached to Fricka were those that held that the goddess possessed certain divine magic that allowed her to exercise control over some routine matters of society life. Such beliefs are very much in the pattern of heathen Germanic religious thought which placed each of its gods in a mortal form and then caused each to move about in an existence that essentially duplicated that of human life but which was, always, on a plane greater than the life of man. Thus it was that the gods of Teutondom were able to bring about or to achieve certain numerous and diverse ends or results by means of specific powers that they held, powers that mankind was incapable of exercising, controlling, or effecting. Fricka's magic, if indeed 'magic' is the proper word to apply to her divine function, was related to *marriage*, and indirectly, to children who were born through marriage. Some scholars of Teutonic mythology believe that Fricka's magic was that of simply administering the oaths of marriage. The mythical literature is not entirely clear in this regard, but the inferences throughout the Eddic writings seem to convey more the idea that the goddess is really a presider over marriage, that is the guardian of such vows, rather than their administrator. Viewed in this manner, it can be said that Fricka was the Goddess of Marriage, or, perhaps, Goddess of Wedding Vows.

There is ample if indirect evidence to support the idea that Fricka was indeed the Goddess of Marriage. The literature speaks of men and women who are about to marry and who seek (but not invoke) Fricka's blessings on their union. However, in one of the poems of *The Poetic Edda* it is from a certain *Vor* that a blessing on a marriage is sought. Most scholars are agreed that this Vor is not a second goddess of marriage, but rather, like Hlin and Gna, another name for Fricka. In other situations that are presented in the Eddic poetry there are those believers who are already married but who implore a resolution by Fricka because they are experiencing difficulties in their union. Even childless couples occasionally called upon Fricka to intervene in their dilemma, to request that the goddess allow them to have children. In some regions of Teutondom, those few areas in which it was believed that Fricka could heal wounds, children that had been born of marriage were often taught to beseech the goddess to cure them of their illnesses.

The mythical association of Fricka with marriage was a concept that was universal throughout all of the heathen Germanic world. It was, however, also a belief that, in time, expanded beyond the single idea that made her the divine guardian of marriage, beyond even the belief that Fricka was the deity who protected the sanctity of the union of man and woman. This second facet of Fricka's godhood was a kind of tangential matter, the result of those activities that were biologically innate to mankind, but which most cultures tend to associate naturally with marriage.

This additional feature of the Fricka godhood was concerned with sexual intercourse! It must be understood that this aspect regarding the nature of the Goddess of Marriage was really more folkloric in character, that is, a popular consideration among certain strata of Germanic societies, rather than a sensitive manifestation of serious religious belief. It was because of this folkloric quality of the matter that mythologists have tended to avoid its consideration, or -- if the subject comes to the fore -- to give it only passing mention. Reference to this coloration of the Fricka domain is appropriate here, however, not only because the related beliefs were so widespread throughout the early Teutonic culture, but also because they were somehow so persistent throughout the centuries that there are certain remnants extant yet today, in our modern-day English-speaking culture. Then too, there is also the possibility, or is it probability, that this feature of the character of Fricka had some effect on her development as Wagner brought her into his *Ring*.

The inference that Fricka was the deity most concerned with sexual intercourse is projected more by linguistic evidence than it is by literary matters. Although there are isolated passages in the Eddic writings that touch upon the subject, some of which make pointed reference to Fricka's sexual behavior, the linguistic matters clearly show that Fricka is at least the divine overseer of physical love, if not its goddess or guardian. This linguistic evidence takes the form of words and terms, some of which continue in use in modern English, that are derived or developed out of Fricka's name and which are popularly sexual in meaning. The Nordic name for this goddess, -- *Frigg* -- and her southern name -- *Fricka* --, both of which are doublets of *Frico*, have as their root word the proto Indo-European *prij* ("love"). (This is the same term that allowed for the development of *Preapus*, the name of the god in Asia Minor who was charged with male generative powers.)

It is out of the northern and southern names for the goddess that no less than three separate English terms developed. Each of these words, semantically, is overtly sexual in nature, each is an acknowledged vulgarism, and each has made a heavy imprint in the culture of the English-speaking peoples. The first of these words is directly related to the Nordic name for the goddess and is found today in modern English as the verb *to frig*. This word, considered to be quite obscene in some areas, is used in the United States to mean 'to perform the sex act,' or 'to copulate with.' British English more often gives the verb the meaning of 'to masturbate.' A second but related word also developed along with the verb form: this is the term *frigging*, which is used both as an adjective and as an expletive, and always with a vulgar sexual connotation. These two terms became quite ingrained in the language and culture and they remain there today although the passage of time and repeated usage over the years has diminished somewhat the unlimited vulgarity they once conveyed. Today, these two words are thought of more as slang than as vulgarities.

The third of this trio of obscenities that is related to the name of Teutonic Goddess of Marriage is that term that shows a definite linguistic relationship with the southern or German form of her name, that is, *Fricka*. The English word is *prick*, a vulgarity meaning "penis," which was found in Old English as *prica*, in Middle English as *prikka*, and as *pric* in Middle Dutch. (The semantic as well as morphological relationship of this word to the proto Indo-European *prij*, meaning "love," is obvious.)

There seems to be little difficulty in reasoning, or at least surmising, how each of these three terms with sexual connotations developed with an obvious relationship to the principal goddess of Teutondom. In the first regard, societies have always viewed the physical union of man and woman as an act that has a direct and primary association with marriage. In many regions of the contemporary world, a marriage is not considered legal unless and until the marriage vows are consummated. Thus, there was in Fricka's godhood a natural, and indeed, an expected association and relationship with the physical act that is acknowledged to be the true fulfillment and execution of the marriage vows. Yet, at the same time, the act of sexual intercourse has always aroused scatological interests, prurient concerns that tend to concentrate on the act itself. These considerations have given rise to physical gestures by means of distinct parts of the body, to vocal utterances, and to specific language, all of which in one way or another make reference to the act of sexual intercourse. Most of these expressions have been of a coarse nature, and, in the course of time, have been excluded from the accepted social conduct of societies. Many, however, have remained and continued in use in one form or another, in one or another groups of each culture. It would be logical to assume that any, or at least some of these expressions, whether of accepted or of less than tasteful interpretation, would find some link with the deity involved with marriage. That Fricka was that deity makes her, in a sense, a most suitable figure on which or around which to base such conduct. At the same time, the situation becomes more tempting when one understands that the goddess herself behaved at times in a manner that may be viewed in modern terms as sexually arousing, and, further, the myths reveal that this goddess was known to have had sexual relations with gods and supernatural figures other than her husband Wotan. Indeed, there was something more than the tinge of promiscuity in Fricka's divine conduct, there was a conduct that obviously attracted an outward black, and less than savory sexual attitude.

The evidence of erotic thought in the Teutonic myths takes several forms, but in the case of Fricka, there is a broad inference, indeed even the open accusation that she is a sexually promiscuous goddess. This less inviting aspect of Fricka's activities, all of which is displayed within the Teutonic divine framework, can be envisioned most easily by means of a poem that is found in *The Poetic Edda*. The poem, which has been given the title "Lokasenna" ("Loge's Wrangling"), is certainly not the most carnal of the Eddic poems, yet there is a certain definite sensuality that surfaces as the tale progresses. Aegir, a sea-deity, prepares a great feast for the gods. At the festivities, Loge slays one of Aegir's servants, and because of that act he is then driven away, into the forest. The malevolent fire-spirit returns, enters Aegir's hall, and begins to speak in a heated tone about the gods, referring to each one and recounting certain of the past activities of each. When he focuses on Fricka, the malicious demigod accuses her of having been the bed-partner of each of her husband's two brothers, Vili and Ve. Fricka offers no denial of Loge's accusation, although it would seem that she had anticipated something of the sort when she witnessed a heated exchange between Loge and Wotan, and then had counseled that it was better to leave unsaid the stories about what dark deeds each may have done in the past! "Old tales should n'er be told," she cautioned. There is no way to know if Fricka's words are offered as wise counsel, or if they were spoken with the intent to keep secret her past activities. Regardless of whatever purpose Fricka's words may have had, Loge's revealing remarks associate the goddess with a certain eroticism that blends easily with the popular concepts of the relationship of the goddess and sexual intercourse. That Loge's revelation is not merely an isolated remark, or one made in a moment of intense anger, is attested by the fact that the substance of this tale is repeated by Sturluson in his *Ynglinga Saga*, a work that became the opening section of the Icelander's larger masterpiece *Heimskringla*. Sturluson writes that Fricka became the mistress of Vili and Ve during a protracted absence of Wotan, who was traveling at length about the universe in his never-ending search for knowledge and wisdom. Sturluson adds, however, that when the supreme god returned from his journey, he accepted Fricka back as his wife. (It is this incident in Fricka's behavior that has caused mythologists to conclude that *Hlin*, previously mentioned as a possible handmaiden to Fricka, is really another name for Fricka because it was Hlin's duty to protect those men that Fricka has wished to save from danger, and that such an act was one that was actually carried out by Fricka herself in order that she could indulge in continuous sexual pleasures.)

The association of Fricka and base sexual matters was more easily achieved in the heathen Teutonic society than perhaps it might have been in other cultures. The manner in which these early people viewed their gods definitely allowed for a broad, if not unlimited interpretation of divine activities. As has been mentioned earlier, the ancient Germanic culture endowed its gods with a physical makeup that was not unlike that of man. Although it can be said that the gods of many other societies also have been seen as having human form, those of Teutondom were not only human in their physical presentation, but they existed as an extension of mankind itself in that they displayed a nature that was basically identical in character and structure to that of man. Thus it was that the gods of Teutondom were not really supernatural beings who were capable of effecting what might be termed the "marvelous" or even the "miraculous." Rather they were divine beings whose human abilities were simply larger and greater than the equivalents in mortal life. Teutonic godhood lay rooted in the belief that the deities realized matters that were essentially a part of the human experience -- or at least those that the people considered to be a part of their experience -- but which were matters man himself was incapable of achieving or attaining. The Teutonic gods were essentially human, but of a more perfected character; they were deities whose positive qualities exemplified the fantasies of mankind, but they were gods who, like man, also had negative qualities. In the overall view, the gods of Teutondom led lives that duplicated human life, but -- at the same time -- they were gods that were possessed of powers that man considered natural to himself but which were just beyond his physical or mental reach. Thus it is that the early Teutonic gods ate, slept, talked, laughed, and cried, but they also brought about rain and lightning and thunder. The gods of Teutondom felt pain and sorrow, but they also changed from one guise to another, at times by means of their own will and at other times by means of some external magic. The Germanic gods loved and hated, they became angry, they waged war, but unlike man they gained their victories through the magic of their weapons rather than by means of a warrior's skill. These gods, like men, had been born, they married, they conceived and they bore children, and they were destined to die. Fricka was one of these gods: her divinity was her supernatural guardianship of marriage, a condition in which the sex act is primary. It was by a natural analogy, then, that her name came to be associated with that act in its purely sexual context, and the linguistic manifestations of that association naturally came into existence as expressions of heathen Teutonic societal thought and culture.

With human life as the pattern for the existence of the Teutonic gods, it was a natural step from the husband-wife relationship of many of the deities to that of parenthood. Fricka and Wotan were no exception to this accepted belief. Unfortunately, the mythical literature is often unclear as to the figure who bore certain of Wotan's children, but there is one being of the Teutonic divine hierarchy about whose mythical parenthood there is no doubt. This figure, this acknowledged and recognized son of the supreme god and the primary goddess of Teutondom, is Balder.

Balder was the favorite son of Fricka, and he was much beloved by Wotan. This god was a soft-spoken god, always merciful in his affairs, and he was to become the most respected divine being of all Teutondom. Balder was destined, however, to have but a brief existence, at least a brief existence in the divine world of Wotan and the other gods. Early in his life, Balder suffered an untimely death. This god's demise came about at the hands of his blind brother, Hod, who killed the god by hurling a sprig of mistletoe through his body. (In the death of Balder, Hod, -- whose mother is unnamed in mythical literature -- was the innocent victim of the cunning Loge.) Balder's death caused great sorrow throughout the land of the gods. Fricka was beside herself and Wotan was extremely angered. If the Allfather vigorously sought the return of his son, he also desired to avenge his death. When Wotan learned of Balder's death, he begat a son with Rind. (Rind is named as a goddess in *The Prose Edda*.) This son was named Vali, and his mission was to seek out and to slay Hod. (The death of Balder is viewed as the first of a series of disasters in the universe that ultimately resulted in the downfall of the gods. Curiously, both Balder and Hod are 'raised,' survive the destruction of the gods, and then live in the new world, but removed from all evil and corruption.)

Such, then, is the composite depiction of the goddess Fricka as presented in the two *Eddas*. It would be from this total picture that Wagner would draw what he considered to be the significant features and qualities for the Fricka of his *Ring*. It is obvious to the student of both Wagner's drama and the Eddic writings that the composer was selective in the matter of the divine attributes that he wove into the role of this deity. For those who give serious consideration to the Fricka figure in the drama, it is equally evident that Wagner's choices were directed by what he considered features and qualities that were complementary to the character as a dramatic figure, and, at the same time, complementary to the thematic development of the story that he had created for the gods.

In the matter of Wagner's Fricka, that is, the nature of the goddess as she moves in and about the *Ring*, it is perhaps prudent to indicate from the outset the minimal number of mythical beliefs that seemed to be of little or no dramatic or thematic value to the composer as he developed this deity as part of the drama's *dramatis personae*. First, Wagner envisioned no need whatsoever to involve his goddess with children, and neither did he note a need that she be served by handmaidens. Such activities would not further his thematic cause. If he gave thought to Fricka's mythical activity as a goddess-judge, it was no doubt only minimal consideration, because it would be to the Allfather Wotan that he would grant the power to make determinations and decisions. It was imperative that this activity lie within the parameters of Wotan's forces because it was to be a decision of the supreme god that sets into motion the major developments of the drama.

Wagner also rejected Fricka as Earth Mother. He realized that such a concept merited inclusion in his drama. After all, such a belief was basic to a culture that existed in what may be called a nature-oriented ambience. Yet, for his own theatrical reasons, he disallowed Fricka this concern and created his own figure, his Erda, to be the 'mother of all things.'

The rejection by the dramatist of these few mythical qualities of the goddess Fricka automatically infers that he allowed each of the other numerous beliefs associated with the goddess to figure in the total character that would evolve in the *Ring*. Such is true if the profundity of each feature is not brought into question. Wagner knew, for example, that in the myths Fricka is only seldom, if ever, concerned with relative substantial matters, those matters that required divine action or judgment by the gods, and he was also aware that her appearances in mythical literature are relatively few. He thus restricted Fricka's involvement in *Ring* matters to what is essentially only one major thematic element, that of attempting to protect the vows of marriage which she believed were broken by the Siegmund-Sieglinde relationship, and he limited her appearances to only three of the drama's thirty-six scenes.

Wagner believed that the mythical relationship of Wotan and Fricka, that is as husband and wife, was imperative to his drama. Although he would not give parenthood to the couple, he did expand on the matter of familial relationships by giving Fricka certain ties that had not existed in the myths. In the *Ring* the goddess becomes a sister to Donner, Freia, and Froh, and these four then were made cousins to Loge. It would seem that Wagner believed that this brother-sister arrangement would enhance the idea of dramatic unity of thought among the gods and also make more pointed the gods' concern for Freia when she is detained by the giants. The exact reason for Wagner's decision to make Loge a cousin to the four gods has never been offered. It may have been that Wagner sensed that some kind of relationship of the six major supernaturals would make the dramatic unity of his poem even more intact and compact.

Wagner had sensed early on that Fricka's elevated position within the divine hierarchy of early Germanic religious thought had been due, in large part, to her status as Goddess of Marriage. If, at first, such a charge might be viewed as somewhat awkward if not difficult to weave into the argument that he envisioned, it would soon become a matter that he would use to great advantage as he went about developing the argument of his drama, converting it -- as he did -- to a substantive theme. It is in the opening moments of the second act of *Die Walküre* that Fricka identifies herself as the custodian of marriage ("Ehe Hüterin"), after which she defends most forcefully the sacredness of the wedded state. Then, it is with equal vigor that she decries her husband's sexual union with a mortal woman, the result of which was the origin of the Volsung clan. The goddess proclaims that the offspring of that relationship, the brother-sister pair of Siegmund and Sieglinde, are the "sensual fruit of sin," and she further declares that the incestuous union of that pair is an evil that violates her sacred charge. A careful examination of the substance of Fricka's words reveals that the concern is only slightly associated with early Teutonic beliefs, and even then, of scant significance. In fact, both of Fricka's allegations are really foreign to the heathen Teutonic concept of acceptable personal conduct. The myths of ancient Teutondom frequently tell of extramarital activities, with only minor concerns being shown, and, further, the act of physical love between brother and sister is recorded in the Eddic and saga literature without the slightest hint of incestuous stain. Thus it is that all that Fricka has criticized is not early Germanic in essence, but rather a product of Wagner's own dramatic thought, and, in a broader sense, exemplary of the Christian thought that abounded in nineteenth-century Germany. This fusion of the heathen goddess and matters that were completely acceptable to Wagner's contemporary society was one of the composer's methods of drawing a public into the exposition of his drama and, at the same time, causing that public to view his Fricka as a goddess of elevated dignity as well as a force that should be recognized and considered with all seriousness. There can be no doubt that Wagner's dramatic plan was a success.

The presentation of Fricka as the guardian of the marriage vows is, at one and the same time, a reflection of mythical reality and a thematic means by which Wagner could invest his goddess with yet another of her counterpart's qualities. As has been stated earlier, Eddic literature shows the goddess to be capable of offering protection to those whom she believed to be in danger. (The literature reveals that this protection was Fricka's through her handmaiden, Hlin, although it is entirely possible that the word *Hlin* is merely another name for the goddess, in which case it is the goddess herself who has this power.) Wagner, the dramatist, was careful to incorporate this quality into his Fricka, if only in a most subtle manner. As Goddess of Marriage, it is natural that Fricka deem the love-bond between Siegmund and Sieglinde as wrong and evil as well as an affront to Sieglinde's legitimate husband, Hunding. The goddess is aware that Hunding will seek to avenge the wrong that has been done him, and that such action will be in the form of a physical confrontation with Siegmund. In Fricka's eyes, the offended husband faces an obvious danger. The goddess then seeks out Wotan, who is responsible for the present state of affairs, and asks that he withhold his divine aid from the Volsung at such time as he and Hunding will face each other. Wotan at first refuses his wife's plea, but Fricka then forcefully details the situation and demands her husband's word that he will do as she asks. Wotan hears Fricka's words, and he understands the truths that she speaks, that by allowing this brother-sister union he has violated the criteria that govern moral mortal existence. Although it goes strongly against his will, Wotan is thus forced to succumb to his wife's arguments. The Allfather then reluctantly orders that Siegmund be given no aid when Hunding seeks to avenge his honor. Readers of the *Ring* are well aware that in the combat that takes place, Wotan ultimately fulfills his word, and that Hunding slays the Volsung, an act made entirely possible by the powers of the goddess Fricka. In effect, throughout this entire episode, Fricka is offering divine protection to Hunding, not so much directly to him, but rather indirectly, through Wotan, who must accede to his wife's demand because of the basic truths that she speaks. Thus it is that Wagner's Fricka is possessed of the same divine power as her mythological source.

The matter of the love and union of Siegmund and Sieglinde, and Fricka's involvement in that situation, allowed Wagner an approach to yet another aspect of the goddess that is found in the myths. During the lengthy scene in which the *Ring's* Fricka berates her husband for creating the Siegmund-Sieglinde affair, the goddess slowly becomes disturbed and disconcerted. Wotan also reacts on an emotional level. While it is mythically true that Wotan often sought his wife's ideas on certain matters, it is quite accurate to consider the present situation as something more than a "consultation." It soon becomes altogether clear that the disagreement between the two will reach a climactic level. Each of the gods eventually becomes somewhat unrestrained, but especially so Fricka. Neither Fricka nor Wotan is found in a similar emotional state in the myths, and neither is either of the gods ever presented as intemperate beings. However, the Teutonic mythology acknowledged that Fricka and Wotan often held views that were in opposition to each other, and that in these numerous cases the two often fell into arguments.

Wagner knew of the frequent domestic clashes between Wotan and Fricka. With such knowledge, he was able to draw on mythologic reality in order to compose the argument that he places in his drama. Furthermore, that mythical reality allowed him a way by which he could advance thematic matters and his storyline, and, at the same time, enhance the mythical ambience that he so earnestly sought for his drama. In the end, if the details of this Fricka-Wotan encounter are momentarily disregarded, Fricka is clearly visible as an unflinching, inflexible defender of her cause, and she demonstrates a wisdom that is characteristic of the goddess of the myths. It is in her manner and in her words that she projects the dignity of a goddess of rank.

There was, however, yet another mythical facet of Fricka's godhood that attracted Wagner's attention. The Eddic literature makes specific mention of Fricka's fondness for jewelry. Wagner understood that this matter was relatively insignificant in the total character of his *Ring* goddess. However, because he sought to saturate his drama with a mythical authenticity, that is, provide an ambience that reflected as much as possible the mythicalness of early Teutondom, he was careful to consider any element that might contribute to that end. He reasoned that Fricka's attraction to jewelry was an attribute that would not detract from the overall role that he had given her, and there was the indisputable fact that the major property of his drama, the gold ring, was indeed jewelry! Thus it was that Wagner wove into his poem, if only in a most passive manner, the association of Fricka and jewelry. This aspect of the goddess is revealed in that scene of *Das Rheingold* in which there is a discussion of Alberich's gold, at that moment when Loge tells of the ring that the Nibelung has made. Wotan states that he has heard rumors about this ring. Fricka then interrupts and abruptly asks if this circlet can be worn by women as a golden jewel! It is by means of those few words, spoken by the goddess herself, that Wagner attached to his Fricka this pertinent if secondary aspect of the mythical deity. There seems to be no thematic need for Fricka's inquiry, and it is quite possible that some readers of the drama will conclude that Wagner weakened somewhat the continuity of his argument when he introduced this element of the Fricka character, especially so when the purpose is merely that of enhancement of the mythical ambience. Such would seem to be true when, at first glance, there seems to be no relationship between Fricka's fondness for jewels and the other more serious dramatic and thematic matters that are unfolding. However, Wagner soon shows his skill in making everything integral by causing Loge to answer the goddess, saying in effect that with the ring she would be able to keep her wandering husband at her side. Loge's words become a kind of consolation to Fricka who has shown great concern about the errant ways of her husband

and they also allow for the element of Fricka and jewelry to become a part of the story.

There are several additional mythical beliefs of ancient Teutondom that were attached to the goddess Fricka. Wagner was obviously aware of these beliefs, and given the fact that he had devoted so long a period of time to his study of the Germanic myths, those beliefs and concepts were probably deeply ingrained in his mind. However, these beliefs gave him little or no serious concern regarding his drama's Fricka because of the manner in which he envisioned that this role was to mesh with others of his argument. The mythical literature, for example, tells of Fricka's dwelling, Fensalir, calling it by name and making reference to its grandeur, Wagner had no need to include such a matter in his poem. After all, in his *Ring* it was the great fortress Valhalla that would serve as the home of *all* of the gods and, further, it was Valhalla that would be central to his argument. It was not so much that he felt it necessary to avoid the association of any specific dwelling with the goddess, but rather that Valhalla in this case was of far greater importance, and he did not wish to detract from that importance by including another building of strength and beauty. To assist him in his dramatic plan, he went so far as to have Fricka approve of the construction of Valhalla because she firmly believed that such a home would entice her husband to refrain from taking those many journeys on which he wandered at length through the universe.

It was in a similar manner that Wagner treated another aspect of the Fricka godhood. In the myths, this deity is the Goddess of Wedlock, a factor that he retained for the Fricka of his *Ring*. If the composer brought the mythical title to his goddess, he would pay little attention to the mythical ideas regarding marriage, and, as briefly stated previously, he would apply to this aspect of the godhood of his Fricka certain ideas and concepts of marriage that were essentially contemporary to his day, that is, ideas and concepts that were a part of a his own modern-day morality. Thus it is that there is no possibility that Wagner's Fricka can reflect the sexual mores that are part of the goddess of the myths, and quite to the contrary, the character of the *Ring* goddess argues for virtue and moral stability. Wagner's Fricka, then, is able to speak at length on the necessity of fidelity in marriage, and she is able to defend the matter of Hunding's moral rights as the husband of Sieglinde. This same Fricka can also censure her husband for his errant wanderings, and she can view Valhalla as a means by which she and Wotan can enjoy together the domestic bliss that should generate from marriage. (Despite voluminous writings, both by the composer and scholars throughout the world, this particular aspect of the Fricka godhood, as found in the *Ring*, has never been explored in any expanded way or in any depth. It would seem, however, that Wagner anticipated some societal reaction to the sexual matters included in his drama, and that the reaction to the matter of the brother-sister union would be exceptionally strong. In that light, it would seem safe to state that Wagner was, in effect, presenting matters that he had found in the myths, but also he was using his Fricka as a means to project a point of view that was at once comfortable in the society of his day and which was also befitting of the goddess of his drama.)

It is obvious to the reader of the mythical literature and the *Ring* that Wagner utilized many of the beliefs regarding the goddess of Teutondom in the development of his Fricka. The similarity of the two deities is evident, and any variances in the characters are, at least to this point, of minor consequence. However, Wagner wrote into the role of Fricka one substantial attribute that is not at all associated with the goddess of myth, a quality that is not even suggested in the myths simply because it was not a consideration throughout the length and breadth of ancient Teutondom! This feature is of Wagner's own design, a dramatic creation that he adapted from the religious thought that was attached to other major Teutonic deities, and from the ritualistic practices that the people of the time carried out as they sought the favors of those other gods. For the Fricka of the *Ring*, Wagner developed a *cult*, a religious veneration that had been denied the goddess of mythology!

Wagner was well aware that the ancient Teutonic peoples did not worship Fricka with the same intensity or fervor that they worshipped other principal gods. Fricka reigned over a specific domain, (marriage), and her blessings in that domain were often sought, but her powers, unlike those of the other major deities, were not those that determined the outcome or result of any primary and essential aspect of existence. It is true that the people believed that Fricka was aware of the fate of all living things, but she did not participate in the determination of that fate. Fricka had no role in the course of life, she was incapable of granting life or death, and she had no control of those elements of nature that were fundamental to the quality of life. Fricka lacked such powers, and therefore the society of the day could not and did not dedicate to this goddess the rituals that were considered necessary to the worship of those gods who were believed to hold such control. The Fricka of mythology was never the honored recipient of any of the rites of the ancient Teutonic people. Neither did those people offer incantations to the goddess, and they did not sing charms to her. It is mythical fact that Fricka, in many ways, was not looked upon by the ancient Germanics as a true goddess, an actual goddess, as an authentic being of the Teutonic divine hierarchy.

Wagner sensed that the activity generated by a cult was the kind that offered great dramatic possibilities. He believed that such activity could enhance the theatricality of his drama. And of major importance to him, he believed that such activity, given the proper setting, would contribute to the overall mythical ambience that he strove to achieve. He reasoned further that if such an activity were related mythically to Wotan and to other major gods, so too would it be appropriate for the principal goddess of Teutondom, the wife of the Supreme God, the Goddess of Wedlock.

In his *Ring*, Wagner gave evidence of this cult of the goddess Fricka in two distinct ways, both of which are to be found in the last of the four dramas, *Götterdämmerung*. The directions for the stage setting of Act II of this work state that a rocky height shall rise in the background, and on that height there are to be visible three altar stones, one each for Fricka, Wotan, and Donner. In the early Teutonic way of life an altar stone was any large rock that the people had dedicated to a god or goddess and before which the people could make their individual or group supplications. If the stone were of sufficient size, specific rites or rituals would also be carried out. The altar stones of Wagner's *Ring* could not be large stones. He had not intended that any rite was to be performed. Rather, their purpose was that of being stones that were readily seen as well as readily recognized symbols of the worship of each of the three gods. From a theatrical point of view, each of these altar stones contributed physically to the setting itself, while -- at the same time --

each altar stone served as a definite acknowledgement of the religious significance of the god to whom it had been dedicated. (It should be noted, however, that Wagner hesitated to allow his Fricka to have a religious status that equaled that of either the great Wotan or the powerful Donner. To indicate that this goddess, his Fricka, did not hold a religious status that was equal to that of either of these gods, he directed that her altar stone be placed on a level *lower* than that of the stones of the other two gods!) It was, nevertheless, by means of these altar stones that Wagner, admittedly in a somewhat moderate and measured manner, created for his Fricka a cult of worship much as that enjoyed by the other principal gods of Teutondom.

Wagner then went beyond the silent, passive state of a stage setting with three altar stones, one of which was to symbolize the cult for his Fricka. Now he resorted to dialogue to put forward the cult for this goddess, and to ensure that his created cult would have religious stature, he caused this dialogue to endow his Fricka with a religious standing that was equal to that accorded the respected and much venerated *Triad* of Teutondom. It is in that same second act of *Götterdämmerung* that the dramatist plays out the scene. Gunther is about to arrive at the Gibichung Hall with his bride Brünnhilde. Hagen summons the vassals to give welcome to the pair. As part of the celebration that Hagen wishes to arrange, he orders that animal sacrifices be made, sacrifices that are intended to invoke the respective powers of the gods and to cause them to look with favor on the Gibichung and the former Valkyrie. Hagen's words concern a much-practiced heathen Teutonic religious rite that focused on the sacrifice of animals as a means for pleasing the gods, and as a means for seeking the divine help and aid of those gods. Specifically, Alberich's son asks that a goat and a boar respectively be slaughtered in dedication to Donner and Froh. For Wotan he would sacrifice an ox and in Fricka's honor, Hagen asks that a sheep be slaughtered.

Wagner's choice of goat and boar as the animals of sacrifice for this duo of Teutondom's most revered gods was not an arbitrary one, but rather a reflection of his intense desire to duplicate, whenever possible, the mythical reality of the ancient Germanic peoples. Each of those animals is directly associated with the god for whom it was to be sacrificed. The sacrifice of a goat was always made in honor of Donner, the God of Thunder and

Lightning and who was also called *Lord of the Goats*. The association of this creature and Donner came through the god's habit of never riding a horse, as did most of the other gods, but rather traveling everywhere in his chariot that was drawn by two he-goats. Further, each night Donner fed on these goats, and then, on the following day he raised them to life by means of the magic of his mighty hammer, Mjollnir. The association of Froh and a boar was as equally accepted as the previous association. This god owned a boar, a very special animal, an animal that had been made for him by the dwarfs. This unique creature had golden bristles that lighted up the night. Froh's boar, which drew the god's chariot, could run through the air and through water faster than a horse.

The association of Fricka and sheep, however, was not a matter that had been developed in the ancient society and recorded in its myths. The association of Fricka and sheep was a creation of Richard Wagner solely for inclusion in his drama of the *Ring*. As he had created a cult for this goddess, in imitation of those cults that that were evident for other gods, so too did Wagner find it necessary to develop for his Fricka an animal of sacrifice, in imitation of those other animals that were slain in ritualistic worship of the gods.

Wagner's choice of the sheep as the animal to be sacrificed to honor the Goddess of Marriage has never been explained, and even today, the reasons for that choice remain somewhat of an enigma. The composers extensive familiarity with Teutonic mythology, which he had derived from many years of serious study, obviously had made him aware that neither the mythical literature nor cultural history indicates or even suggests that there was any association of the goddess with sheep. Indeed, he also probably understood that there was no record, either historical or mythical, that sheep were thought to be symbols of any religious significance, or that their magic, if indeed there was a belief that this animal possessed any special powers, had stirred or stimulated any of the gods to act in behalf of petitioners. Yet, in this instance, as in other examples of Wagner's created mythical matters, it would seem that there was some grounded reason for his choice. There are historical documents that refer to, and occasionally describe, certain religious practices that were carried out by the early Teutonic peoples. Some of these practices included animal sacrifice, at times when the occasion was not of any special significance and no specific god was to be honored or invoked. These rituals, carried out in a rather routine manner, did not require a specific species of animal as the sacrifice, and in such cases the sheep usually became the object of this religious slaughter. These sacrifices utilized the sheep because it was at once numerous and to be found throughout the region, and because *its flesh was edible*. It should be noted here that the sacrifice of any animal was followed by the drinking of its blood and the consumption of its meat, and therefore, the only animals that were sacrificed by the heathen Teutonic peoples were only those whose flesh could be eaten. Wagner without doubt sensed that it would be unwise, at least from a dramatic point of view, to include or even make reference to the latter practices, yet he also felt that allusion to sacrificial acts enhanced the mythical ambience of his work. Thus, as he brought the matter of sacrifice into his poem, he attempted to duplicate to the extent possible the matters as he had found them in the Teutonic past and therefore, if other gods were to have a cult and to be honored by sacrifice, so too, should Fricka be the recipient of such homage! And, if the myths specified the association of certain animals with each god, so too must such an association exist for Fricka. Thus it was that Wagner dug deep into the cultural practices of the early Germanic peoples and extracted the sheep as an animal of sacrifice which, if unrelated religiously with the mythical Fricka, was nevertheless a creature common to the practice and very much an animal that had its place in heathen thought and its supporting rites.

(Wagner also resorted to cultural practices in his selection of the ox, or bull-ox as it was commonly known, as the sacrificial animal for Wotan. In the earliest times of the heathen Teutonic peoples there was no specific sacrificial animal that was associated with Wotan. However, later in that history, male cattle, and especially the bull-ox, were almost always the animals sacrificed in honor of the god. This creature was a respected beast, its flesh was edible, and its meat was a favorite food among the people. Such a status within the social groups led Wagner to cause this animal to become the animal that he would have sacrificed for the Supreme God of Teutondom.)

The time required for Hagen to utter his words regarding the animal sacrifices to the gods is of brief duration, and it is entirely possible that their significance is lessened if not lost in the dramatic din and commotion of this act of *Götterdämmerung*. However, Wagner was quite cognizant of what he had done, and as he continued the composition of his drama, he included a second instance of the association of Fricka and sheep. As with the first, this later relationship is somewhat fleeting, yet in its own way it makes its contribution to the mythical theatricality that pervades the work. The scene occurs in *Die Walküre*, the second drama in order of presentation but a work which Wagner wrote some four years after the completion of *Götterdämmerung*.

Unlike the first reference to the association of Fricka and sheep, the second is found in the form of a stage direction which, if carried out, is followed by action on the stage itself. Wagner wrote that as Fricka enters the scene to confront her husband about the Siegmund-Sieglinde-Hunding situation, the goddess is to ride in a carriage that is drawn by two male-sheep!

Such, then, is the first goddess of heathen Teutonic thought and the depiction of that deity that Wagner developed in his *Ring* drama. When the latter is viewed as a total character, there is no doubt that she is the essence of the goddess of early Germanic times. This Fricka of the *Ring* envelopes the major attributes, characteristics, qualities, and functions of the goddess that occupied so important a position within the hierarchy of the Teutonic gods. It was only natural that Wagner's Fricka would not be a mirror image of the Fricka of myth. Some aspects of that mythical figure would make no contribution, either theatrically or dramatically, to the story that Wagner wished to tell. When those matters of mythical belief that Wagner excluded from his goddess are studied carefully, it will be quickly noted that they are of less than primary importance or consequence in the existence of that goddess as a ranking deity. Yet, it is possible to accuse Wagner of an overindulgence in his portrait of the mythical Fricka, an accusation that focuses on an excess of religious meaning that his Fricka-goddess exudes by means of the cult that he created for her and the practice of animal sacrifice in her honor, both of which were not hers in Germanic beliefs. Some scholars of the ancient religious practices of the Teutonic peoples and of the accompanying religious thought staunchly maintain that when Wagner gave Fricka a cult and a sacrificial ritual, he was manipulating the realities of that religious thought and that the person who comes to know the Teutonic gods through the *Ring* will receive a completely false perception of the goddess. There is a certain validity to such an argument, but it is equally true that the composer's action in this regard actually enhanced the importance of the goddess, or -- in another light -- Wagner's action in no way denigrated the Fricka of old and neither did his action remove from her any of the regard in which she was always held.

The conclusions in this matter remained divided. There are those who praise the development that Wagner gave to this goddess, and there are those who attack his work. What is paramount to all else, however, is that Wagner's Fricka thinks and speaks and acts as does the goddess of old, and, as a *Ring* deity, she brings into the modern age the personage of that goddess of old who once held a rather formidable influence over the minds of the people she served.

III

DONNER

Of the many gods of the ancient Teutonic world, there was one who not only exerted an incredible and profound influence in the religious thought of the early Germanic people, but who also enjoyed a unique and intense cultural popularity entirely unknown to the other deities. This divine figure was Donner, the German name for the deity whom Snorri Sturluson called "the foremost god," the god who is depicted in *The Poetic Edda* as "the warder of the earth," the god who was often viewed as the superior and supreme god of Teutondom, the god who was frequently accepted as the ranking god of the Teutonic world.

In the collective mind of the ancient Germanic people, Donner's powers were as extensive as they were awesome, a concept that gave the god a unique and special authority. This command, this dominion in the heathen Teutonic world is summarized in the religious belief that held that Donner was one of the three gods who, more than all the other gods, dominated all forms of life and nature. This trio of divine beings was looked upon as the *Triad*, and its members, -- Wotan, Donner, and Froh -- were thought of as the most capable, the most powerful, and in some ways the most feared of the gods of Teutondom. Of these three gods, Wotan was, in the overall picture, the principal and supreme god, the acknowledged *Allfather* of the universe. At times, however, and especially in certain regions of the early Teutonic world, Donner was accepted as the ranking god, at once because of the forces unique to his divine command and also because of the tangible effects and results that these forces had upon daily societal life. Donner was frequently invoked by the people, especially on those occasions in which there was a need for relief from some overwhelming distress. It was believed that Donner not only had the power and divine might to grant the most difficult of requests, but he was also more accessible than Wotan, more a god of the people than was the Allfather.

Donner was a deity who was universally accepted throughout all of Teutondom and, therefore, his name was a part of each of the several Germanic languages that emerged in that area. In the original Old Norse the name was pronounced *Thor*, a name and a pronunciation that continues relatively unchanged in contemporary Scandinavia. (The initial letter of this original name is a letter that does not exist in the English alphabet but which has the sound of English "th".) In Gothic the name was *Thunr*, while in Old Saxon and Anglo Saxon (Old English) the name had become *Thunar* and *Thunor*. Middle English had changed the name to *Thoner*. Old High German called the god *Thonar*, which later became *Donar*, and then *Donner* in modern German.

Donner was also known by several secondary or bynames. The practice of attaching numerous cognomens to individual gods was regularly carried out by the early Germanics, but it was a practice that was usually reserved for the deities of highest divine rank. Donner, of course, was one such god, and most of his bynames were really descriptive terms that were indicative of one or another of his powers or his activities in the universe. One of these secondary names is, however, somewhat unique, and its use is of significance in an understanding of the religious beliefs of the people regarding this god's position within the divine hierarchy of ancient Teutondom. The name was *Asathor*, which literally means "Thor of the Gods." The impact of this name lies in the term *asa*, which was a Germanic word derived from the word *Aesir*, the name of the race of divine beings that was worshipped throughout Teutondom before the advent of Christianity. The word was synonymous with *god*, and when used with that meaning it could have served as a prefix to the name of each of the other deities. However, the term is found affixed only to the Nordic or northern name for Donner, and in such use it obviously carried a broader and more profound meaning, one more of the nature of 'god of gods,' or perhaps 'holiest of gods.' The lack of a precise translation of the word *asa* does not detract from the elevated concepts of the god Donner that it infers. Such usage, in its own way, is also significicant for an understanding of why, in face of the influx of Christianity into the Teutonic world, Donner's godhood continued to remain strong and prominent while the religious importance of the other gods steadily decreased.

Donner was a god of early origin. It was, at least in part, because of that lengthy period of divine existence that Donner came to be a god of stature and rank throughout all of the Teutonic world, and the true national god of those people who inhabited what today is Norway. From the beginning Donner was a god with whom the people felt at ease, an earthy god for an earthy people. He was invoked both by individuals as well as groups; statues were erected in his honor; images of him were carved in wood and stone; animal sacrifices were carried out as a means of asking his special favor; toasts were drunk to him; his name was used in curses; there was even a rune* that bore his name. Additional testimony that attests to the divine position in which the people, both ancient and modern, have held this god is evidenced in the numerous times his name has been attached to distinct items: cities, mountains, an insect, a plant, an herb, a natural element, and even as a name for male children. Then, of course, there is the day of the week that bears his name, *Thursday* (*Thor's Day*) in English, *Donnerstag* (*Donner's Day*) in German, a day that once was of special religious observance in the ancient Teutonic world, a day that was holier to the people of the time than is Sunday in modern Christianity.

The belief in familial relationships among the gods was a feature of the old Teutonic religious thought. There are some questionable arrangements, but it seems more the rule than the exception that each of the Teutonic gods, at least the major deities, was related in some manner to one or another deity. These relationships could have been through blood ties or through marriage. The Eddic literature relates, for example, that Wotan and Fricka are husband and wife, and Froh and Freia are brother and sister, the children of Njord, a god of wind and sea.

Donner was not excluded from the concept of divine relationships. Despite the fact that there is historical evidence that Donner was invoked and worshipped in certain regions of Teutondom before the religious presence of Wotan, the myths picture Donner as the son of the Allfather and the goddess Iord ("Earth"). Each of the *Eddas* also identifies Donner as the offspring of the supreme god, and at one point in *The Prose Edda* this identification is achieved indirectly, when Donner himself states that he is the brother of Meili, who in turn was depicted elsewhere as another son of Wotan. (Meili is a relatively obscure figure in Teutonic mythology. Although he is represented as Wotan's son, he has no role in the religious belief of the people.) Curiously, this father-son (Wotan-Donner) relationship of two of the most celebrated gods of the heathen Teutonic world generates scant attention in the myths and, further, this relationship has little if any bearing on Donner's activities, his powers, or his functions.

Donner, like many of the gods, had a wife. This wife was Sif, who is regularly viewed as a minor goddess of fertility and the emblem of a ripened cornfield. Sif had had a previous marriage, a union in which she bore Ull, the God of Archery. (Donner thus becomes the stepfather to Ull.) Sif's only prominence in mythology comes about through the tale in which the malicious Loge cuts off her hair. In this story, Donner becomes so angered and enraged at Loge's act that he demands that the demigod find a means by which Sif's hair can be replaced. Loge approaches the sons of the dwarf Ivaldi, who make new hair out of gold. The magic that is put into this hair allows it to grow on Sif's head. (Ivaldi's sons are the same dwarfs who forged Wotan's famed spear, Gungnir, and the magic ship, Skidbladnir, that belonged to Froh.)

Donner was also a father. He and his wife Sif were the parents of a daughter named Thrud ("Strength" or "Power"). Little is known of Thrud, and she is mentioned and named in only one poem of *The Poetic Edda*. Donner also had fathered two sons. They were called Magni ("Might") and Modi ("Courage" or "Wrath"). The mother of Magni, and presumably of Modi also, was the giantess Jarnsaxa ("Iron Cutlass). (This giantess is not the same Jarnsaxa who is named in *The Poetic Edda* as one of the nine mothers of Heimdall, the guardian of Bifrost, the Rainbow Bridge.) The most significant mythological fact regarding these two sons of Donner is that they survived *ragnarok**, the downfall and destruction of the gods, and at their father's death they inherited all of his possessions. (It has been suggested that the names of Donner's three children -- Strength or Power, Might, and Courage -- are words that depict the overall nature of the god himself.)

Donner was like many of the other Teutonic gods in that he had his own personal dwelling. Donner's mansion, and indeed it was a mansion, was called Bilskirnir ("Strong"). This dwelling had 540 rooms and Sturluson writes that this most magnificent of structures was the largest house known to man. Bilskirnir was located in Thrudvangar ("Plains of Strength or Plains of Power"), the region that Donner governed. Donner lived in his mansion until his death. At such time as the god was not on one of his numerous and frequent journeys, he would leave Bilskirnir to attend the Council of the Gods that was held daily by the World Ash Tree. To reach the Tree, Donner would wade four rivers (Kormt, Ormt, and two named Kerlaug) rather than cross the Rainbow Bridge, as did the other gods. Donner hesitated to cross the bridge because it became too hot for him as it stood in the sun.

Donner was distinct from the other gods of the ancient Teutonic peoples in that he was a deity of unusual strength and physical might. By means of such power he literally dominated all living creatures. *The Poetic Edda* a calls Donner "the strong one" and Sturluson states that he was "the strongest of gods and men". The god also had a temperament that, in its way, was equal of his strength. Donner was irascible and testy, and he was easily angered. Often, at the slightest provocation, he "rose in swelling rage", and on such occasions the combination of his great strength and his furious wrath caused the nearby mountains to shake and quiver.

Donner was known as "the slayer of giants". The god traveled extensively, searching out this formidable enemy of the gods. When the god came face to face with one of the giants, he usually vented his wrath and anger in a confrontation, and then used his power and strength to slay the enemy. One of Donner's many victims was the giant who had made a pact with the gods to rebuild Asgard, the Land of the Gods, after it had suffered much damage during The First War. (It was this mythical tale that gave Wagner much of the story that he put into *Das Rheingold*.) On another occasion, Donner slew Thjazi, the giant who had abducted Idun, the guardian of the Apples of Eternal Youth. Donner also fought and killed the giant Hrungnir who had a three-horned heart and a head of stone. On one journey to the East, Donner stood guard at a river and used his strength to prevent the giants from invading the Land of the Gods. It was these battles, along with numerous other successful struggles with the giants, that early on gave rise to the mythical belief that Donner had killed enough giants to allow mortals to be free of this terrible enemy. According to the myths, it was Donner who made it possible for mankind to survive and continue its existence on earth.

The giants were not the only beings that suffered the might of the famed god. The "bold one" as he is called in the Eddic poems, once fought at length with Midgardsorm, the monster-serpent that lay in the sea and whose body encircled the earth. The myths also recount the many battles that Donner had with the *berserkr*, all of whom he quickly subdued and killed. (The Old Norse word *berserkr*, from which is derived the modern English word "berserker," was a product of the two words *bjorn* ("bear") and *serkr* ("shirt") and denoted one of those wild Scandinavian warriors who was subject to fits of frenzy when in battle and who then howled like beasts, foamed at the mouth, and gnawed the metal rims of his shield.)

The unusual strength that served Donner in his many battles with the numerous enemies of the gods was used to wield one of the most distinctive weapons to be found in all of Teutonic mythology. This object, whose concept is still vivid in the minds of many modern day Germanic peoples, was really more an implement, or a tool, than an instrument of physical combat. This item was Donner's hammer, Mjollnir ("Crusher" or "Mauler"). This hammer was an object that was capable of several feats of a magical nature and these qualities were so prized that the gods considered Mjollnir to be the most valued treasure in the universe. The esteem that was given to this hammer is frequently evidenced in the myths and most vividly displayed by means of an entire poem in *The Poetic Edda* that tells of the rescue of Mjollnir by Donner after it had been stolen by the giant Thrym. This poem, which is titled "Thrymskvida" ("The Lay of Thrym") is one of the two most famous poems in the *Edda*, and has been called one of the finest ballads in the world.

Mjollnir had been forged by Eitri, who was aided in his work by his brother Brokk. These dwarfs were the smiths who had fashioned Froh's special boar and Draupnir, the magic ring of gold that belonged to Wotan. Mjollnir had a rather short handle, and it could be folded and then carried about in a pocket. This hammer was very hard and it could not be broken. After Donner threw Mjollnir, it always returned to the god's hand. When Donner used this hammer as a weapon, it hit every target at which it had been aimed, and it was this quality that assured the god of victory in every instance. It was, of course, with Mjollnir that Donner slew the many enemies that he faced, and -- in time -- the hammer came to be called "the lover of killing." But, as the god used Mjollnir in several ways, it was something more than a weapon in his hands. Because of the unique magic that had been forged into Mjollnir, the hammer could consecrate corpses, and it could raise the dead. Donner also used Mjollnir to hallow brides at their wedding and the hammer took on a most important role when he functioned as the God of Thunder, a matter which will be discussed later in this chapter.

Mjollnir survived *ragnarök**, that catastrophe that became the downfall of the gods and signaled the destruction of the universe. Unlike the other treasures that belonged to the deities and which perished in the fire and flood that overwhelmed the universe, Donner's hammer remained intact, suffering no serious damage. Upon Donner's death at *ragnarök**, Mjollnir passed into the hands of his sons, Magni and Modi, who also survived the conflagration.

Donner also possessed two additional magical items. Both of these objects were unnamed and although each had certain magical qualities, the mythical literature does not reveal that either figured in the god's activities in any prominent manner. The first of these items was a pair of iron gloves that Donner wore and which allowed the god to keep a firm grasp on his hammer. The second of these two items was a belt which, when worn, doubled the god's natural strength.

The mythical literature reveals that Donner was known as "the charioteer of the gods." Such a designation arose naturally because the god rode in his chariot as he sped about the universe. If it was characteristic of the gods of Teutondom to make numerous and frequent trips throughout the world, in the main, such travel was made by horse. The myths, however, imply that Donner never rode on horseback, nor did he ever travel on foot. The god always traveled in his wagon which was drawn by two male goats, one of whom was named "Tooth-Gnasher" and the other was called "Gap-Tooth." (Froh also had a chariot that was drawn by a special boar and Freia's wagon was drawn by two cats.) Donner's goats also served the god in a second capacity: they became his foods. Sturluson writes in *The Prose Edda* that once, while on a journey, the god consumed his goats and then, the next day, raised them back to life by means of his hammer in order that he could continue his journey. Shortly after the god had raised the goats, he noticed that one of them was lame. When Donner eventually learned that the animal had been injured by the son of a farmer whom he had invited to share the meal and who had split the goat's leg bone in order to get at its marrow, his anger could not be contained. He flew into a rage and became so furious that he took the youth, who was named Thjalfi, and his sister Roskva in retribution and made them his bondservants. (Some students of the Teutonic mythology contend that Donner's goats were the *only* food that the god consumed!)

The continuous association of Donner and the goats that pulled his chariot became a prominent aspect of the god's mythical life. The myths frequently refer to this association, calling Donner "the goats' mighty ruler," and speaking of the god as "Lord of the Goats." This relationship of Donner and his goats was quite popular with the early Germanic people and it was a relationship that soon became firmly established in all the regions of Teutondom. The statues that the people erected in honor of Donner, as well as the drawings, paintings, and images that were made of the god often included a goat. This creature even became a kind of symbol for the god. The conspicuousness of the goat in all of Donner's activities became so permanent that it was only natural that this animal ultimately would have some role in the religious rites or rituals that the people carried out as they rendered homage to the god. Although it can be said that heathen Teutonic religious conduct did not include what might be called formalized ritual, there was one act that was common to all the heathen Germanic peoples, an act that was usually practiced when large groups, or even tribes, sought the favor of the gods. This practice was that of animal sacrifice, and as the people invoked Donner, as they attempted to cause the god to act in their behalf, as they attempted to have the god's magic work for them, they regularly offered an animal as a sacrifice. Of course, the animal that the people slaughtered in an attempt to please Donner was the goat!

The several concepts that have been presented thus far as part of the composite picture of the mythical Donner blended admirably, and that fusion allows for a facile understanding of this interesting god. This picture shows Donner to be a god of unusual strength, an aggressive god who was given to antagonistic behavior. That picture also shows that Donner was possessed of a temper that was easily aroused, one that showed itself as rage and anger. This forward nature of the god was enhanced by the magic that was present in his mighty hammer, the weapon with which he killed his many victims. In addition, it has been shown that Donner traveled continuously throughout the universe, usually to seek out his foes and then to do battle with them, and the impetuousness of the god during these journeys was such that he would speed across the heavens as fast as his goats could pull his chariot.

The total overall mythical portrait of Donner was one of the most vivid and most impressive concepts that had developed in early Germanic societal thought. The fusion of the several attributes then allowed for the formation of yet another belief, a concept that in its own way seemed to match the blustery nature that Donner exhibited and, curiously, one whose manifestations can still be evidenced in certain of today's Germanic societies. This additional feature was related to that early Teutonic habit of associating a god, at least the major deities, with some facet of nature. Froh's natural attribute, for example, was sunshine, Wotan often served as a kind of 'god of rain,' and Heimdall was custodian of the rainbow. It is true that such associations usually related a deity with some gentle or beneficial aspect of nature. (The people associated the giants with the more destructive of nature's forces.) In the case of Donner, however, any association of the god with a facet of nature could only be acceptable if that nature somehow matched the complete character of the god.

The heathen Teutonic peoples found it appropriate to relate their god Donner to one of the wilder forms of nature. If these people invoked the god's name and often sent their prayers to him, and if they beseeched him to cause the rain to fall and thus assure the fertility of their lands, these same people were, nevertheless, most fearful of the nature that Donner could create when he was angered. They knew that when Donner's ire had been raised the clouds gathered together in giant forms, then rolled ominously as they turned black and darkened the sky. The people then knew that the heavens foretold of the violent storm that the angry god was about to cast upon the earth. At those times that Donner's "divine wrath" reached its peak, he would race his chariot through the heavens and its speeding wheels caused sparks to leap out and rumbling thunder to be heard. During these wild rides, the god would use all his might to throw Mjollnir. He used such strength that the hammer split the air and a great clap of thunder was heard for miles around. Then, when Mjollnir struck its target, it hit with such force that a giant spark lighted the sky. The spark was lightning. On occasion, the god had become so angry that he threw huge stones about the heavens and they too, like Mjollnir, caused thunder and lightning as they vented the air and hit their mark. These stones came to be called *Donnerarte*, which meant literally "thunderbolt."

The beliefs that related Donner to this ferocious nature were so vivid and so much a part of the Teutonic culture that appropriate vocabulary became a part of several languages. In English, the word *thunder* was derived from the Anglo Saxon name for the god, *Thunor*, which in turn is from the Old Norse *Thor*. In the southern region of the Teutonic world, Donner became the God of Thunder and Lightning and the German name for the god, *Donner*, became the word for *thunder*, along with numerous compounds that were formed with the name: *Donnerschlag, Donnerstrahl, Donnerwetter*. The concept of Thor-Donner as thunder and lightning and violent storms is an early Teutonic association that even today remains very much a part of certain Germanic cultures and their languages.

The god Donner, like all the Germanic gods, was fated to die. Just as he and the other deities married, conceived children, slept, ate, drank, and performed all the activities that were natural to human life, so too did the gods of heathen Teutondom have to face death. The death of the God of Thunder was essentially a physical reflection of the manner in which the god had lived. Its story, as well as that of the fated deaths of the other gods, is told in the most famous as well as the most important of all the Eddic poems, "Voluspo." In this fascinating work of some sixty-six stanzas, the Volva (Wise-Woman) speaks to Wotan, who has sought her out. After telling the Allfather of the past, of the creation of the universe, of the beginning of time, of the origin of the dwarfs, of the origin of mankind, of the World Ash Tree, of the great war between the Aesir and the Vanir (Wanes) races of gods, of Wotan's secrets, she then reveals the details of the final doom and destruction (*ragnarök**) of the gods and their universe.

The Volva tells of the beginning of this violent struggle. She recounts that she saw the Valkyries as they assembled, that she saw Balder, the favorite son of Wotan and Fricka, slain by his blind brother Hod. She then tells that the river Slid rushed through the poisoned vales, that the cock crowed to awaken Wotan's army that lived in Valhalla, that Heimdall sounded a warning of impending danger. The World Ash Tree began to shake, she says, the giants began to groan and the dwarfs who lived in the earth began to roar. The enemies of Wotan and his cohorts then converged on the gods. Hrym, the leader of the giants, came from the East, Loge -- guiding a ship that carried the people from Hel -- came from the North, and Surt came out of the South leading his army of fire-giants across the Rainbow Bridge into the Land of the Gods. The gods now came forward, prepared to meet the enemy and to do battle with these formidable foes. Wotan fought and was killed by the wolf Fenrir, the monster-son of Loge. Froh was slain by Surt. Donner confronted the World Serpent, another offspring of Loge. In this struggle, Donner killed the serpent, but before he died, he breathed his venom on the God of Thunder. Donner turned away from the serpent, took nine steps, and then, overcome by the poison, the god fell dead. As the three gods die, the sun turns black and the earth sinks into the sea. Hot stars fall from the sky, steam hisses all about, and flames leap from the earth into the heavens. Donner, Asathor, the Lord of the Goats, the warder of the earth, the God of Thunder dies as the universe is consumed by fire and flood.

The Donner that Wagner brought into his *Ring* is a dramatic figure that mirrors the essence of his divine counterpart of Teutonic mythology. Wagner's god, however, appears in only one of the four music-dramas, and then only briefly. (Donner's entire role consists of 179 words.) With such restrictions of time and brevity of dialogue, it would seem difficult if not impossible for a dramatist to develop a full characterization of any figure. Yet, Wagner's thorough familiarity with the thought, beliefs, and concepts of the ancient Germanic people, and his total understanding of the particular role that Donner had held in the religious life of these people, allowed the composer to overcome the matter of the god's brief involvement in the argument and to invest his Donner with the significant traits and attributes of the Donner of old. Wagner's compositional skills were such that even as he developed a full and total Donner, he was also able to cause his god to become an integral figure in his tale of the gods, gold, and heroes.

Wagner understood that it would not be necessary to incorporate into his Donner each and every attribute of the mythical figure. Certain of those traits and functions did not lend themselves to his story and therefore could make no dramatic or thematic contribution to the argument. Wagner realized, however, that he must exercise care in the matter of his Donner because his figure not only had to project the divine stature that was unique to this singular god, but his divine strength and powers had to be evident, his divine functions had to be pertinent to the story, and the god had to be viewed as a necessary dramatic factor in the movement and activities of the deities. It was imperative, then, that the composer select with the utmost care those mythical aspects that he was to give to his Donner.

At the outset, Wagner was able to eliminate certain factors that were associated with Donner's mythological being. He was aware that the god's origin was of no concern or importance to the body of his tale. Wagner also felt that the concept of Donner as the warder of the earth was of no practical use in his *Ring* story. If that concept were to be included in the argument, there was the possibility that such a representation would detract from the significance of the supreme god, Wotan, and he knew that the supremacy of Wotan had to be retained. The composer also concluded that it would be impractical to employ any of the secondary names that had been attached to the god, regardless of whatever their relevance in the myths.

In his mind's eye, Wagner envisioned how the remaining attributes of the mythical Donner could be incorporated into his *Ring* deity. First, above all else, there was that mythical fact that Donner was a god of great authority and high rank, a god who at times and in certain parts of what is today Norway enjoyed a status that was equal to that of Wotan. Such a position was a clear indication of the god's divine dominion and sovereignty, and Wagner obviously understood that it was imperative that this concept somehow should be conveyed. The society of another day had viewed Donner as a member of the Triad, that is, Wotan, Donner, and Froh, the trio of gods that essentially governed the universe. Wagner did not see any place in his drama in which the Triad *per se* could be accommodated, either as a theme or simply as a matter of dramatic ambience. A "Triad," as it had existed in societal thought, would weaken the fundamental authority of the god Wotan who, in the dilemma that he creates, must make those decisions that will restore the authority of his godhood. Yet, Wagner found a way by which he could present his tale of the gods and, at the same time, acknowledge the societal belief in the existence of the Triad. The composer's resolution was both simple and subtle. He would not include the Triad as a cultural entity in and of itself. Neither would he cause the Triad to function in any way. He would not call it by name and no reference to it would find its way in his drama. Rather, its presence would be felt by means of the gods that he would include in the *dramatis personae*, that is, the gods of his *Ring* would be three in number and they would be those gods that were looked upon in earlier times as the Triad -- Wotan, Donner, and Froh. Wagner obviously reasoned that the presence of this trio would not only infer the existence of and indirectly make reference to that famed Triad, but the individual roles that each god would play in the drama would reflect the respective divine position that each held in the German concepts and, at the same time, the trio would represent the collective powers that the heathen Germanic mind had given the deities.

It should be noted here that Wagner was convinced that with his *Ring* he was creating a *national* work of art, a drama that would project the true qualities of the German character and personality. In such light, if he felt that he must include the three major gods of the Teutonic world in his work, he must give them the divine authority that was theirs in German thought. Therefore, he gave little heed to the mythical fact that both Donner and Froh, in scattered parts of Teutondom, held a greater authority than did Wotan. Wagner resorted to the beliefs of his native soil, and his Wotan was to be the King of the Gods, the 'high one,' the supreme god, while his Donner and Froh would be gods of high, but nevertheless lesser, rank. (This attempt to project a German nationalism is also evidenced in the names that Wagner uses for his gods, as well as the those of all the figures in his drama: regardless of whatever had been their Nordic names, Wagner's figures bear only German names.)

It was in a manner similar to his treatment of the popular concept of the mythical Triad that Wagner was able to dramatize yet another concept of the god Donner. In the myths Donner is a "god-judge." He is one of those select deities who meets daily at the World Ash Tree to counsel and then, according to individual judgments, to make all decisions regarding the universe. The story that Wagner envisioned for his *Ring* does not offer an opportunity for the gods to meet in council, and there is no point in the drama in which the gods, as a group, are to make a decision that effects the functions of the universe. There is, however, a need in the drama for an important decision to be made, but a decision that is essentially Wotan's to make. The dilemma arises when the Allfather must decide what is essentially the fate of Freia who has been taken by the giants. Wotan must determine if he should seek the return of the goddess, and then to do so by means of the theft of the Nibelung gold from Alberich. Donner, along with Fricka and Froh, have listened to the plan laid out by Loge. The three have weighed its merits and each has judged it to be the course that should be followed. They urge Wotan to put the plan into action. In this relatively short scene in *Das Rheingold*, Donner functions as a "god-judge," if only indirectly. Indeed, his thoughts on the matter are inferred, but, nevertheless, his decision is obvious, and readers of the *Ring* can recognize the importance of that decision and also sense that the god's input reflects a degree of keen judgment.

As with the matter of the Triad and that of Donner as a god-judge, Wagner also had his thoughts regarding the familial relationships of his gods and goddesses*. He would accept the principle of relationships, as included in the mythical literature, but he would disregard the several family ties that are recorded in the Teutonic myths, and in their stead place his own created kinships. Wagner obviously believed that the relationships that he had devised afforded him greater dramatic unity in the overall argument and, at the same time, that these blood-bonds intensified and made more plausible the deities' desire to extricate themselves from the entanglements caused by Wotan's pact with the giants. Thus it was that the composer rejected the mythical belief that Donner was the son of Wotan and Earth, and he ignored the concept that Donner was the husband of one of Teutondom's goddesses.

Wagner also laid to one side the ancient belief that parenthood was a part of Donner's existence. Wagner saw his gods in a different light: his Donner, Froh, Freia, and Fricka would be brothers and sisters, and through Fricka's marriage to Wotan, Donner would become the Allfather's brother-in-law. This relationship, singular to the *Ring*, becomes a subtle means by which the pleas of the gods for the rescue of their sister become more concerted and take on a greater degree of sincerity and urgency. These blood-relationships that Wagner devises are of no real consequence in the development of the story of the *Ring*, and they seldom, if rarely, are made the subject of outside attention or notice. There is no doubt, however, that they are distinct from mythical thought, and they uniquely serve the purpose for which they were created.

There is one additional relationship that Wagner created for his drama which, in its own way, also contributes to the sense of dramatic unity by helping to draw the supernaturals into a kind of family unit. This relationship is one that unites the four brothers and sisters, Donner, Froh, Fricka and Freia, with the *Ring's* Loge. Wagner had patterned his Loge after the supernatural figure that is found in the myths, and in following the mythical line he was very much aware that ancient beliefs did not view this cunning spirit as a god of Teutondom. For that reason, Wagner could not give true divine status to his Guardian of Fire, and neither could he make him a part of the brother-sister bond that he had created. Yet, the composer also knew that throughout the myths Loge is constantly in the company of the gods and, in one way or another, he is repeatedly involved in their activities. Wagner brought this factor into his drama, but he also obviously felt a need to project the intensity of the familial relationships as much as possible, thereby conveying a greater unity among the principals. A familial tie would again become his method, but now such a bond had to be one that would not seriously violate mythical beliefs. The relationship was to be present, but it could not be direct or primary. Loge could not be a brother to the four deities, and neither could he be a husband or a son to the goddesses. Wagner solved his problem: his Loge would be a cousin to the four!

There was yet another concept regarding Donner that Wagner brought into his *Ring* but which, like the familial relationships, he did not transfer exactly as it existed in the myths. The subject now was that of Donner's dwelling. The reader of the Teutonic myths soon comes to understand that the heathen Germanic people were especially concerned about the homes in which their gods resided. The myths speak repeatedly to this matter because, with few exceptions, each of the principal gods of Teutondom resided in his or her individual hall or home. Each residence of a deity was given a name, as was the region of the universe in which each abode was located. As might be expected, each of the gods' homes was a large, lavish structure, and each usually boasted some distinguishing feature. Of course, Donner had his home, Bilskirnir, the structure with 540 rooms, in which he resided when he was not away on one of his numerous journeys. However, as Wagner brought the gods together and caused his drama to tell the story of their collective plight, the situation was such that it would be dramatically impractical for each of the deities to establish and maintain residency in an individual home. Yet, the concept of the divine dwellings was always central to Wagner's thoughts, and if each of his deities could not have his own separate abode, at least there could be one luxurious hall in which all resided. This plan would achieve two ends: a hall of the type that he envisioned would allude, if figuratively, to the mythical fact that the gods regularly resided in an imposing structure, and, secondly, the dramatic projection of a kind of communal life for the gods would infer a sense of unity and purpose among them, the same kind of unity that was inferred by the blood-ties that he had created for these divine figures.

Wagner's plan of a single residence for all the gods instead of individual and separate dwellings, as in the myths, was easily realized. He would make Valhalla the Home of the Gods! Wagner understood quite well that the Teutonic structure known as Valhalla had never served as a residence for any of Teutondom's gods. He was also aware that mythical belief reserved this mighty structure as the celestial home of the *einjerar*, the fallen hero-warriors who had been selected to have an afterlife in which each would become members of Wotan's army, the army that one day would defend the gods against their enemies. The composer also knew that Wotan frequently visited Valhalla, especially at "eating and drinking time", and also that it was from this noble temple that the King of the Gods sent his ravens each day to gather news of the world. The Valhalla of the *Ring* was to be the Valhalla of myth, but it was also to be something more. Wagner's Valhalla was to be fundamental to his drama, an ideal if you will, a desire, a lure, the object of Wotan's dreams, the stimulus for the Supreme God to make a pact with the giants for its construction, without regard for the price that must be paid. The fundamental relevancy that Wagner attached to his Valhalla caused this famed structure to take on added prominence in the drama as well as a significance that made it primary to his tale. With such import established, Wagner knew that the substance of this great hall could be enhanced even more if the regency of the universe were to be carried out from within its walls. Thus it was that he made his Valhalla the home of all the gods. With the decision to make Valhalla the residence of the gods, Wagner automatically realized certain other ends. Obviously, he was complying, at least in his own way, with the Teutonic penchant for housing the gods; at the same time the presence of the deities in Valhalla gave the hall a singular dramatic prominence as well as an additional measure of majesty and nobility. Wagner's decision regarding his Valhalla also afforded a tangible and appropriate place in which the gods would await the end that would ultimately overcome them and the universe. Wagner was most conscious of what he was doing, and Valhalla, the Hall of Fallen Heroes, became the Home of the Gods, the home of Donner and his kin.

Although Wagner's decision to use Valhalla as the dwelling place of the gods satisfied the thematic needs of his drama, and also contributed to its mythical ambience, it is apparent that the composer's interest in the mythical matter of individual homes for each god was more than casual. For whatever reason, Wagner apparently felt that he must include in his *Ring* some acknowledgment of the existence of such a concept in Teutonic belief. He accomplished that goal by including in the dialogue of the second scene of *Das Rheingold* a reference to specific residences for both Donner and Froh. The reference occurs when Loge enters and then responds to Wotan's plea that the demigod help the gods in their dilemma. The Guardian of Fire comments that a home, and the domesticity that a home affords, hold no attraction for him. (Such a remark is entirely appropriate to Loge because, after all, this maleficent spirit is not a god and therefore he does not think or feel as a god.) He then adds that Donner and Froh have pondered this matter, but he cautions the pair that if they are to know the fruits of love and marriage they must first acquire a dwelling, an abode in which such life can be realized. Loge's few words have no bearing on the development of the argument, and it is most probable that they are passed over in any analysis of the drama. These words are, however, part of the dialogue and the allusion that they make to mythical beliefs about the gods and their homes is unmistakable. Regardless of the indirectness of these words and their subtle reference, they represent Wagner's concern regarding a mythical matter, they demonstrate his attention to mythical detail, and they become yet another example of the composer's intellectual fidelity to the mythology of his people, the mythology that served him as the source for his own tale of the gods.

Until this point in this discussion, the mythical aspects of the god Donner that Wagner incorporated into his drama probably were -- at least in his mind - of less than prime importance in the development of his *Ring* story. There were, however, other factors from the ancient mythology that Wagner considered of first order, features, characteristics, traits, and functions that distinguished Donner from the other gods who populated the divine hierarchy of Teutondom. Wagner was drawn to these facets of Donner's existence. He realized that such characteristics could not be slighted or neglected, and -- curiously - he understood that they were concepts that could not be overstated or exaggerated. Wagner molded his God of Thunder after the mythical counterpart and the Donner that roams about in the *Ring* is really that god who also roams the worlds of the ancient Teutonic universe.

First, and perhaps the most prominent among the matters that come from mythology, was Donner's great strength which, when coupled with his aggressive and impatient temperament and his relish for combat with giants, caused the god to stand out as one of the truly unique deities of Teutonic mythology. Donner was a god of great might and power, a god whose anger and wrath are easily stirred, a god whose hatred of giants is easily discernible. These qualities are quite evident in the Donner of Wagner's *Ring*, and they make themselves known by means of dialogue and by certain movements that Wagner requested in his stage instructions. The drama's first reference to Donner's strength is really more an inference than an outright reference.

The moment arises in *Das Rheingold*, at that point when the frightened Freia enters, seeking help against the giants who pursue her. The goddess approaches Wotan and Fricka, and then she cries out to Donner (and to Froh), pleading that they come to her aid. Fafner and Fasolt then appear and they press their demand that they be given Freia for their work on Valhalla, as promised. Donner and Froh rush in, and Freia again cries out and rushes to Froh who shelters her. The wrath and might of Donner then become quite apparent as the god places himself between the two giants. The god's anger has been aroused; he lifts his hammer in a threatening manner and then he tells the brothers that in the past he has dealt with giants and that he has given many of them their just reward which -- in this case -- is death. The scene continues and ultimately the giants agree to accept the gold of the Rhine as their payment. Later, however, as they contemplate the gold that Wotan has turned over to them, they lament the loss of the fair goddess, and to lessen their sadness Fasolt demands that the gold be piled around Freia to hide her from his view. As Loge and Froh place the treasure around Freia, Fafner pressures them to wedge together the lumps of gold. He looks for crevices; he looks for openings; he demands that a chink be closed. Donner is unsettled by the giant's demands and his anger is again stirred. Fafner once again directs that more gold be piled on the heap. Now Donner cannot hold back. He dares Fafner to fight with him. Fafner's answer only irritates Donner more and he then raises his hammer to strike the giant. At that point, Wotan intercedes and then announces that Freia has now been hidden by the gold. Wotan's words restrain the God of Thunder.

The hatred that Wagner's Donner has for the giants is reminiscent of the hatred that the mythical deity of old had for the same race. Yet, it must be remembered that the Donner of mythology not only held a powerful enmity for these beings, but also that he did not hesitate to come forward in a confrontation of any kind. (In one of the myths, Donner even threatens the Allfather Wotan.) For reasons that are fairly obvious, the *Ring* Wotan must be the supreme and dominant god; his divine authority must not be challenged in any form. It is he who will make the decisions which then will be the stimuli for all that follows, and for this reason Wagner could not allow his Donner to exercise authority as perhaps he did in other times. However,

Wagner very much desired to shape his Donner in the mold of the god in the myths, and it was necessary therefore to show the god as a fearsome being. If Donner's confrontations with Fafner and Fasolt projected that image, the composer sensed that such an image could be enhanced by means of additional incidents of similar nature, and if not against Wotan or the other gods, certainly against the crafty Guardian of Fire. Thus, Wagner caused his Donner to come down heavily on Loge, to confront the wily spirit, and then to threaten him. This incident also occurs in *Das Rheingold*, shortly after Donner has faced the giants. Loge appears and quickly denies that he had made any promises to Wotan that he would resolve the god's dilemma with the giants. Fricka then admonishes her husband for trusting this rascal and Froh thinks that a better name for Loge is *Luge* ("Falsehood" or "Lie"). For his part, Donner bristles with rage and he approaches Loge in a threatening manner. He alludes to Loge as a fire-spirit and then he says, in effect, that he will put out his flame, he will extinguish him.

Donner's threats were always given added emphasis by means of the great hammer that he carried. Wagner was aware that this hammer was of prime importance in the development of his *Ring* god. The dramatist had learned early on that in the myths Donner and his hammer were essentially inseparable; he knew also that the hammer was capable of several acts that contributed to Donner's significance as a god; he also realized that these magic powers that the early people had associated with the hammer were the very factors that had caused the people to view the hammer with awe, with respect, and at times even with fear. Wagner also was aware that Mjollnir was probably the single most important object that had found its way into Teutonic mythology, at least the most significant if adjudged in part by the number and kinds of references that were contained in the myths. In addition to the ways in which Donner used his hammer, the myths had detailed its origin, they had described it, and those same myths had told how it had survived the destruction of the universe*. Wagner was also aware that there was in *The Poetic Edda* one lengthy poem that was dedicated to the story of the theft of the famed hammer, and Donner's attempts to regain possession of it. The question that was in Wagner's mind, therefore, was not one that pondered the matter of Donner's possession of the hammer, but rather which of the celebrated hammer's several mythical features and functions were relevant to the hammer that his Donner would carry. This concern was a major consideration because the Donner of Wagner's drama was to appear only briefly and the hammer would be seen only at such times as the god participated in the story. It would be necessary, then, to display Mjollnir's qualities, whatever they were to be, in a relatively short period of time.

In its final form, Wagner's *Ring* reveals that the composer chose to exclude all of what may be termed broadly the 'features' of the mythical hammer. The dramatist obviously felt that the origin of the hammer and the mythical fact that it was short of handle were matters of a secondary nature, matters that could offer no dramatic or thematic contributions to his story. At the same time Wagner sensed that there was no need for the hammer of his drama to possess that magic that allowed it to be made small, to be folded, and to be carried in a pocket. After all, the Donner of the *Ring*, unlike the god of the myths, was not to journey about the universe, and therefore such a feature would be essentially superfluous material in his tale. It is also possible that Wagner believed that such an attribute, assuming that it somehow had to be demonstrated, would serve to defeat the need that his hammer be as visible as possible at all times. It was for similar reasons that Wagner chose to exclude the magic that allowed the hammer to return to its thrower and that which caused it always to strike its target. Wagner was aided in the last exclusion by the fact that in his drama there would be no need for Donner to throw his hammer because the god's confrontations with the giants were really all face-to-face. Lacking such features, it was only logical, then, that Wagner exclude from his argument the iron gloves that Donner wore when he cast his great hammer.

Wagner also elected to leave the hammer in his drama unnamed. There can be no doubt that Wagner's studies of the Teutonic myths had revealed to him that the people of that ancient era regularly gave names to each of the major possessions of the gods. He had learned, for example that Wotan's spear was named Gungnir, and that the god's ring was called Draupnir (Dropper). He was aware that Froh's magic ship was named Skidbladnir ("Wooden Bladed") and that the famed necklace that belonged to Freia was called Brisings ("Twiners"). The fact that Donner's hammer also had a mythical name could not have escaped his notice. Wagner sensed, however, that the role that the hammer had in his drama, like that of Wotan's spear, was really secondary in both dramatic and thematic importance to that of the great sword that Siegfried wields. To project that importance, he had named that sword *Notung*. (In the *Eddas*, this sword is called *Gram*, while in *Nibelungenlied* it is known as *Balmung*, the latter being the name that Wagner gave the sword in the first drafts of the *Ring*.) To give names to the hammer and to the spear would have made these items, psychologically at least, as significant as the hero's weapon. To avoid that possibility, then, Donner's hammer and Wotan's spear remain without names.

There is one additional mythical matter associated with Donner's hammer that Wagner omitted from his drama. The feature that the composer now chose to exclude was the hammer's survival of the destruction of the gods and its passing into the hands of the god's sons. Wagner concludes his *Ring* with the death of the gods, when the flames of Siegfried's pyre seem to reach into the heavens and there to consume Valhalla where the gods have gathered to await their doom. Although the drama, as well as the music, infer that an undefiled world, free of corruption, is now to follow, the actual presentation of that virtuous new world is not a part of the drama itself. The matter of the hammer's survival of the old world and an existence in that world that follows is, therefore, never a factor to be considered as a possible element in the *Ring*.

Wagner's primary interest in Donner's Mjollnir, at least for its role in the *Ring* drama, lay in the hammer's higher magic, that is, in those of its functions that may be considered to be truly of a divine nature. As he went about the business of developing the finished poem from his initial sketch, Wagner understood that his tale did not contain any incident that called for consecration of corpses or for the raising of the dead. From the beginning, then, these mythical qualities could be totally disregarded.

It is quite possible, however, that Wagner gave some thought to a second great magic that was attached to Mjollnir. This magic was that which gave the hammer its mythical power to hallow brides. There were, after all, three 'brides' (in four unions) in his *Ring* story: Sieglinde as the bride of Siegmund, Gutrune as the bride of Siegfried, and Brünnhilde as the bride of both Siegfried and Gunther.

There is, nevertheless, at least one factor in each of the first three 'marriages' that effectively prohibits the use of the hammer to consecrate the 'bride.' At the time that Sieglinde becomes the 'bride' of Siegmund, the Volsung is actually the wife of Hunding. (Perhaps the word *bride* is inappropriate in the Siegmund-Sieglinde union.) The union with her brother will occasion an act of infidelity, an act of adultery which also is, at least in the context of modern day thought, an incident of incest. Obviously, under such circumstances, the use of Donner's hammer to hallow the bride would be entirely inappropriate.

There is an equally serious factor that rules out the use of Donner's hammer to bless Gutrune as the bride of Siegfried. The union of this pair comes about by means of a devious scheme that Hagen and Gutrune arrange. Siegfried's attraction to Gibich's daughter is initiated only because the unsuspecting hero accepts from her a potion that erases from his mind the memory of his love for Brünnhilde and the love-vows he made with her. All evidence in the myths indicates that Donner's hammer could not extend sanctification to a bride who achieves a union in such a manner. If, however, such a situation were not sufficient to exclude consecration by the hammer, certainly the dramatic fact that Siegfried has already joined with Brünnhilde would negate any such blessing. Wagner was correct to disregard any possibility of the use of Donner's hammer in this situation.

As Gutrune sought to be joined with Siegfried by devious means, so too did Gunther resort to an underhanded scheme to take Brünnhilde as his wife. His act is one of deception, one in which Siegfried, drugged by Gutrune's potion and thus unaware of his prior union with Brünnhilde, disguises himself as Gunther and forces the former Valkyrie to accept him as husband. Such a marriage as this, that is one in which the use of force comes into play, coupled with the open reluctance of the intended bride, is hardly one in which the blessing of Mjollnir could be invoked. It is almost superfluous to add that prior to this action, Brünnhilde had joined herself with Siegfried.

The fourth marriage-union of the *Ring*, that of Brünnhilde and Siegfried, is one on which the revered blessing of Mjollnir would have been mythically correct and appropriate. This union occurs before each of the pair becomes entangled with others, that is with Gunther and Gutrune respectively. It is a union that really begins to form at that moment after young Siegfried has penetrated the fire that girds the mountain and then lays eyes on the form that lies inert before him, a form that is really Brünnhilde who has been placed in a sleep of banishment by her father, Wotan. Siegfried eventually awakens Brünnhilde with a gentle kiss, and as the maid greets her new world, she and her awakener slowly become more and more attracted to each other. The emotions of the pair are stirred and a mutual love that is now born eventually becomes the love-bond, the 'marriage' if you will, of Brünnhilde and Siegfried. The vows that each of this pair declares are made naturally, the result of a deeply felt, sincere love. The marriage that these vows symbolize is one of choice and of desire, and the consumation of such a union can be viewed as the apex of a true love-union. This is a marriage in the full meaning of the word, a union that is made with honesty, faithfulness, and purity. This marriage-union of Brünnhilde and Siegfried is, therefore, the kind for which the blessing of Donner's hammer is very much in order. Had he chosen to do so, Wagner would have been *mythically* correct in this instance to use the high magic of his god's hammer.

Wagner understood that it would have been mythically correct to use Donner's hammer to bless the union of Brünnhilde and Siegfried, but he chose not to dramatize such a scene. Oddly enough, when the circumstances that surround the marriage-union of this pair are examined carefully, there is present ample *dramatic* justification for Mjollnir's absence. The union of Brünnhilde and Siegfried climaxes the final moments of *Siegfried*. The scene begins in quiet calm. As the awakened Brünnhilde and the startled Siegfried look upon each other in the glowing light, each is moved in a manner never before experienced. Their first words come slowly, tranquilly, yet as the two come to know each other, they begin to reveal their feelings and they then begin to speak in more passionate terms. Each begins to sense a driving force that is drawing each toward the other. Each word of the dialogue and each note of the music becomes a carefully constructed expression in sound of the emotional state and the emotional reactions of the lovers as they build to a fevered intensity and ultimately erupt in a supreme moment of abandonment, that moment in which each gives himself totally to the other. It is at this point that the mythical magic of Mjollnir would have added a certain culminating dramatic finality to the scene. Wagner chose not to introduce Mjollnir, an introduction that he sensed would present a second impact, a distinct thrust that would have been of a disrupting nature. The injection of Mjollnir and its magic at the climactic moment of this scene would have interrupted the essential matter of the scene, that is, the matter of Brünnhilde and Siegfried and their newly discovered love that leads to the ecstasy of each. It is that ecstasy that is the substance of the entire scene, a scene that has been presented carefully, both poetically and musically, from its innocent origin to its orgasmic, emotional end, all by means of a continuous, unbroken, ever more intense elaboration. An interruption of any kind, and at any place, in the scene would have created a breach in the fragile thread of emotional reaction, a hiatus that would have destroyed both the thematic and the dramatic continuity of thought. If that gap were caused by the hammer, attention would be drawn to it and such focus would attach to it a significance that is unmerited in the total theme. At the same time, the attention that would center on the hammer would, in all probability, engender yet another element of dramatic concern, a diminution of the central importance of Siegfried's sword which, in this very scene, cut the strands that bound Brünnhilde's breastplate as she lay sleeping. (It should be remembered that in the earlier scenes of this music-drama, Wagner strove diligently, both with words and music, to invest this sword with an aura of majestic nobility.) Wagner sensed the exclusiveness of this final scene of his drama, and he also felt the need for an absolute continuity. Rightfully then, he excluded anything that might mar that continuity, and although the appearance of Donner's hammer in the scene would have been appropriate as well as mythically correct, it is nowhere to be seen!

Wagner's exclusion from his drama of these several features of the mythical Mjollnir did not divert his attention from what may be considered to be the two dominant, and indeed most prominent, qualities of the hammer. The first of these two qualities is its use in the myths as a weapon. In these tales, the hammer was the "mauler" or the "masher," as its name denotes, the weapon with which Donner confronted and threatened his numerous opponents, the weapon with which he slew so many giants. Wagner recognized the fundamental importance of this aspect of the hammer's existence in the life and the world of the gods. That recognition necessitated a similar use of the hammer in his *Ring* drama. Thus, as in the myths, so too does the Donner of the *Ring* employ his hammer as a formidable weapon. Although Wagner's Donner does not slay any of the gods' foes, the storyline does call for Donner to have several confrontations with the giants Fasolt and Fafner, confrontations in which the god strongly threatens the two brothers. There are even moments in the drama when the dialogue or even the god's actions infer that he is about to use the hammer to do battle with these giants. There can be no doubt, then, that in the *Ring* Donner's hammer is very much a weapon, a weapon that its master uses, or at least threatens to use, at each and every moment during his meetings with the giants.

The second distinctive quality of the Mjollnir of myth that Wagner felt compelled to attach to his hammer was a feature that not only set the instrument apart as one of the most unique in all of Teutonic mythology, but one that also contributed greatly to Donner's status as one of the primary gods of Teutondom. This quality was that of the hammer's power to produce thunder and lightning. The myths relate that Donner often became furiously enraged. Frequently, when the god's wrath was stirred, he would use his great strength to throw his hammer through the heavens. As the hammer streaked across the sky, it split the air, making a wide path in the heavens. As soon as the hammer had passed, the two great volumes of air rushed into the void to join each other. The noise that was made on impact was thunder. Then, when the hammer came down to earth it struck the ground with such force that a giant spark flashed throughout the sky. That spark, that flash, of course, was lightning. This magic -- the thunder and the lightning -- that resulted from Donner's hammer was so accepted, so thoroughly believed in early Teutonic thought that any depiction of the god, in any form, was incomplete if it did not include the hammer and also associate the pair with thunder and lightning.

Wagner was very much aware of the magic that allowed Donner's hammer to produce thunder and lightning. He also sensed the unusual dramatic potential that this magic offered. It was only natural, then, that he somehow include this potential in his *Ring*, that he somehow bring into his poem and then into his music this truly extraordinary quality that was so universally associated with Donner and his hammer. Wagner found the place, the exact spot in his drama for Donner and his hammer to carry out their magic. The scene occurs in the final moments of *Das Rheingold*, as the gods prepare to make their initial entrance into their new celestial home, Valhalla. The mighty castle is veiled in mist and hidden from view. Donner mounts a rock. As the god tilts his head skyward and looks into the heavens, he begins to swing his hammer in a great arc, back and forth, back and forth. The god increases the power of each swing, and when his strength has reached its peak, he brings the hammer down heavily on the rock. A blinding flash of lightning leaps from the rock into the heavens, and a violent clap of thunder is heard. The mythical Donner, as the God of Thunder and Lightning, and the mythical Mjollnir and its magic, most dramatically take their places in the *Ring*.

Wagner's spectacular dramatic and musical presentation of the mythical might of Donner and his hammer occurs but once in the *Ring*. This single depiction, however, allowed the composer to demonstrate what is without doubt the primary mythical magic of the hammer and, at the same time, to complete the character of the god who owned and wielded it. It is tempting, nevertheless, to assume that Wagner had been moved to develop such a scene by a few words of dialogue that he had written into his *Götterdämmerung*, which is the last of the four *Ring* dramas in order of intended performance, but the first in order of completion. In the second act of this drama, Hagen assembles the Gibichung vassals in order that they may honor the return of their lord, Gunther, and his bride Brünnhilde, who had been won for him by Siegfried who had used the magic of the Tarnhelm to take Gunther's form. As the act progresses, Brünnhilde becomes aware that somehow she has been the victim of deceit, and she then accuses Siegfried of dishonor. The drugged hero then attempts to defend himself. The controversy becomes more intense, and ultimately each of the two swears an oath that the story that each has told is the truth. The stories, of course, are contradictory. The vassals witness this heated argument. They are bewildered by the conflicting accounts, and they are at a loss to determine which of the two has told the truth. These vassals are torn in their loyalty to Brünnhilde, who is to become their sovereign's bride, and their love for the hero whose deed has won for him their mistress Gutrune. In the center of this fray is Gunther, who believes that his honor has been stained. The confused vassals finally call upon Donner to help them, to bring on his thunder and lightning that will render silent the disgrace that has befallen them. The vassals' words are few and their prayer is brief, and neither the god and his hammer nor the magic of that hammer appears in response to the words of Gunther's men, yet the reference to the might and magic of Donner and his hammer is unmistakable! Wagner apparently sensed the dramatic and musical potential of this brief scene, and as he composed the drama in which Donner is a principal character, he decided to make the god's thunder and lightning a visible and audible part of his tale.

The vassals' call to Donner for his divine intervention is an act of invocation. This plea to the god is Wagner's attempt to weave into his story a representation of a cultural practice that was quite common in the life of the early Germanic tribes. These heathen peoples often turned to a specific god or goddess to seek aid or assistance, or even special favors, in a given matter or in certain situations. The deity upon whom they called was, naturally, that god whose powers could fulfill the request. Donner was one of the gods frequently invoked because the rain that his storms always caused was needed in agricultural endeavors. More often, however, these people sought the fearful noise of Donner's thunder to frighten an enemy or, as with other beliefs, the god's lightning which could bring injury, even death, to a foe, or at least wreak some destruction on that foe's property.

Wagner's use of invocation, although quite brief and passing, is appropriate to the drama's situation. The vassals had been incited by Hagen. As they hear the conflicting stories of Brünnhilde and Siegfried, and the accusations of deceit, betrayal, and faithlessness, they are confused. They do not know which of the pair to believe and therefore they cannot determine to which their allegiance should be given. The emotional conflict of these people demands resolution, and they turn to the gods for help, in this case, Donner.

Wagner's use of invocation achieves three separate and individual dramatic ends. In the first regard, the fervent plea of the vassals to Donner, which is the invocation itself, is patterned after a religious practice that was regularly carried out in early Teutonic culture, and with that invocation Wagner again demonstrates his remarkable faithfulness to mythical matters. In the second regard, the few words uttered by the vassals reflect a sense of mythical antiquity, the primordial ambience that Wagner was so intent on weaving into his drama. The third achievement of this invocation concerns itself with Donner. By means of the vassals' words, certain of the concepts regarding the god are accurately mirrored and his powers find a new and distinct use. In effect, the plea gives another dimension to the Donner of the *Ring*: he is not merely the god who creates thunder and lightning, but a deity who can also bring those aspects of nature to the aid of mankind. The plea thus becomes an enhancement of the *Ring* characterization of the god, which in turn makes him a more faithful counterpart to the great god of Teutonic myths.

The invocation to Donner that is made in the second act of *Götterdämmerung* does not arise altogether unexpectedly. Wagner prepared for this scene, or at least he made indirect reference to it, by means of the stage setting that he developed for this act. As a part of this setting, the composer directed that three *altar stones* be included. Each stone was to honor a specific god, one of which was Donner. (The two other altar stone were directed to Wotan and Fricka.) Altar stones were special objects to the early Teutonic peoples, objects that were reserved for the observance of prayer, religious rites, or sacred ritual directed to a specific god. The altar stones that are found in the *Ring* become physical reminders that such ritual was carried out, and also a reminder that the god involved was honored, invoked, and worshipped. Wagner's altar stones, like those of the distant past, are silent stimuli to prayer, and those in his drama, in their own way, seem to anticipate some kind of plea to the gods, or at least to one of the deities. (It is interesting to note that one of these three altar stones is inappropriate, mythically speaking. Of the three gods honored by these altar stones, one -- Fricka -- was not worshipped by the ancient peoples. Fricka was never invoked, nor were prayers and the accompanying ritual directed to her. She was never the subject of the religious practices of these tribes. Wagner never revealed why he placed an altar stone to honor Fricka in the stage setting, but it is logical to assume that he was very much aware that the goddess had no serious standing in the religious beliefs of earlier times, and that the reason that he included her in this manner, that is by means of an altar stone, was really another means by which he sought to enhance the concept that this goddess was a persuasive power in her own right, and especially so in those affairs that fell within her domain.)

The use of altar stones as part of a stage setting is yet another demonstration of Wagner's attempt to have his drama reflect as much as possible the beliefs and religious thought of the ancient people of his culture. The detail to which he resorted in these attempts is often minute, and in the case of the placement of these stones that detail is evidenced in the instructions that he wrote as part of the stage directions. Wagner directed that the altar stones that are dedicated to Wotan and to Donner were to be placed on the same level, that is, side by side, and the stone that is to honor Fricka was to be located on a level below that of the other two. Wagner's obvious intent in this arrangement of the altar stones was to indicate the respective divine rank of the gods, a rank that was demonstrated in numerous ways in the myths.

Wagner's reasons for the specified placement of the altar stones is at once mythically correct and, at the same time, rather questionable. The placement of the altar stone to honor Fricka is easily explained. This goddess was limited in her powers, and she was restricted in her control of those powers. Fricka did not command with the same authority as her husband or Donner. The placement of her altar stone on a level beneath those of the two gods accurately symbolizes her position or rank in the divine hierarchy.

It is Wagner's placement of the altar stones of Wotan and Donner on the same level that raises some questions and also initiates some conjecture. As was pointed out earlier, Wotan, in the main, was considered to be the high god of Teutondom, the main deity throughout all of the Teutonic territory. Such beliefs were completely prevalent in what is today Germany where Wotan was accepted as the Allfather, the Supreme One, the ranking god of all the gods. Donner was a popular god in that region, but nevertheless, he was of lesser divine rank than Wotan. The practical application of these mythological facts would necessitate that this divine rank be observed and in the placement of the altar stones, Wotan's altar would have been located above those of all other gods. Yet, in the Scandinavian region of the heathen Teutonic world, the gods were sometimes viewed in a different perspective. Such was especially true regarding the religious standing of Wotan and Donner. In this north country Donner was, on occasion, accepted as the most powerful of the gods, and he was often venerated as much or more than Wotan. An application of this concept would have allowed Donner's altar stone to be placed on a level higher than that of Wotan. It is logical to assume that Wagner never considered Donner to be a more powerful god than Wotan! However, if the composer was desirous of using German beliefs and concepts as much as possible in his "national work of art," as he stated on numerous occasions, why did he not utilize the German beliefs regarding divine rank, and thus place the the altar stones of his stage setting accordingly, that is the stone for Wotan on a higher level than that of Donner? Or, phrased differently, why did Wagner equate the divine rank of Donner and Wotan by the placement of their respective altar stones on the same level? It cannot be said that Wagner was unaware of the southern and the northern religious concepts and beliefs, their similarities as well as their differences. His years of study and reading had made him quite knowledgeable in such matters. However, he never addressed the question, and therefore the answer lies completely in the realm of speculation.

Wagner was familiar with the Nordic concept of the Triad. As explained earlier, the Triad was that trio of gods -- Wotan, Donner, and Froh -- whose powers were separate and distinct, but essentially complementary, which in turn made the three equal in divine rank. It is perhaps reasonable to assume that Wagner considered the equality of Donner's membership in that celebrated Triad coupled with his prominence and the enormous popularity that he enjoyed throughout Teutondom which, of course, included Germany. As a result of such consideration, it is entirely possible that

Wagner concluded that Donner merited some additional recognition in his drama, and that such recognition could be achieved by means of the placement of his altar stone on the same level as that of Wotan. Such an arrangement had no effect on the drama itself, and neither did it detract in any serious way from the divine position that he was giving to Wotan, his King of the Gods. Then again, it is quite possible that there may have been other reasons for his directions as he wrote them. Finally, it is entirely possible, although highly unlikely, that Wagner made an initial mythical error, and for whatever reasons that mistake was never brought to his attention. In the end, however, all the potentials are conjecture because, as stated above, Wagner never volunteered an explanation!

Curiously, Wagner did not include an altar stone for the third equal member of the Triad, Froh! The exclusion of a stone for this god may seem, at first glance, to be a demonstration of Wagner's personal selection of which specific mythical matters he was to bring into his tale. It is also possible that Wagner had given serious thought to the mythical Froh and an altar stone in his honor and concluded that there was mythical thought or belief about the god that justified a decision to omit this reference to him.

Froh, like Donner, was a deity who also had a popular following among the early Teutonic peoples. Froh was looked upon as a gentle god, a noble god. He was the god of light and sunshine, a god of zephyrs, a god of soft rain. With such a divine nature, it is possible that Wagner sensed that Froh was not representative of the explosive situation that develops in his drama -- as were Wotan, Donner, and Fricka -- and therefore an altar stone in his name would be inappropriate in the setting. It is also possible that yet another mythical concept of the god figured in Wagner's plan for the setting of his stage, a mythical concept that is available to the student of these early myths, but one that is not too often discussed. The several powers that were associated with Froh made him a god of fruitfulness in nature, a god of fertility in that the light and sunshine and gentle rain that he brought produced an abundance of crops and other foodstuffs. The belief in Froh's godhood in matters of fertility in nature somehow was transferred to human life when matters of fertility there were uppermost. Froh came to symbolize this human fertility and this aspect of his godhood was depicted in the many carvings and pictures in which the god is shown with an erect penis. Wagner knew of this side of Froh's godhood and obviously sensed that he should approach the matter of Froh in his drama with some caution. In the end, Wagner was content to have his Froh serve only as the *Ring's* Guardian of the Rainbow.

The altar stones that Wagner placed in his drama also served in a capacity other than merely as visual symbols of worship through invocation. These stones became physical reminders of a fundamental element of early Teutonic ritual worship, *animal sacrifice*, to which reference has been made earlier. Invocation of the gods was frequent, and such worship, especially when carried out by groups or entire tribes, usually included animal sacrifice, a ritual in which altar stones were put to practical use. The sacrifice of animals was performed for any of several reasons. A primary belief held that the gods were pleased by sacrifices, that their attention was more easily gained than in any ritual that did not include a sacrifice. It was also believed that a sacrifice rendered the gods more inclined to grant a request, a plea, or a prayer. Another belief held that a plea or request was ennobled by a sacrifice, and thus such a plea was more acceptable to the gods.

The matter of animal sacrifice was of serious concern to the people. Their purpose was, of course, to gain the attention of a god, and then by sacrifice, to induce that god's divine powers to act on their behalf. This seriousness of purpose is reflected in the requirements that were rigidly enforced regarding the animal that was to be sacrificed. Primary in these requirements was the mythical belief that specific breeds of animals were sacrificed to individual gods. The animal to be slaughtered had to be one that mythical beliefs held to be closely associated with the god whose favors were sought. Each sacrificial beast had to be a male animal. Only those in the best of health were chosen for the ceremony, and then only those that had shown strength, courage, and virility in life. A final requirement held that the animal to be sacrificed had to be *one whose flesh was edible*.

It was during the act of sacrifice that the altar stone came into service. The ritual was usually performed in a grove of trees. The altar stone was placed at the base of the largest and strongest tree. The selected animal was then hung, head downward, from the branches of the tree, its head located directly over the altar stone. Once slaughtered, the beast's blood drained onto the altar stone and then was taken up by the celebrants. The pleas and prayers were uttered during the act of slaughter and the gathering of the animal's blood. When the rite was completed, the animal's blood and meat were prepared for consumption.

Wagner included sacrifice in his *Ring* poem, but only by reference. He sensed that it was not necessary to make sacrifice a part of the stage action, but he understood quite well that the element of sacrifice, like that of invocation, would reflect mythical authenticity. He also believed that animal sacrifice would contribute to the dramatic characterization of the god or gods that were being honored. He also was of the opinion that both the characterization and the ambience could be enhanced if the words that were to be delivered were the correct words, delivered at the correct time.

Wagner had placed the altar stones in the setting for the second act of *Götterdämmerung*, and it was in that same act that animal sacrifice became a dramatic reality. In the scene in question, Hagen calls the vassals to assemble and to make ready to welcome their leader Gunther, who will soon arrive with his bride, Brünnhilde. Hagen tells the vassals that the gods must be honored if they are to give their blessings to this marriage. He then adds that they are to honor the gods with sacrifices, one animal each for Wotan, Froh, Fricka, and Donner.

It is by means of Hagen's words that Wagner was able to realize a dramatic reference to the societal-religious practice of sacrifice which in its own way subtly increased the mythical ambience of his drama. It was also by means of Hagen's words regarding the intended animal sacrifices that Wagner was able to include yet another element that conveys even more the ancient ambience and which, at the same time, demonstrates further the composer's astute awareness of heathen Teutonic thought. As Hagen continues his address to the vassals, he designates specifically the kinds of animals that are to be sacrificed. He directs that the best of bull-oxen is to be slaughtered for Wotan, after which the blood is to be poured on Wotan's altar stone. He orders that Froh be honored by the sacrifice of a boar, and Fricka's blessing will be sought by the sacrifice of a sheep. To gain Donner's favor, a goat will be slain in the god's honor.

Wagner's inclusion of a goat to be slaughtered to honor Donner was not a matter of his own design, but rather an accurate reflection of actions and beliefs of the Teutonic past. Animal sacrifices to Donner were indeed a part of the rituals that the ancient people celebrated, and at such rituals it was always a goat that they offered to the god. The association of Donner with a goat, as already has been pointed out, was one of long standing, and that association had total acceptance throughout all of Teutondom. Such an association had come about because of the belief that Donner possessed two goats that drew his chariot through the heavens, often at such great speed that the wheels of the chariot ground against the clouds and the noise that resulted was thunder. It is also mythical belief that on occasion Donner's two goats served him as food, and that when he needed the animals in order to continue his journey, he raised them with the magic of his hammer Mjollnir. It was also this mythical association that gave rise to the popular name for the god, *Lord of the Goats*. (This association of Donner and the goats remained prominent in societal thought well into the Christian era, and remnants of that association can still be discerned from time to time in the present day.)

(It was also the mythology that gave Wagner the basis for Hagen's words that stated that a boar was to be sacrificed to honor Froh. The association of that god with a boar was well documented throughout the myths. However, Wagner did not find in the myths any animal associations for Wotan and Fricka, that is, associations with those kinds of animals that could serve as sacrificial animals and which he could cause Hagen to name. Thus, it became necessary for the composer to create his own associations in order to complete the concept of the ritual that he wished to depict in his drama, and that necessity caused him to resort to the cultural history of the early Germanic peoples. His search, ultimately, was relatively successful for in that history he found a weak but acceptable basis for naming the bull-ox and sheep respectively for Wotan and Fricka.)

There is one additional matter that must be considered in order to make complete the comparison of the Donner of myth and the god that Wagner made a part of his *Ring*. The matter that now becomes pertinent is this god's death, or more specifically, the manner in which he dies in the myths, and in the drama. As discussed earlier, Donner's mythical death came about in the celebrated last battle of the universe.* Each of the principal gods of Teutondom individually fought an enemy, and all perished. The foe that Donner faced was the World Serpent. The God of Thunder valiantly struggled with this great monster of the Teutonic world and, ultimately, he killed him. However, in his last gasps of life, the serpent breathed his poisonous spittle on the god who then collapsed and died as he was walking away from the beast. The intensity of this extreme form of death in the myths is not unlike that which is sensed as the god of Wagner's drama meets his end. What is quite different in the *Ring*, however, is the *kind* of death that befalls the god.

In the final scene of *Götterdämmerung* the gods sit forlornly in celestial Valhalla, awaiting the doom that they know is to come. On the shores of the Rhine, near the Hall of the Gibichungs, Brünnhilde stands beside the slain Siegfried, praising him as the worthiest of heroes. She removes the ring from his hand, and as she places it on her finger she cries out to the Rhinemaidens that they shall have their ring again, after its curse has been removed by the fire that will consume her and the Volsung hero. The ex-Valkyrie then seizes a torch and casts it on Siegfried's pyre. As the flames take hold, she greets Grane, the valiant stallion that once was hers and which she had given to Siegfried as a love-gift. Brünnhilde mounts the horse, and together they bound into the fire. The blaze becomes intense, and the flames seem to envelope everything in their path. Soon, the hall and all that surrounds it are ablaze, and then the fire begins to subside, and a great cloud of smoke is seen. At that moment, the Rhine overflows its banks and Hagen, who has been watching Brünnhilde, plunges into the waters to retrieve the ring for himself. The Rhinemaidens drag Hagen into the depths of the river which slowly returns to its bed. A red glow slowly appears in the heavens and as the clouds disappear, Valhalla is seen, engulfed in flames. Slowly, the home of the gods is consumed by the fire, and the gods -- Donner, as well as Wotan, Fricka, Freia, and Froh -- perish in the conflagration. The twilight of the gods is at hand!

(It should be noted that Donner's death as well as that of the other gods of the *Ring*, was not a part of Wagner's original story. For the first version of this drama, which was titled *Siegfrieds Tod* (*Siegfried's Death*), Wagner prepared an ending in which the gods did not die, rather they survived and were restored to power, their divine forces now to be used for good in the universe. Such a divine state was possible because of Siegfried's rescue of the gold and its return to its home in the Rhine. Some time later, Wagner returned to his poem and rewrote Brünnhilde's final words. This revision became the ending as we know it today, a revision that altered considerably the interpretations of the story and one which allowed him to retitle his work to *Götterdämmerung* or *Twilight of the Gods*.)

Thus, Donner, the God of Thunder, the God of Lightning, the Lord of the Goats, the warder of the earth, the burly, brusque fighter of giants, dies, both in myth and in the story of the *Ring*. The manner in which he dies is at variance in the two tales, but the end, the god's fate, remains the same. There are perhaps those who would question Wagner's deviation from the early beliefs regarding the manner of the god's death, but the composer's dramatic purpose must always be a consideration when such a question is raised. Wagner never intended to dramatize the specifics of the end of this, or any of Teutondom's other gods. Rather, he wished to have that end as part of a greater, more extensive and more significant picture. The death of all the gods in his drama was to serve as the climactic symbol of the end of a corrupt and chaotic universe, a world that was to be followed by a new and virtuous life which had been made possible by the deed of a great champion. The death of Donner and the other gods is primary to his tale; the manner of those deaths is secondary. Wagner chose to have his gods meet their doom together, consumed by the same fire that would make way for a new and undefiled world.

This, then, is the god Donner of Wagner's *Ring*. The god's role in the drama is brief and relatively secondary, yet in a very real sense it resembles more closely that of its counterpart in myth than does that of any of the other *Ring* deities. Wagner's Donner is the fiery, tempestuous god of myth who is easily provoked; he is the ancient god who persistently confronts and fights the enemies of the gods; he is the god who is invoked, the god to whom the people direct their pleas and for whom they offer sacrifices; he is the god who wields a mighty hammer; he is the god of nature who brings storms and thunder and lightning. There is little of Wagner's Donner that is not found in ancient Teutonic mythical belief. If Donner's words in the *Ring* are few, and if his involvement in the argument of the drama is of relatively little import to the main elements of that story, he remains, essentially, a substantial double of the god of old.

IV

FROH

It is not unusual for many, if not most, of the followers of the *Ring* to look upon the role of Froh as one of the lesser roles of Wagner's powerful dramatic and musical masterpiece, *The Ring of the Nibelung*. If either the amount of time that this god participates in the drama's argument, or the number of words in this character's dialogue is the criterion, then such a judgment is valid. Froh appears in only two scenes of the first of the four dramas of the tetralogy, and his entire verbal contribution is scarcely more than one hundred words, less than that of his colleague Donner, who appears at his side, and less than that of Forest Bird in its single, brief appearance in *Siegfried*. It is also equally true that Wagner's God of the Rainbow Bridge is only indirectly involved in the matter of the gold, which is the central matter of the only drama in which he appears. To belabor even more this god's brief involvement in matters of the *Ring*, he has absolutely no thematic relationship or connection with the Wotan-Brünnhilde-Siegfried involvement, which is the principal dramatic line of Wagner's tale. However, the inclusion of Froh in this tale of the gods and the Volsungs, and the dramatic depiction that Wagner makes of this figure that he drew from the ancient Teutonic divine order of things is, in a larger sense, a reflection of the composer's awareness of the prominence in Teutonic mythology of one of its most celebrated deities, as well as vivid testimony of his intimate familiarity with the significance of this god in this early heathen thought.

Froh was one of Teutondom's most influential gods. It was he along with Wotan and Donner who formed what is commonly known as the *Triad*, the trio of the most important of early Teutondom's deities. This "exceedingly powerful god," as he is called in *The Poetic Edda*, stands in the forefront of the religious rites, rituals, and practices of worship that were carried out in all of the Germanic lands. Froh was accorded everywhere a dedication and a devotion of the first rank, but it was also a following that varied somewhat in intensity in certain regions of the Teutonic world. Modern day scholars have concluded that in some areas Froh's divine supremacy even exceeded that of Wotan, the acknowledged *Allfather* among the early Germanic peoples. This latter standing was noted in what may be called Scandinavia, especially Sweden where numerous relics of his cult have been uncovered and where in later years his name was used to designate the supreme being of Christian beliefs. It was in Iceland where temples were dedicated to this "Lord of Heaven," and where there remain today places that were named in honor of this god who, as Sturluson writes in *The Prose Edda*, "was beautiful to look at." This truly unique god was also worshipped by the Anglo-Saxons who frequently used his name as the equivalent of *lord*, a usage that is found in much of the Old English poetry, including the epic poem *Beowulf*. The degree of acceptance and relative significance of this god is also evidenced by the early development of a rune* that became an integral facet of the religious thought of all these ancient peoples. This rune was originally symbolized by the mark *F*, which appeared in the Germanic, Old Norse, and Old English *futhark* (runic alphabet) and which remains as the letter *F* in alphabets of today.

The term *Froh*, as a name, is a singular one, unique as it is to the *Ring*, and yet it is but one of the several variants by which the god has been known at different times in various regions of the Teutonic world. In the original language of the Teutonic peoples, and mainly in what is today Iceland and Norway, the name of this god was *Freyr*, the name by which he is most often known because that is the name that is used in Eddic writings. The word *Freyr* and its several variants can be translated as "lord" (as Freyja/Freia meant "lady"). In English, the name became *Frey*, and in the Eastern branch of the Teutonic peoples, that is the Goths, this god was known as *Frauja*, a word that was once commonly used as a man's name. In Denmark and Sweden, this god was called *Fro*, a word that was carried southward and used in the old German language versions of the mythology. This derivative *fro* had such usage in Old High German that it became a form of personal address, as also did *frea* in Anglo-Saxon. (In Anglo-Saxon, the god occasionally was called *Frea*.) The adjectival form, *frono*, in Old High German was used to denote "lordly" in the sense of 'holy,' and the frequent use of that word was a definite indication of the religious respect in which this god was held. In addition to this sacred quality that was associated with the god, *Froh* was thought of as a gracious and understanding god, one who was associated with happiness, and in time, so popular had he become, his name took on related meanings. Modern German developed such words as froh ("glad", "happy", "joyful"), *frölich* ("cheerful", "joyous"), *frökeit* ("cheerfulness", "gladness"), and the verb *frönen* ("to be a slave of love"). Even English fell under the religious sway of this outstanding divine figure, retaining in modern language the words *frolic* and *to frolic*, which are derivations of this god's name.

It is no secret that Wagner was forced to utilize what is regularly termed the *Nordic* or *Northern* version of the Teutonic myths as the primary source for his *Ring* story simply because there were no known written versions extant that were native to his Germany. Yet, as part of his intent to create a "national work of art", Wagner turned to the German language for the name of each player that he had found in the myths. *Froh* was no exception. The composer took the older name *Fro*, carefully examined the major attributes of the god, and then unceremoniously converted the older name to *Froh*! Wagner became the brunt of some criticism for this action. There were those students of the mythology who sharply attacked the composer for what they called his distortion of the German heritage, as there are today those who do the same. Yet, it is obvious that the composer was not altering the pronunciation of the early name, and that with the word *Froh* he was merely attempting to make the name reflect certain predominant beliefs that the early people had about this god.

In *The Poetic Edda*, Froh (Freyr, Frauja, Fro, Frea, Frey) is called "the foremost of gods", and there is no doubt that he was one of the three primary deities in heathen Teutonic religious thought. Curiously, however, he was in many ways the antithesis of his cohort Wotan, who was very much a war god, and quite the opposite of even the third member of the Triad, the ill-tempered and tempestuous Donner. Froh was not a god of war, he was not interested in battle or confrontation, or the carnage of combat, and, except for his struggle in The Final Battle* of the universe, he performed no act of war whatsoever. On the other hand, however, it cannot be said that Froh was the God of Peace in that he was worshipped or invoked in that vein, but, nevertheless, he was looked upon as a tranquil god, as a peaceful god, and in the main a god whose divine powers were reflective of a such a nature.

Froh's divine powers were concerned with the milder aspects of nature and mankind. He was the god who brought the gentle rain and the sunshine, both of which were necessary for any abundance that the people reaped from their fields, a fruitfulness which in turn allowed for man's well-being and prosperity. These natural concerns of the people, and their belief in Froh's forces, allowed them to look upon him as the God of Spring. (Wagner changed this mythical godhood to that of God of the Fields.) This mythical match of Froh and nature's elements of reproduction and growth gave the people cause to interpret his godhood as one of fertility of the soil, an interpretation which, in time, they expanded to one of fertility in the union of man and woman. It was then that Froh, "the god whom no man hates," was worshipped and invoked in serious matters of love, fertility, and human reproduction. To complement such rather benign attributes, Froh was also seen as a gentle god, a considerate god, but a wise god, one whose wisdom allowed him to be one of the god-judges who sat each day at the World Ash Tree, there to make those decisions that would determine the matters of the world.

The follower of the *Ring* will read, or in the case of a performance, hear, Froh's name before the god actually makes an appearance in the drama. In the second scene of *Das Rheingold*, Freia has fled Fasolt and Fafner, the giants who pursue her with the intent to take her as their reward for their work on the magnificent new home of the gods, Valhalla. The distraught goddess rushes toward Wotan and Fricka, pleading for their help. Then, almost immediately as she makes her plea, she cries out to Donner and to Froh, asking them in turn for their assistance in her plight. Freia's turn for help to her fellow gods is, of course, a natural as well as a logical dramatic move. However, Freia's call to Froh is something more than mere dramatic action. Freia's call to Froh is also Wagner's inclusion, albeit a most subtle one, of yet another mythical belief regarding the powers of this god. In heathen Germanic thought, Froh was the god to whom the people turned for protection from captivity of any sort. According to these beliefs, Froh was the god who was invoked for protection when one wished to be free of a captor, the god who could grant freedom for those who had been made prisoner, liberty to those who somehow had been bound or fettered. It was

Froh, above all other gods, who was the divine refuge for those who needed assistance in ridding themselves of whatever or whoever had deprived them of freedom. Freia's cry for help becomes even more incisive when it is understood, as no doubt Wagner understood, that it was also believed that Froh looked with special attention on those pleas that came from maidens and wives, upon whom he regularly granted his favor of added protection from harm! (Although our concern here is primarily with the god Froh, it should be noted that Freia's call to Donner to protect her from Fasolt and Fafner is also mythically in order. Throughout all of Teutonic mythology, Donner is famed for his many battles with giants, for his numerous journeys to the East, the sole purpose of which was to confront and to slay these enemies of the gods.)

Freia's cry for help, directed first to Wotan and Fricka, and then to Donner and Froh, is a call of one deity to other gods of the same world, a cry to others, all of whom are bound together by the mythical fact of their divinity. The godhood of this quintet of beings is sufficient reason for this dramatic display of unity and cohesiveness. Yet, Wagner intensified that natural draw of one god to another. He made the relationship of these supernatural beings even stronger than it naturally was by means of a thematic device that was of his own creation. When Freia makes her plea for help, she includes in her frightened words some terms that are indicative of a familial relationship that is not altogether an accurate reflection of ancient beliefs. When the goddess addresses Fricka, she calls her "sister," and she calls Wotan "brother-in-law." Then, as she cries out to Donner and to Froh, she calls them "brothers." These few words of desperate imploration do more than expose dramatically Freia's fear and anxiety, they also reveal that Fricka, Freia, Froh, and Donner are brothers and sisters, and further, that Wotan and Fricka are husband and wife! Ancient Teutonic beliefs did not include such a relationship, at least not one that is so complete as that found in the *Ring*. In the myths of Teutondom, Wotan and Fricka are indeed husband and wife, and Freia and Froh are brother and sister. However, that is the mythical extent of the familial ties among these five deities. There are no other blood lines or marriage ties that relate any of these gods. (It is important to be aware that in both of the *Eddas*, Donner is called the son of

Wotan and Iord ("Earth"), a relationship that is not regularly made prominent in the myths. This relationship is usually viewed as one of the many that become possible because of the mythical fact that Wotan is the *Allfather*, that is, the father of *all* things.) Wagner duplicated the Wotan-Fricka union, and, also that of Freia and Froh, which for reasons of his own he extended to include Donner and Fricka. The composer never indicated the thought that compelled him to establish this created relationship that is unique to his drama. It would seem that he sensed that such a relationship as he had developed was one that brought the gods together in closer unity, and also brought them together in a manner that was not only dramatically acceptable, but one that also spurred the move by Freia to seek aid as well as the reaction of the other gods to offer aid. It seems reasonable to assume that Wagner also sensed that he was not wandering too far afield in forming this relationship because certain similar relationships had existed in the myths and, further, the relationship that he had placed in his *Ring* did not interfere in any way with the thematic development of his story. (For reasons also unexplained, Wagner extended this supernatural relationship and the matter of familial unity by making Loge 'cousin' to Donner, Froh, Freia, and Fricka.)

In the Teutonic myths, Froh and Freia are the children of Njord. This is a brother-sister-father relationship that is mentioned frequently throughout the two *Eddas*. It seems that Njord was a chief among the Vanir (Wanes) gods, a race that some scholars believe may have been a cult, perhaps nothing more than water spirits, that developed among the sea-people of the Baltic region. Little is known about the Vanir, other than that they were neighbors of the Aesir deities, of which Wotan was the supreme god. Early in the time of the world, the Vanir and the Aesir waged what has been called 'the first war.' The two races of gods fought fiercely, but it soon became evident that neither could defeat the other. Finally, this great war was concluded with a pact of peace that required an exchange of certain members of each race. For their part, the Aesir were to deliver to the Vanir the god Honir and Mimir. (Honir was a god who was to survive *ragnarök** and to have the gift of prophesy in the new era and Mimir was the guardian of the Spring of Wisdom.) The Vanir were to turn over Njord, a matter on which there is total agreement in all the myths. There is, however, some mythical disagreement on the matter of Njord's activities, or more precisely, when certain actions took place, and it is in these contradicting myths that the births of Froh and Freia are recorded. According to Sturluson in *The Prose Edda*, after Njord was given over to the Aesir gods, he married Skadi, the daughter of the giant Thjazi. This union proved to be unpleasant because each of the pair was displeased with the other's home. This prose version of the myths then states that after Njord's marriage with Skadi was ended, Njord fathered a son, Froh, and a daughter, Freia. It is obvious that such chronology makes Njord the sole hostage that was taken by the Aesir and places the births of Froh and Freia after their father was accepted into the race of gods that was dominated by Wotan. The verses of *The Poetic Edda*, however, present a different account of these events. According to the poetry, Froh was born of a union of Njord and his unnamed sister, a birth that took place *before* Njord had been turned over to the Aesir gods, and, therefore, before his marriage to Skadi. The Eddic verses do not speak directly of the birth of Freia, although she is acknowledged in these verses as the daughter of Njord and there is also the implication that she was born of the union of Njord and his sister, and at the same time as Froh. (The mythical characteristics of Froh and Freia are quite similar, and frequently identical. This mythical fact, coupled with the great probability that Freia was born of the same birth as her brother, has caused most mythologists to look upon this pair as *twins*.) Students of the Teutonic mythology have long considered the concepts, the beliefs, and the thought that are related in *The Poetic Edda* as more authentic in their basic qualities and in their details than those that are presented by the often lighthearted Sturluson in his prose writings. It is for this reason that the manner and time of the birth of Njord's children are generally accepted as those presented in the Eddic poetry, and, therefore, it is the trio of father, daughter, and son that the Vanir gods handed over to the Aesir in order to comply with the terms of the pact of peace. This version of the birth of the two gods, that is, the version offered in *The Poetic Edda*, takes on added authority when it is noted that the same Snorri Sturluson who apparently somehow depicted an incorrect time and manner of Froh's birth, gives a second version of this matter in his *Ynlinga*

Saga, which is really the opening chapters of his celebrated *Heimskringla.* In this work Sturluson's details essentially support the poetic version that Froh and Freia were born of the union of Njord and his sister, and the belief that the father and his children become the hostages that are delivered over by the Vanir.

(The subject of Froh's mother is not a primary concern in these pages, but it is, nevertheless, a topic that has provided mythologists an opportunity to study an interesting yet puzzling situation. There is general agreement among students of Teutonic mythology that *The Poetic Edda* presents the account of Froh's birth that is accepted as an accurate version of early Teutonic beliefs, that is, that his mother was Njord's sister. It is that same *Edda* that also offers a clue to her identity, a clue that reaches us through Froh, or rather through the god's name. In one of the Eddic poems, a servant calls the god by a hyphenated name, a practice that is only infrequently followed in those writings (e.g., Utgard-Loki, Asa-Thor). The name that is used in the *Edda* is *Ingunar-Freyr.* This name is used only once in the *Edda,* and there is no further reference, either direct or indirect, to the prefix word, which, of course, permits several questions to go unanswered. What, indeed, is the purpose, if any, of the prefix word? What is the significance of *Ingunar*? Does the prefix word have any special meaning? Some linguists who have given attention to this matter have advanced the idea that *Ingunar* may be the genitive of a woman's name, *Ingun,* and because the name is here associated with Froh, it may very well be the name of the god's mother, and that of Njord's sister.)

The reader of the Teutonic myths will quickly discern that Froh was not originally of the Aesir clan. In *The Poetic Edda* the god is born a Vanir and later is handed over to the Aesir as part of the pact of peace that had been arranged. In *The Prose Edda* there are two versions of his birth, one that duplicates that found in the Eddic verses and a second that states that he was born at a later date, but still the offspring of the Vanir god Njord, about whose origin and background there is no doubt. Regardless of which of these versions is a more accurate account, and it is always possible that each was an accepted belief in some region of the vast Teutonic territory, Froh (and his sister Freia) went on to become accepted in mythical beliefs as if they were true Aesir! Their activities, their functions, their relationships, and even their divine powers became integral to the divine hierarchy that dominated ancient Teutonic religious thought. Not only did Froh and his sister become primary and ranking gods in their own right, each also acquired a mythical standing and a cult that on occasion ranked them higher than Wotan and his wife Fricka in certain areas of Teutondom! The follower of the *Ring* quickly becomes aware that Wagner not only accepted these prevailing beliefs about Froh and Freia, but that he also intensified them in his drama by enlargement of the sphere of mythical relationships, causing the pair to be related by blood to Donner and Fricka and by marriage to the Allfather Wotan.

There were other mythical matters that Wagner had to consider as he prepared the poem that was to be his *Ring* drama, one of which was the dwelling places of the gods. In the Teutonic myths Froh is the only one of Wagner's gods who does not possess a stately and magnificent dwelling. In mythical beliefs, Wotan's home is *Valaskjolf* ("Shelf of the Slain"). Fricka's home is called *Fensalir*, while that of Freia is known as *Sessrymnir* ("Rich in Seats"), which is located in Folkvang ("Field of the Folk"). Donner's home is *Bilskirnir*, which is located in Thrudheim ("Place of Might"). Each of these homes is a mighty dwelling, and the myths in their own way tend to make much of the fact that these gods possess such resplendent abodes. However, these same myths do not assign a dwelling to Froh, and further, they give no reason why this ranking god is so unlike the other deities in that he has no abode of his own. Wagner was conscious of this mythical reality, and because he was intent to incorporate into his *Ring* whatever he could of early Teutonic beliefs, he makes mention of this condition, if in a subtle and almost inconspicuous manner. The incident occurs in *Das Rheingold*, shortly after Loge first appears. This wily demigod, who becomes Wagner's Guardian of Fire, addresses Wotan regarding the god's great castle that stands high in the heavens. As he tells how he has inspected this stately building and how he has found that the work that the giants have put into it has been well done, he makes a brief reference to Donner and to Froh and to certain matters regarding dwellings and love. Loge says that these gods have thought of home and shelter ("Dach und Fach"), and that if they would know love, they must first have homes. These remarks are of little thematic consequence in the development of the *Ring* argument, and it is quite possible that the casual reader of the drama may give them little if any attention, or possibly even find them enigmatic. However, as Froh's actions toward his sister were an indirect depiction of his role as a divine protector, so too are Loge's words indicative of certain other mythical realities regarding his god, mythical realities of which Wagner was well aware and which, if they could play no real role in the thematic development of his argument, he was nevertheless determined that somehow he would bring them into the work. Loge's few words about Froh and his thoughts of home and shelter reflect just such an intent. Of course, Wagner had no serious concerns about which god had which home, or even that Froh had no mythical dwelling place. He simply did away with individual homes for each of the gods and housed all of them in that celestial fortress that Loge had inspected, and which would bear the name *Valhalla*.

Loge's few words concerning home and house, love and courtship are especially appropriate when Froh is a consideration, not only because he is the only of Wagner's gods who does not enjoy a dwelling, but also because he is the only deity of the Teutonic myths who experienced a serious love affair. This incident in Froh's divine existence is the subject of an entire poem, "Skirnismol" ("The Ballad of Skirnir"), in *The Poetic Edda*, and Sturluson tells the full story, with only slight variation, in *The Prose Edda*. The storyline, in brief, is as follows: Froh enters the noble dwelling of Wotan, the Allfather. Once inside this stately mansion, the god seats himself in Hlidskjolf ("Shelf of the Slain"), the place from which one can see everyone and everything that happens in the nine worlds* that make up the universe. (Wagner not only made Valhalla the home of all the gods, but he also brought into the fortress that place in Wotan's home from which the Supreme God looked down to view the happenings of the universe.) As Froh looks out over the world, he looks down into Jotunheim ("Land of the Giants") and there he sees a lovely maiden, Gerd. The god is immediately smitten by Gerd's beauty, and he is overcome with love. Froh orders his aide, Skirnir, to journey to Gerd's home and there to speak to her on his behalf. Skirnir is most willing to do Froh's bidding, but he requests two items from the god: his horse and his sword.

Froh immediately grants both requests and Skirnir makes his way to Gerd and there speaks for Froh. Gerd, whom *The Poetic Edda* later calls Froh's "wife," rejects Froh's proposal. Skirnir then seeks to turn Gerd's mind in his master's behalf by making her a present of "eleven apples all of gold." When Gerd refuses this gift, Skirnir then offers her a ring of gold. Gerd again refuses. Skirnir's ire is aroused at these rejections, and he draws the sword that Froh had given him. He makes some serious threats to Gerd and then, by means of his magic staff, he begins to place a great curse on her. As Skirnir progresses with the curse, Gerd finally agrees to meet Froh in a nearby forest nine nights hence where, as she says, "Gerd will there grant delight." Skirnir hurriedly returns to Froh and tells the god what the maid has said, and when and where she will meet him. Then he repeats Gerd's words, that she will "grant delight." Froh is quite excited and anticipates the fulfillment of his love rather joyfully. He is somewhat distraught, however, because he is forced to wait what he believes is a long time before he can be with his love. The emotional strain is clearly shown in the last stanza of the poem, which is perhaps the most moving of all the Eddic verses. Froh laments:

"Long is one night, longer are two;
How then shall I bear three?
Often to me has a month seemed less
Than now half a night of desire."

Loge's isolated and thematically inconsequential remarks in the *Ring* regarding Froh and his dwelling, and love, if enigmatic to those unfamiliar with the mythology, are in reality a subtle but unquestionable indication of Wagner's thorough familiarity with the early Teutonic beliefs that formed the basis and framework of his drama. Although the composer did not choose to shed any light on Loge's remarks by the inclusion of some significant matter extracted from "The Ballad of Skirnir," the existence of an entire poem devoted to Froh and his love for a maiden points up most clearly the relevance of the god within the Teutonic divine hierarchy, and the contents of that poem further justify Wagner's choice of Froh as one of his five gods. One notes, for example, that Froh had access to Wotan's dwelling, a privilege certainly not accorded other gods! Froh also possessed the golden apples, which is a matter that can only be interpreted as somehow related to the celebrated and prized apples that the gods consumed in order to preserve their youth. The second gift that Froh sends to Gerd, the ring of gold, is not just any ring. It is, rather, *Draupnir* ("Dropper"), that ring whose magic allowed it to drop eight rings of equal weight each ninth night, and the ring that was one of Wotan's treasured possessions. Unfortunately, the myths do not reveal how it came about that Froh had access to Wotan's home, and neither do these tales reveal how the god had "apples of gold" or how Wotan's ring came into his possession. Yet, it is mythical fact that the god went freely about the Allfather's residence, and he had apples that infer the magic fruit of the gods, and he had in his possession Wotan's ring and felt free to give it as a gift. Such matters become an unequivocal indication that Froh held a status somewhat equal to that of the Supreme God himself. (It should be remembered that in some areas of Teutondom Froh was looked upon as a god higher in rank than Wotan.)

There are two additional items that are a part of "The Ballad of Skirnir" which in their own way bespeak further the mythical importance, prominence, and indeed the rank of this celebrated divine figure whom Wagner called Froh. The first of these items is the horse that Skirnir had requested of Froh in order that he could carry ourt his mission on the god's behalf, a request that the god had granted. As is usual with the items that were possessed by the gods of Teutondom, Froh's horse had its own kind of magic, a magic that made it unique even among the horses of the gods: Froh's horse could run through the darkness of night at full speed and, if necessary, it would be able to penetrate the "magic flickering flames." (The Eddic poem implies that Gerd's home is encircled by fire.) That Froh should possess a horse is in keeping with the mythical beliefs that horses were the animals most used by the supernatural beings, including the gods, in their travels. (*The Prose Edda* calls numerous of the horses of the gods by name.) Yet, of all the mythical horses that are used by the gods, even those that are called by name, there are only two that receive special mention of any sort in the Teutonic myths. One of this duet is, of course, the horse that belonged to Wotan, Sleipnir, the most famed horse of the universe, the animal that receives mythical attention quite frequently. The second horse of all

Teutondom is that unnamed creature that belonged to Froh, and which figures in this poem about the god and his love.

The second of the two items that Froh gave to Skirnir in order that he could carry out his mission of love is yet another example of the marvels that were associated with this ranking god of Teutondom. The item in question here is the god's sword. Froh's sword was a very special weapon in mythical beliefs, special in that it held a magic that was unique among all the swords of the Teutonic world. Froh's sword, when placed in the hands of a worthy warrior, could fight by itself! Throughout the "Lays of the Gods", which is that section of *The Poetic Edda* that contains the mythical lore of the Germanic peoples, reference to this sword is often made, and of all the swords of Teutondom, that which belonged to Froh was the only one of its kind. It was a weapon that received mythical respect, as well as admiration, and it was one of only two swords that is granted such prominence in the myths of Teutondom. (The other sword that is of special regard in Teutonic thought is the one that a mysterious stranger thrusts into the trunk of a tree. The stranger is, of course, Wotan, who has appeared in one of his many guises, and that episode itself is readily recognized as one that Wagner brought into his drama.) It should also be noted that Froh's sword plays a significant role in the god's mythical death, a role that comes about not because of the sword's presence, but rather because of its absence. Froh's decision to grant Skirnir's request, that is, to allow him to have the sword as he travels to the Land of the Giants on the god's errand of love, as versified in "The Ballad of Skirnir", is to prove to be a most serious mistake. Froh's decision essentially determines his fate at *ragnarok**, his destiny at the destruction and downfall of the Teutonic gods. When the fated moment of The Final Battle* is at hand, Froh has no weapon with which to defend himself against the enemies of the gods. The god's first combat is with the giant Beli, whom he slays with his fist. However, when he faces Surt, the leader of the Fire-Giants, Froh, the weaponless god, is killed.

The followers of Wagner's *Ring* will no doubt note that the composer did not bring into his drama any of the unique treasures that belonged to Froh, that is, the special horse and the singular sword, or those that were in the god's possession, that is the apples of gold and the ring Draupnir.

Certainly, however, their quantity, coupled with the special magic that was associated with each, is a considerable reflection of the weighted mythical thought that was attached to this god. Such beliefs inferred not only the overall divine power with which Froh was invested, but also the authority and control that he was thought to have. These items, however, were not the only objects that Froh controlled or possessed and which so accurately portrayed the elevated divine status that he enjoyed. There were others which, if Wagner also chose to exclude them from his drama, nevertheless served to enhance the divine status of the god in the religious thought of the early Germanic society and which also allowed an intensification of the conclusion that Froh was indeed one of the ranking gods of Teutondom.

Another of Froh's possessions, and one that illustrates the god's might and authority, was an enormous ship. Froh's ship, this "best of ships" which is mentioned in both *Eddas*, was called Skidbladnir ("Wooden Bladed"), and it was one of three prized treasures that were made for the gods by the sons of the dwarf Ivaldi ("Mighty"). (The two other items that Ivaldi's sons had made for the gods were Gungnir, Wotan's magic spear, and the golden hair that was worn by Sif, the wife of Donner.) Froh's ship was so large that it could easily accommodate all of the Aesir gods and their weapons, and when it sailed upon the seas it always received a fair breeze. Despite its size, when not in use, Froh's ship could be folded and kept in a pouch.

Of Froh's numerous possessions, however, none was more a reflection of this god's divine grandeur and authority than one that he had received as a gift from the hands of the gods themselves. This gift, which in itself is awesome to contemplate, even by the standards that Teutonic mythology had established for its gods, was an item that not even the supreme god, Wotan, the Allfather of the heathen Teutonic people, could possess. Briefly stated, the gift was an entire world, one of the nine worlds* of the universe! This gift from the gods is revealed in a poem in *The Poetic Edda* that states that in ancient times the deities of the universe gave Froh, the "bright god," the world of Alfheim, the Land of the Elves. According to the poem, this was a "tooth-gift," which referred to the social custom of presenting a child with a gift when it cut its first tooth, a custom that is still to be found in some regions of Teutonic Iceland. Unfortunately, the Eddic poem gives no further details about the gift, and there is no additional pertinent information regarding this gift in the rest of Eddic literature, hence there is no way to ascertain in what way Froh used this gift, if indeed he used it at all. The gift of an entire world, nevertheless, is singular throughout all of the mythical literature, Froh is the only god who owns such an item, and as a possession it obviously is one that has no equal!

Of all the items associated with the god Froh, that is, the apples, the ring, the sword, a horse, a ship, and the world of Alfheim, and the magic that the god acquired through their ownership, none achieved the mythical significance of a belief that developed because of yet another item that was associated with this remarkable god. The item that fomented this belief was an animal, a boar, and the belief that developed around this creature and the god was to become so extensive, so strong, and so persuasive in early Germanic cultural thought that it could not have escaped Wagner's attention; he seemed to sense that somehow, in some way, it should be made a part of his poem. Although this belief could make no thematic contribution to his drama, it was indeed one that would enhance the overall mythical ambience that the composer knew was necessary to his work, and which he sought so sincerely to duplicate.

The boar that belonged to the god Froh was a very special animal, a creature that receives more attention in the Teutonic myths than any other animal, with the possible exception of the most celebrated horse of the universe, Sleipnir, the animal that belonged to Wotan. Froh's boar was named Gullinbursti ("Goldbristle"), and the first facet of its uniqueness was that it was the only undomesticated animal that the gods of Teutondom possessed. (Even Wotan's two wolves, which he fed each day in Valhalla, and his two ravens, which he sent out daily to gather the news of the world, were essentially domesticated animals.) A second characteristic that contributed to this animal's singularity was that it was not an animal of biological origin, as were the numerous other animals that inhabited the world of the gods, but rather Gullinbursti was a creature that had been created especially for Froh. It is in *The Prose Edda* that the details of the origin of this renown animal are presented. According to the author of this *Edda*, Gullinbursti was the creation of the brothers Eitri and Brokk, the dwarfs who forged the two other treasures which, along with Froh's boar, were considered to be the most prized possessions of the gods, namely Wotan's gold ring Draupnir, the same gold ring that Froh sends to Gerd, and Donner's mighty hammer, Mjollnir. The dwarfs had fashioned Gullinbursti from a pigskin that they had heated in their furnace. When the dwarfs had finished their work, the animal's body was covered with bright bristles of gold, which gave the animal its name and which kept the creature illuminated at all times. The magic of Gullinbursti was that he could run through the air and over the waters of the oceans, and his speed was faster than that of a horse. Gullinbursti was also put to the task of drawing Froh's chariot, and the animal is specifically mentioned in that capacity when Froh attended the cremation of Wotan's favorite son, Balder.

The association of Gullinbursti with a divine figure, and especially a relationship that involved a god of such rank and divine prestige as Froh, permitted the boar an elevated and privileged status and position in Teutonic mythical beliefs. This status early on gained solid roots within the Teutonic culture, and the boar, as an animal, quickly became a creature of some importance among the people. From the earliest of times the people saw in the boar the essence of growth, development, and reproduction. They knew of this animal's penchant for rooting with its snout, and because Froh brought rain and sunshine to the fields, this culture conceived that the two worked together to bring about an abundance of crops, and in a larger sense, the fruitfulness of nature. Out of this concept, two lesser but nevertheless sturdy beliefs emerged. The first accepted the boar as the sign of fertility, and the second gave the boar the honor of having taught man how to plow!

The close relationship that the boar had with a god of the religious following that Froh enjoyed was a natural cultural stimulus for that animal to be perceived in a special light, to be accepted as a symbol of other matters that were pertinent to the society. Early warriors and chiefs began to use the boar as their personal as well as their family symbols. This practice was quite widespread and it persisted through the years, and in later times the royal lines of several Teutonic countries adopted the boar as part of their royal crests. A similar development occurred when the boar was looked upon as food. There were many who thought of the boar as a very special food, the kind reserved for royalty, or at least to be served only on special occasions. As a result of this kind of thought there developed throughout Teutonic lands the belief that the roast suckling pig was the food of the gods, a food that should grace only the truly great banquet halls of Teutondom. The epitome of this concept was clearly evident when the famed edible of the gods, the apple, was added. (This belief that the flesh of the boar was a food that was intended only for the select few was furthered, without doubt, by the mythical belief that the slain heroes who had been chosen to be received in Valhalla ate only the meat of a boar that was prepared each day, and then later raised in order that it could be served as food the next day.)

The mythical association of Froh and a boar, and the cultural practice of preparing this animal as food, gave rise to yet another custom among the Teutonic peoples, especially among those of the northern regions of Teutondom. As amply evidenced in the previous paragraphs, Froh was a highly venerated god, a deity whose magic was often invoked, a deity whose mythical favor was often sought, and the custom that was developed apparently was believed to be a more concrete means by which the people could gain the god's attention. At such time as a boar had been prepared for a banquet, the participants -- before seating themselves at the table -- would swear individual vows, pledges, and even oaths, each one of which took on an almost sacred quality, pledges that bound the celebrants to their fulfillment. Following these words, the boar was then appropriately dedicated to Froh. This kind of ceremony was practiced on the belief that the act of swearing vows upon the boar was a way of assuring that Froh would look kindly upon the participants and in turn would work his magic in their behalf. In the beginning this custom was regularly observed at various times of the year, but in time it became almost a ritual at the arrival of the new year.

The consecration of a boar to Froh during the feast of the New Year was analogous to the sacrifices that were common to earlier Teutonic practices. Animal sacrifice, as a means of pleasing, placating, or appeasing the god, or of securing the benefits of his divine forces, was a regular part of the religious ritual of the early people of Teutondom. These rites of sacrifice, which were readily accepted and frequently practiced by the people, were looked upon as the most solemn form of worship and devotion, and were considered to be the most elevated display of belief in the respective gods. The sacrifice of an animal was the single highest societal honor that could be given to a god, and when the god to be invoked or honored or favored was Froh, it was only natural that the animal to be sacrificed would be a boar. (It should be noted that specific kinds of animals were sacrificed to certain gods, and the only animals that could be sacrificed were males whose flesh was edible.)

The matter of animal sacrifice as practiced in the early heathen culture, coupled with the mythical attention that the Eddic literature gave to the association of Froh and a boar, and as well to boars in general, apparently were sufficiently persuasive to cause Wagner to conclude that some aspect of the theme of a boar was appropriate for his *Ring*. The composer obviously understood that such a theme could not become primary in his story, and as drama one expanded into four separate works, it was most evident that the matter would remain secondary to major themes and topics. Yet, Wagner was always desirous of creating a mythical ambience, a dramatic environment that essentially mirrored early Teutonic thought, and the theme of Froh's boar and related concepts loaned themselves ideally to this intent. The composer deemed that the opportune place to include this matter was in the second act of the first poem that he would write, *Götterdämmerung*, at that point when Hagen arouses the vassals to give welcome to their leader Gunther and his bride Brünnhilde. Hagen desires that the gods look with favor on this union, and to that end he requests that sacrifices be made to these gods, as part of the wedding celebration. Hagen orders that oxen be sacrificed to Wotan, and that a goat be slaughtered for Donner. He states that a sheep must be sacrificed to console Fricka, and of special interest at this point, he says that a boar must be offered for Froh.

Neither Hagen nor the vassals elaborate or expand on these requests. The storyline of the drama moves along on in a spirited manner, wholly as if the requests for sacrifice were integral as well as natural to the celebration at hand. It is quite possible that a casual reading of this section of the *Ring* might allow for Hagen's words to be disregarded, or at least passed over, much in the manner that Loge's reference to Froh and a dwelling and love were overlooked, ignored as it were in the deluge of the poem's more significant concerns. If Hagen's words are in fact studied, it is then possible that the reader of the *Ring* who is unfamiliar with the myths that form that drama's foundation might easily conclude that these declamations represent a form of dramatic color, a means by which the dramatic excitement of the scene might be heightened. Yet, it remains that Hagen's request is not a spurious matter; his wishes are not a matter that Wagner devised to lend show or to add perspective to his drama. Rather, Hagen's words are a reflection of the mythical beliefs and the cultural practices that were part and parcel of the heathen Germanic thought and behavior, and, at the same time, they are also a further indication of the composer's intimate knowledge of the mythology that served him so well as he created his version of the story of the gods.

Froh's single instance of dramatic prominence in the *Ring* arrives in the climactic final moments of *Das Rheingold*. Wotan has settled the matter of his payment of the gold to the giants and he is ready to lead the gods in their initial entrance into their new home and fortress, Valhalla. The deities stand on the mountain-top, their great castle hidden from view by the veil of mists that surrounds it. Donner slowly mounts a rock, and he then begins to swing his mighty hammer. He soon garners all his strength to bring the hammer down upon the rock, creating a loud clap of thunder and a flash of lightning that streaks through the sky. The clouds suddenly disappear, and Valhalla stands majestically in the heavens. The God of Thunder then calls to Froh, asking that he show the gods the pathway (*Weg*) to the fortress. Froh, the Guardian of the Rainbow Bridge, stretches out his hand and a great rainbow appears. It arches high in the sky and reaches from the feet of the gods, out and over the deep valley, to Valhalla. Froh then turns to the gods and bids them to cross the bridge. Accompanied by some of the most sonorous and expressive music of the *Ring*, the gods then begin to make their way over the rainbow, into their new home.

The Rainbow Bridge that Wagner's Froh brings forth and which his gods use as their pathway to Valhalla is a prominent feature in Teutonic mythology, one which has a significant role in the existence of the gods. In the myths this bridge of colors is known as *Bifrost* (some scholars refer to it as *Bilrost*), a name that Wagner disregards totally in his drama. The mythical function of Bifrost is to serve as the roadway that connects Asgard, the Land of the Gods, with other parts of the universe. The gods cross Bifrost daily as they make their solemn journey to the World Ash Tree where they meet in council and make their judgments. The Rainbow Bridge is also the pathway that Wotan uses to reach other parts of the universe as he travels about in his persistent search for knowledge and wisdom, or as he seeks to observe all that transpires in the universe that the gods have made. However, the *volva*, the wise woman, has predicted the ultimate doom of the gods, and she has also said that in that destruction the Fire-Giants, those formidable enemies of the gods who live in Muspellsheim, Land of Fire, will come from the south, and following their leader Surt they will cross Bifrost to confront the gods in The Final Battle*. Wotan listened intently to the *volva*, and then sought to prepare for that fateful day. The Allfather gathered a large army that he housed in Valhalla, and the gods made ready in part by posting one of their own as watchman. This god who would be ever alert would reside at the Rainbow Bridge, and he would sound a warning should any enemy attempt to cross Bifrost to gain entrance to the Land of the Gods. This Guardian of the Rainbow Bridge, the warder of the gods, was *Heimdall*, one of the primary deities of early Teutonic religious belief.

Heimdall was a most holy god. The early people of Teutondom called him the *White God*, a term that suggested that he was the *God of Light*, a godhood that probably arose out of the need for the presence of the sun in order for the rainbow to be visible. The myths state that Heimdall was the son of Wotan and nine women who were, at least according to *The Prose Edda*, sisters. These same myths also reveal that Heimdall had been made with the "strength of the earth, with ice-cold sea, and blood of swine." This warder of the gods could see one hundred leagues by day and night, and his hearing was so sensitive that he could hear the wool on a sheep and the grass grow. Heimdall lived in a house that stood at the end of Bifrost, from which he could observe all who crossed the bridge. The *volva* who had predicted the destruction of the gods also had said that when the enemies of the gods approached the Rainbow Bridge, to cross over into Asgard, Heimdall would sound an alarm on his special horn, an instrument that lay hidden in the World Ash Tree and which was to be used only to signal a warning to the gods. In time, The Final Battle* would take place and in that struggle Heimdall would fight with Loge and the two would slay each other.

Wagner's designation of Froh as Guardian of the Rainbow Bridge is a major deviation from the mythical realities of heathen Teutonic beliefs. The composer never spoke the matter of his replacement of Heimdall as the guardian, and therefore any explanation is merely speculation. It seems appropriate, however, to assume that Wagner was guided in this action by two factors: theatricality and thematic economy. He was aware that Bifrost was an integral part of the mythical universe, serving, as it did, the daily existence of the gods, and becoming, as it did, a factor in their final doom. Without doubt, he sensed that the Rainbow Bridge, if utilized properly, could provide a dramatic scenic impact of considerable intensity. He did not place his rainbow bridge in the destruction that comes to the gods and their universe, as it was found in the myths. (The poem of *Götterdämmerung* had been completed some three and one-half years before he began the sketch of *Das Rheingold*.) Rather, he envisioned the bridge as a valuable dramatic property in that poem which would be populated only by the gods and other supernatural figures, where it could serve as the pathway for the gods to that new home that he had provided for them in the sky.

Wagner obviously understood that this bridge, like other mythical items that held some special magic, must have one of the gods as its owner or keeper. Yet, he was fully aware that Heimdall had been one of the less colorful figures among the major gods of Teutondom. He also had long known that Heimdall's cultural following had not evoked the religious enthusiasm that had developed around the gods of the Triad. He knew that the divine powers held by Heimdall were not nearly so extensive or so conclusive as those of Wotan, Donner, and Froh. His Wotan of the *Ring* possessed and controlled the magic of the great spear; his Donner retained that of his mighty hammer. It was only the Froh of his *Ring* who had not been invested with any of the properties that were the marks of the Teutonic gods of rank. At the same time, he sensed that the introduction of yet another god, one not nearly so mythically significant as his Froh, might be thematically unwise, especially if it were accomplished merely to bring forth a single bit of mythical magic. Such a figure would necessitate additional matters of plot in order to intertwine him into the story, and those themes and actions and their related characterization would only dilute, if not seriously weaken, those that were primary to his tale. Wagner also realized that the presence of another god could cause serious distraction from the primacy of his trio of deities. There was no real need in his *Ring* for Heimdall and, on the other hand, his Froh was in need of a magic property. The result, of course, became the arrangement in the *Ring* as we know it: Froh, the God of the Fields, would also become Guardian of the Rainbow Bridge.

It seems clearly evident that Wagner's choice of Froh as one of the gods of his *Ring* resulted more from the god's standing within the religious attitude of the early Teutonic culture than from a dramatic need of his mythical functions or activities. It is also obvious that Wagner showed little concern for the many and varied details about Froh that are found in the *Eddas*. Yet, ironically, it is the sum of those details that point up this god as the principal and primary god that indeed he was. Wagner felt no need to consider this god's origin, albeit questioned as it was, or to dramatize any of Froh's main divine functions or the many activities in which he participated, or to refer to any of the several items of magic that he controlled. Then, to add mythical color to his otherwise individual characterization of this god, he invested him with the powers of a lesser god of Teutondom! It can be argued, however, that despite Wagner's arrangement of mythical tangibles and despite Froh's rather low dramatic profile throughout the *Ring* story, and despite the god's insubstantial thematic contribution to that story, Wagner's Froh emerged as the important Teutonic god that the mythology shows him to be.

In the *Froh* of the *Ring*, one finds the essence of the Teutondom deity of early times. Wagner's Froh projects the pacific and temperate qualities that were his divine trademark. Wagner's Froh is a god of tranquility, a protector, a god of bounty and fruitfulness. If the qualities are drawn more by subtle reference, by innuendo perhaps, than by overt participation in the matters of the story, they are, nevertheless, very much a part of that story. It is obvious that Wagner adapted and adjusted the Nordic version of the religious thought that once was dominant within Germanic culture. It is also true that Wagner's Froh does not display the intensity and the proportion of the earlier god, and in that sense he is a god unique to the *Ring*, but above all else, Wagner's Froh is indeed that once mighty god of ancient Teutondom.

V
WOTAN

The most powerful divine being of ancient Teutondom, the Allfather of the universe, the supreme god of the heathen Teutonic peoples, was Wotan. This god was the all-pervading deity in pre-Christian Germanic religious beliefs, the god whose cult was practiced by all of the early tribes, the god to whom these ancient people had given limitless divine power and authority which, in turn, permitted him to exercise a religious control that dominated practically every aspect of the lives of these people as well as the existence of the world that they inhabited. At the zenith of his religious powers, Wotan was so revered --and so feared -- that the simple act of calling aloud his name could produce an emotional experience that was so intense for some of these early people that they could be transported beyond what can only be called the limits of normal mental and emotional day-to-day reality. Wotan was, without question, the *All-Mighty* of the ancient Germanic world. It was this god whom the people so intensely invoked that Wagner brought into his *Ring*, the god for whom he caused an altar stone to be erected and animal sacrifice to be included in his drama, much in the manner of the early heathen Teutonic people. It was this god and the dominance that he held over all of Teutondom that Wagner was to make the protagonist and principal force in his *Ring*.

The belief and faith in Wotan as the Supreme God of the Germanic peoples remained relatively intact for a period of several centuries. The cultural and societal devotion and dedication to this god was unshaken until the advent of Christianity, which began about 800 A.D. in what today is modern Germany, but which did not reach Scandinavia until the end of the spectacular, incredible Age of the Vikings, that is, about 1100 A.D. It is true, however, that during this lengthy period there were two other gods who, at certain times and in specific regions of the Teutonic world, would garner a religious significance that rivaled that of Wotan. In southern Norway the God of Thunder, known there as Thor but called Donner in Germany, was much venerated because of his special powers, and in southern Sweden, Froh, who was called Freyr, had his unique niche in religious beliefs. Yet, throughout the many years, in all of the vast area of Teutondom, and among all the numerous but varied clans or tribes of peoples, it would really be Wotan who was the ranking god, the primary essence of all religious belief of the heathen Germanic peoples.

There is both a linguistic history of the name of this important god of Teutondom as well as a history of his mythical origin. The latter is essentially straightforward and unquestionable while the former probably raises more questions than it answers. This linguistic history of the word *Wotan*, if interesting, is very much fragmented, and really unsubstantiated. As mythologists probed the Teutonic past over the years, several theories regarding the origin and development of this god's name surfaced. Each of these theories is distinct in and of itself, yet each projects an attractive credibility. Curiously, however, when these ideas are viewed collectively, one with the other, they reflect a certain similarity, a kind of relationship that is immediately recognized.

Some students of language believe that the word that was first used as a name for the god was *Voden*. (This name is found, if only once, in *The Prose Edda*.) Theorists speculate that this word was derived from Old Norse *vada* (pronounced *vatha*), which was a term that denoted "fury", "rage", or "wrath". Each of these meanings, in one way or another, is exemplary of this god and each can readily be associated with his character, and thus the *vada-voden* relationship seems to offer a most acceptable basis for the origin of the name. Those scholars who expound this theory lend added support to their idea by citing the variations of the god's name that developed in several of the southern Germanic languages, each of which retains the meaning of the original Old Norse word: Gothic - *Vodans*; OS - *Wuodan* and *Wodan*; AS - *Woden* and *Othan*; OE - *Woden*; Frisian - *Weda*; OLG - *Wodan*; OHG - *Wuotan*. This last cited variation, that is *Wuotan*, underwent additional development and later became *watan* and *wust*, both of which survive in modern German as *wuten* ("to rage", "to be furious") and *Wut* ("rage", "fury", "frenzy"). Wagner used a form of the last cited item, in reference to the *Ring's* Wotan when, in the fourth scene of *Das Rheingold*, he causes Fricka to call the god "Wütender". (The sound represented by the ON initial *V* was indicated by the letter *W* in the majority of the southern Teutonic languages.)

The variations of the original *vada* that developed in the languages of the northern region of the Teutonic world were somewhat different. In the Scandinavian tongues, the initial "V" sound was not preserved, and thus *vada* became *od*, -- a byname of the god -- which in turn allowed *Voden* to be rendered as *Odinn*. (A variation found in early Icelandic is *Odur*.) In time, *Odinn* became *Odin*. (In earliest language, the letter *d* in these words was originally pronounced *th*, thus *Odin* at one time was pronounced *Othin*. During the period of development of the Germanic languages, some changed this voiceless interdental into a voiced alveolar consonant which was written and pronounced much like the English *d*.)

A second theory regarding the origin of the word *Wotan* is equally interesting, if less accepted by linguists. This theory proposes that the term is a development from an earlier word which, apparently, has not been preserved, a term that conveyed the idea of "penetrating movement." This concept can be associated, metaphorically at least, with the manner and actions of the tempestuous god, Wotan. Those who accept this theory support their claim by declaring that the original *vada* eventually became the modern German *watan* and its English counterpart *to wade*. (It is interesting to note that one of Wagner's earliest ideas regarding the first scene of his drama, which he partially developed in written form, was to have Wotan *wading* about in the waters of the Rhine River.)

There is yet a third theory of the origin of the word *Wotan*, a recent proposal that must be considered hypothetical pending yet to be uncovered supporting linguistic evidence. This theory proposes that the word *Wotan* is a development from *witan*, which -- in its time -- meant "understanding," or "sagacity." This theory also suggests that *witan* was derived from the original *vada* which, in addition to "wrath," "rage," and "fury," meant "intoxicated" in the sense of "frenzied" or "enthusiastic with understanding." These concepts apparently were carried over into *witan* and then into *wotan*, a term that supposedly depicts the god as "intoxicated with learning and understanding." (There is tangential support for this idea in that the early word *witan* survives in English as the plural of the OE *wita*, which meant "sage" in the sense of "wise," and which is related to OHG *wizzo*, which had a similar meaning. In OE *witan* was a verb that meant "to know," and in Anglo-Saxon England the word was used to refer to members of the king's advisory council, the *witenagemot*.)

It is essentially a matter of linguistic inclination, or perhaps orientation, as to which of the theories regarding the development of the word *Wotan*, if any, is entirely or even partially correct. Each is persuasive in that each of the several distinct meanings that are attached to the original term and to its variations can be readily associated with Wotan, or are representative of some aspect of his divine manner. Disregarding momentarily the matter of origin and linguistic development of the word, what remains indisputable is the relevancy that the god's name maintains in modern Teutonic culture, whether it be the Scandinavian *Odin* or the German *Wotan*, both of which are used extensively in their respective geographical regions. In the twentieth century the term *Odin* is used almost exclusively in English, the result of a popularity that is apparently rooted in the widespread awareness and familiarity with the history of the Vikings. At the same time, it is interesting to note that many of those who refer to the god as Wotan often relegate the term Odin to a distinct and unrelated culture!

Unlike the speculation that surrounds the matter of the origin of Wotan's name, the origin of the god himself raises few questions. This origin is depicted in *The Poetic Edda*, which is accepted as the principal as well as authentic record of heathen Teutonic beliefs and, therefore, the basis for all authoritative statements about the religious concepts of the early Germanic peoples. The verses in this manuscript state that once, long before the world existed, there was only the intense cold of the north and the heat of the south, between which lay a vast space that was called *Ginnungagap* ("Yawning Gap" or "Yawning Chasm"). As time passed, the cold and the heat came together, and the ice and the frost then began to melt. Slowly, out of the rime that this condition produced, a cow emerged. This creature was called *Audhumla*, and she began to lick the ice blocks of Ginnungagap. At the end of the first day the hair of a man appeared. Audhumla continued to lick the ice, and by the end of the second day the man's head was visible. As the third day ended, the entire body of the man had appeared. This being was Buri, who then had a son, Bor, who, in turn, married Bestla, a giantess. This union produced three sons: Odin (Wotan), Vili, and Ve.

Unlike this trio's Wotan, who was to become the major god of the Teutonic race, Vili and Ve were not to have any serious role in the religious beliefs of the early Germanic people. Actually, little is known about these two brothers of Wotan, and they are mentioned by name in only one poem of *The Poetic Edda*. However, the scant attention that Eddic literature gives to Vili and Ve did not persuade Jakob Grimm, the eminent German mythologist, that these brothers were merely passive beings in the heathen religious scene. Grimm claimed that Vili was *Wish*, that Ve was *Will*, and that the two were really one with Wotan. In Grimm's mind this trio of sons born to Bor and Bestla was an early Germanic *Trinity*, three aspects of religious thought united in one godhood. There is no substantial mythical evidence to support Grimm's idea, which is essentially negated by the mythical beliefs that maintain that both Vili and Ve became fathers, and that their sons survived *ragnarök**, the catastrophic destruction that befell the universe, and continued life in the new world in *Vindheim* ("Home of the Wind").

The succinct and relatively unspirited Eddic account of Wotan's birth easily allows for the impression that this event was a matter of minor mythical significance. Such a reaction is strengthened by the attention that the myths give to Wotan's later activities, the extensive accounts of his continuous movement throughout the world, his dominance in all matters of the universe, and the concern that these tales show for the numerous divine forces that he exercised. These various episodes tend to overshadow, both in quantity and in detail, the terse, matter-of-fact record of the god's origin. Wotan's birth, however, was not only a matter of religious importance among the early Teutonic peoples, it was also a necessary component in the acceptance of his divinity. Wagner deemed this aspect of his Wotan of little dramatic importance, apparently because such a matter had no part whatsoever in the story that he developed. And thus it was that the origin of the Supreme God of the *Ring*, and in fact the origin of all its gods, is not depicted or referred to in the drama.

The early Germanic peoples viewed their gods in a rather unique manner. These heathen tribes had no apparent concept of immortality, at least such a concept is not demonstrated in Eddic literature, hence the gods of these peoples did not enjoy an eternal existence. Neither did these ancient peoples have a concept of infinity, and thus it was that while their gods were to have their religious domain, they would hold that domain only for a limited period of time. The Germanic race also believed that their gods had a definite substance and a definite presence that was not unlike that of mortal man, and, therefore, that substance and that presence had a *beginning* and an *end*. Although Wagner felt that there was no thematic need to depict a *beginning*, that is an origin, for any of his *Ring* gods, the concept of their *end* was paramount in his drama, as it was in myth. That 'end' became so significant, so important in his argument that he causes the *Ring* Wotan to make reference to it as early as the second act of *Die Walküre*. This first reference to the end of the gods is made in that scene in which the dejected Wotan speaks to his daughter Brünnhilde, telling her that he seeks to be free from his troubles and his concerns and that now he awaits only one single moment, "The End" ("Das Ende")! A second reference to the destruction of the gods comes in the third act of *Siegfried*, at that moment when the great god of Teutondom tells Erda that he has willed the end for all the gods, an end that is certain to befall them.

The existence of the Teutonic gods, then, was much like that of human existence, that is, the deities experienced birth, life, and ultimately, death. It is mythically true that the gods of Teutondom had strengths and powers that were greater than those of mortals, but that is part of what made them gods. These deities also held a magic with which they could originate, manipulate, or terminate matters that were beyond the control of man. That is another segment of what made them gods. And, these gods lived for a period of time that was longer than the lifetime of man. This was yet another aspect of their godhood. But, throughout it all, these gods of Teutondom lived, functioned, acted, and reacted in manners that were reflections of human life. The heathen Teutonic peoples viewed their gods as human in form, human in nature, and human in character, and like man, they began their existence by means of the same process by which mortal life began, biological conception and birth! (The Eddic literature does not record the origin of each deity. In those cases in which there is no question regarding the godhood of a specific figure, and there is lacking an account of that figure's birth, it is usually correct to assume that the character is not a god of primary rank within the Teutonic divine pantheon.)

The concept that divine existence mirrored that of mortal life was one of the most fundamental and most consistent beliefs of the ancient Germanic religion. In addition to birth, an existence in human form, and death, the gods of Teutondom experienced other matters natural to mortal life. These gods ate and drank, and they loved and hated, they laughed and they cried, they became happy, angry, sad, they sought revenge, and they were generous. Even a casual examination of the *Ring* figures will reveal that Wagner's gods exhibited, in one way or another, each of these human traits and characteristics. Indeed, his Wotan alone -- somehow and somewhere in the *Ring* -- demonstrates each and every one of them. The gods of myth feared and were feared, and they, like mortals, also suffered and endured physical handicaps. These gods also knew joy and suffering through their children because, again like man, the deities married, had sexual intercourse, and became parents. The unions that the gods formed, as well as those of their children, established relationships of blood and marriage that were not at all unlike those of earthly life.

The marriage and parenthood of Wotan, the Supreme God, the All-Mighty God, were exemplary of the basic beliefs that the Germanic clans had formed about the life of their gods. The mythical literature states that Wotan had taken Fricka as wife, a relationship that Wagner carried over into his *Ring*. The myths then reveal that from this union came the foremost of all divine families, that which inhabited Asgard, the Land of the Gods. These offsprings of Wotan were, according to Grimm, lesser gods, all of whom served Wotan, their father, in his supreme godhood. It was in this situation, this parenthood, that the term *Allfather* (*Allfod, Allfadr, Allfader*) came into being both as a form of address to the god, and as a reference to him. This term, however, denoted something more than simply 'progenitor of the gods.' Wotan had been a principal in the creation of the first man and the first woman, and he had been instrumental in the creation of the world in which these mortals lived. It was these involvements, in turn, that accounted for his being called "the father of men" as well as "the father of all things." Wotan, indeed, was the *Allfather*, but in a manner far greater than that proposed by Grimm.

Wotan was very much the Allfather of the universe, but he was also a father in a more personal or immediate sense. Wotan was a father in that way in which mortal men are fathers. With his wife, the god sired two sons, each of whom was to achieve prominence in the divine world. The first of these offsprings was Balder, "the fairest of the gods," who was of special favor to his mother and who was to become the most beloved of all the Teutonic gods. However, Balder died an unexpected death at the hands of the second son, Hod, who was blind. The gods knew that they really should not blame Hod for this death because it had been a death that had been carefully planned and essentially executed by Loge. Balder's death, however, angered the gods, and Wotan's ire became so intense that he sought to avenge it. The god's vengeance was realized through another son whom the god fathered by the seduction of the goddess Rind. This son was called Vali, and it was he who -- one day after his birth -- killed Hod. Balder and Hod later returned to life, survived the cataclysmic end of the world, and lived on in Wotan's battlehall, Valhalla. (Mythologists tend to consider Balder's death as the first in a series of tragedies that culminates in the downfall of the gods and the destruction of the world, or *ragnarök**.)

Wotan was the father of another son, Vidar, whose mother was the giantess Grid. The major mythical feature of this son of the Allfather was his great strength, a strength that was almost the equal of that of the famed Donner. Vidar's might and power were to become paramount as he played out his primary mythical role, that of avenger of his father's death. Wotan met his death in The Final Battle*, in a confrontation with Fenrir, the monster-wolf. When Vidar learned of his father's death, he sought out the god's slayer and killed him. Curiously, *The Poetic Edda* contains two distinct accounts of how Vidar slew this offspring of Loge. There is that tale that relates that a prophetess says that Vidar will kill the wolf by thrusting his sword into the creature's heart. The verses of a second Eddic poem relate the account that mythologists consider to be the more acceptable in heathen Teutonic thought, that in which a wise giant says that Vidar put his great strength to work and with that strength he tore Fenrir's jaws apart. This son of Wotan, like his half brothers Balder and Hod, survived the destruction of the universe.

Wotan was the father of yet another son. This offspring was the celebrated Donner, the *Asa-Thor*, or "Thor of the Gods" as he was known in Scandinavia. This deity, who was to become Teutondom's God of Thunder and Lightning, who was to be venerated throughout all of the early Germanic world, and who was to become one of the three most powerful gods of the Germanic world, was conceived during Wotan's stay with Iord ("Earth"), who -- according to mythical beliefs -- was Wotan's wife and daughter at one and the same time. The myths state that Donner had a brother -- Meili -- who apparently was born of this same union. Unfortunately, little is known about this second son of Wotan who is named in only one poem of *The Poetic Edda* and who receives no mention whatsoever in *The Prose Edda*.

The children of the Supreme God of Teutondom were not all males. Wotan was the father of at least one daughter, an offspring called Saga. Sturluson writes in *The Prose Edda* that Saga is a goddess, but no such depiction is made of her in *The Poetic Edda*. In the latter work, Saga is called by name, but in only one poem, and all that is known about her is to be found in a single stanza. The verses of that stanza reveal that Saga lived in Sokkvabekk ("The Sinking Stream"), a place where cool waters flowed and where she and her father Wotan drank daily from cups of gold. Saga has no role in the mythical activities of the gods and students of the myths have been unable to determine what significance, if any, she had in mythical beliefs. Some scholars have theorized that Saga's name infers relationship to the telling of stories, or possibly to the rendering of accounts of historical matters. Others have proposed that Saga is a hypostasis of Fricka. Despite the scant mythological data regarding Saga, and her apparent secondary position in the Teutonic mythical framework, she is an acknowledged child of the Allfather.

Wagner respected the mythical fatherhood of Wotan. This respect is engendered in his drama, not so much by a duplication of any of the several relationships that are to be found in the *Edda*, and their resultant offsprings, but rather by singular familial relationships that the composer created for his drama and its storyline. Wagner caused the Wotan of his *Ring* to father eleven offsprings. Nine of these children are, of course, the Valkyrie sisters who come into the supernatural world through the god's union with Erda. Wagner's god believed that Erda was the wisest being of the universe, an attribute that he apparently felt would be passed to these nine supernatural figures, and especially to his favorite daughter, Brünnhilde. Wotan's *Ring* wife looks upon these nine sisters with a different eye. Fricka sees the nine as truly wretched creatures, and she treats them with some disdain and no little scorn. The other two of Wotan's *Ring* children are Siegmund and Sieglinde, whom the god fathered through a union with a mortal woman. Fricka views these two as products of her husband's wanderlust and she also believes that this pair should be punished for their union with each other. Wotan sees the brother and sister relationship in a different light, that is, the god of the *Ring* believes, at least in the beginning, that Siegmund will be the hero who will undo the problem that he has brought upon the world.

Wotan's mythical fatherhood -- seven offspring through five distinct sexual unions -- contributes to the concept of the god as the Allfather of Teutondom and, at the same time, subtly infers the god's rather promiscuous nature. Indeed, the Eddic words that refer to Wotan as "the enchanter of old" correctly depict this great god of the universe, and it is equally true that the same powers that gave this god dominion of the universe were the same forces that bestowed upon him what the Eddic verses call the magic with which he could turn a woman's head to his own delight. It is Wotan himself who openly admits that he was able "to master maids," and he once boastfully stated that "seldom shall a young maiden go from me."

The portrait of Wotan as the consummate, but nevertheless promiscuous, persuader is enhanced by the god's numerous extramarital relationships that are recounted in the myths. In addition to those four such unions already noted, that is, with the giantess Grid, with Iord, his seductions of the goddess Rind, and the union with the unnamed mother of Saga, there were others! One tale relates that on one occasion, when Wotan was in the East, a "linen-white maid" granted him "joy." Other verses tell how this god of gods even worked the magic of his "love-craft" on those who rode about at night. (Teutonic beliefs held that witches traveled in the darkness of night on the backs of wolves.) And, in what certainly must be the most unusual mythical union yet, on another occasion, Wotan enjoyed the pleasures of seven women at one time!

Wotan's words regarding his seductive powers, and the mythical accounts of his numerous sexual activities, are the collective cause of an obvious hostility that existed between the god and his wife, Fricka. The goddess never hesitated to express her disapproval of her husband's conduct. Her remarks, on more than one occasion, were cutting and incisive. Wagner's keen sense of the dramatic caused him to conclude that dramatization of this aspect of the mythical god's existence had a place in his *Ring*. As he envisioned the scene, he would be able to depict at one and the same time the tenuous peace that existed between his drama's Wotan and his wife as well as what Fricka considered to be her husband's deviate, lustful behavior. These two significant features of the myths are developed in the *Ring*, mainly in the second act of *Die Walküre*, when Wotan is confronted by his wife whom he calls "... the old storm", and whom he has tried, unsuccessfully, to avoid. Earlier, in *Das Rheingold*, Fricka had berated Wotan because of the agreement that he had made with the giants Fafner and Fasolt, the pact that would reward them with the goddess Freia as payment for their labors on Valhalla. Now, she continues to upbraid her husband for his many travels throughout the universe, away from her. Fricka then vents her ire in a tirade of stored feelings. She criticizes the god for his "lawless love", that union that Wotan once had with Erda and which resulted in the nine valkyries whom she calls "wretched maidens". Fricka then tells of her disapproval of her husband's union with a mortal woman and the resultant Siegmund and Sieglinde. The goddess rebukes her husband for causing Sieglinde to commit adultery, and the brother-sister pair to be guilty of incest. The goddess then refers to her husband's conduct in general, stating that there never had been a situation wherein Wotan had not looked with lust and anticipation. Wotan attempts, if weakly, to defend his actions of the past, but Fricka only asks why, in light of all that he has done, should he show any concern about wedlock and vows when he himself is so often guilty of breaking them! (There are those biographers of Richard Wagner who insist, and with a certain amount of factual history to support them, that the Wotan-Fricka depiction in the *Ring* is based on the relationship that Wagner had with his first wife, Minna.)

Those of Wotan's activities in the *Ring* that Fricka so sternly condemns were not exclusive to the Supreme God that wanders at length through the myths. Other gods and goddesses were known to conduct themselves in like manner from time to time, but there apparently existed among the divine hierarchy an attitude that did not view such activity with too much disfavor. This apparent focus on Wotan seems to come about only because he is the supreme god of Teutondom, and therefore as such he is the god who naturally garners the most attention. Wotan's sexual exploits, however, seem to be integral to his being, that is, they occur frequently and are related in a most relaxed manner, and as such apparently mirror a cultural attitude predominant in that early era. Admittedly, this focus on Wotan allows the depiction of a robust and energetic god, indeed a basic necessity for that figure who would be god of the universe.

There was a third personal mythical relationship in which Wotan was a partner. This relationship, while distinct from that of husband and father, nevertheless produced a family kinship that also reflected cultural patterns that were common to early Germanic society. The relationship was known as *blood brotherhood*. This specific type of familial relationship was a union of two or more unrelated males, each of whom had sworn an oath that he would accept the other as a brother, that he would be concerned for the other's welfare, that he would defend the honor of the other, that he always would be honest and truthful with the other, and that in all ways he would be bound to the other as if in fact the pair was blood related. At one time in the history of the early Teutonic peoples such an oath was made effective and sealed by a pricking of the body and then a mixture of a drop of blood of each individual. (The ancient Germanic society considered an oath of any kind to be inviolable. The failure to fulfill or to obey one's sworn word, or to swear falsely, was one of two unpardonable crimes for which the punishment was death. The second of these two most serious crimes was murder.)

It is Wotan himself who tells of his sworn oath of blood brotherhood. Curiously, this relationship is not one that has been made with one of the deities that make up the Teutonic divine pantheon, but rather an oath that is sworn with Loge, the cunning and crafty schemer of Teutondom. The Eddic literature offers no details about this union of the god and the demigod, other than Wotan's admission. Scholars do not deny the fact of Wotan's admission, but they place a distinct interpretation on the god's words, concluding that the act to which Wotan admits is not one of blood brotherhood, but rather one of *adoption*. In addition, these students of the mythology propose a time-perspective on this act by suggesting that this 'adoption' occurred in the far-distant past, long before Loge emerged as the wily trickster that is depicted in *The Poetic Edda*, in that time when Loge was a being known as *Lodur*, and who most probably was a fire-god.

Wagner included the act of blood brotherhood in the *Ring*, but not as an act that was carried out by any of his supernatural beings. The *Ring* dramatization of the early Germanic cultural practice is found in the first act of *Götterdämmerung*, between Gunther and the drugged Siegfried, after the two had agreed on a plan that will reward each with a wife. Each of the pair cuts himself and draws a drop of blood. The drops of blood are then mixed and the two swear their loyalty to each other and, now as blood brothers, each to defend the other's honor.

In addition to the mythical Wotan's marital ties, his parenthood, and his blood brother relationship, there were yet other facets in the existence of the Allfather that were patterned after specific aspects of human life. These other matters can be grouped together and may be termed *physical qualities*, that is physical features or characteristics that were personal to the figure of this god. These features are relatively few in number, and according to Grimm, they were developed in Scandinavian thought rather than in those beliefs about the god that originated in Germany. Grimm adds that only traces of these physical matters are found in the southern version of the myths, and then only infrequently.

The great god of Teutondom, like Donner, had a beard. The hair of this beard was grey in color and the ON word *Harbard* ("Grey Beard") was a term with which the god frequently identified himself and which became one of the many names by which he was known. In the poem appropriately titled "The Poem of Grey-Beard," a verbal confrontation between Wotan and Donner takes place. Wotan appears in the guise of a ferryman with a grey beard, and is unrecognized by the God of Thunder. The emphasis that these verses seem to place on Wotan's beard, and also on its color, infers that there is some mythical significance, other than that of mere physical description, to this guise that the supreme god takes and which is so effective. It is unfortunate that the myths do not take the matter beyond the poem in question.

A second mythical belief that is related to Wotan's figure concerns the god's clothing. There are verses in the *Edda* that tell of Wotan's blue mantle, a type of cloak and hood that the god wore, apparently on those occasions when he assumed one of the many guises for which he was famed. The association of this cloak with Wotan was quite strong, so much so that like his grey beard, it gave rise to another of the many names by which the god was known. That name was *Grimnir*, or "The Hooded One." And, as in the matter of the god's beard, so too was Wotan's cloak of import in the mythical thought as evidenced by a poem in *The Poetic Edda* that is titled "The Ballad of Grimnir." These verses tell how the mantle was burned when the god, in the guise of Grimnir, was placed between two fires and the flames of one of them touched the cloak.

Wagner gave only passing attention to the beard of the Germanic Allfather, if he considered it at all, but he obviously sensed a mythical significance in the *blue cloak* that the god wore. If he had disregarded Wotan's grey beard, much as he had disregarded Donner's red beard, he deemed it important that his Wotan be dressed in a *blue* robe, the same color robe that the Eddic god had worn! That this action was not merely the result of a quirk of Wagner's mythical thinking is evidence by the fact that he placed his Wotan in a blue cloak, not once, but twice! The first of these two incidents in the *Ring* in which Wotan's blue cloak is involved is rather passive, or perhaps it is more proper to call the incident 'indirect.' In the first act of *Die Walküre*, it is Sieglinde who tells of the time when an old man entered Hunding's house and thrust a sword deep into the trunk of the ash tree that grew there. That old man wore a *blue* cloak, she adds. The second incident, which is far from a passive or indirect reference to the color of the mantle, is to be found in the first act of *Siegfried*, when Wotan, now disguised as Wanderer, makes his first appearance. As part of his stage instructions for

Wotan, Wagner wrote that the god will carry his spear as a staff and he will wear a broad-brimmed hat and a long, *dark-blue* robe! (It is curious to note that Wotan's blue cloak is a matter of some concern, both in Eddic literature and in Wagner's *Ring*, yet, oddly enough, neither of these two masterpieces of its own artistic genre offers any form of explanation as to the significance of the specified color. It is possible to assume, however, that in Wagner's case the use of the color *blue* for this article of clothing reflects the composer's concern for dramatic ambience, a part of his stated intent to create an environment that was totally mythical, a set of conditions that was replete with mythical figures, actions, and settings, as well as properties that were drawn from the ancient Teutonic past.)

There is a third physical attribute of the god which, like his grey beard and his blue mantle, can readily be associated with the ways of mortal life. This feature, however, is related more to the god's person than to his appearance, as were the others. The matter treats of the manner by which the Wotan of myth sustained himself. The Teutonic deities, like humans, consumed food and drink. The Eddic literature mentions several edibles as well as kinds of drink that were available to the gods of Teutondom. There was ox (beef), and pork, salmon, grain, and beer and mead. This same Eddic literature tells how, on one occasion, the gods gathered to eat and to drink, while another Eddic poem pictures most of the gods and some of their children together at a great feast that had been prepared for them by Aegir, a sea-god. A third poem in *The Poetic Edda* describes the voracious appetite of Donner who once ate an entire ox, eight salmons, and then drank two hundred fifty-two gallons of mead, all at one sitting! The myths also tell how each day the Allfather visited Valhalla, and while there he was attended by four Valkyries, who served as Wish Maidens and who brought food and set it before the him. Wotan, however, did not eat this food; rather, he gave it to his two gluttonous wolves, Freki ("The Greedy") and Geri ("The Ravenous"), that sat at his feet. After Wotan's wolves had eaten the food that the god had given them, the Valkyries then brought Wotan his horn of mead, which the god customarily emptied.

The food that Wotan was served and which he regularly gave to his two wolves was food which he would have consumed were it not for one overriding mythical reality. Wotan partook of sustenance on a daily basis, like the other gods, but unlike his divine colleagues, the Supreme God of Teutondom did not eat or dine in the accepted sense of those words. Rather, Wotan, the Allfather of Teutondom, the Supreme God of the Germanic peoples, *gained his nourishment from drink alone*! This feature of mythical thought seems to present an immediate and obvious contradiction within the total sphere of Teutonic mythical belief. Indeed, it is true that one belief held that Wotan derived his sustenance from drink alone, and another equally accepted as well as significant belief held that the Germanic gods, including Wotan, were eternally young because they regularly *ate* those special apples that held that magic and which were in the care of the goddess Idun. There is no immediate, satisfactory response that will resolve this contradiction to the satisfaction of some readers. However, the reader of the Teutonic myths who expects, or even hopes, to find a seamless, unbroken polished train of thought of action in these tales is targeted for early disappointment. The Germanic myths are often unfinished, incomplete in one way or another, often contradictory when viewed within the limits of contemporary standards of logic. An excellent example of this Teutonic mythical contradiction is that Wotan has only drink as food in one tale, while in another story he partakes of the apples of eternal youth. Wagner was obviously aware of these opposing mythical views regarding the god Wotan and the method of his sustenance, as well as the general existence of numerous mythical inconsistencies. He could not, however, be concerned with such matters. Rather, without regard to sustenance of any kind, he brought the apples of eternal youth into his *Ring*, placed them in the charge of Freia, and, when the goddess is held by the giants and their unavailability begins to deprive the gods of their youth, some immediate action is necessary. It is at this point that the magic apples become a primary stimulus to the Supreme God, the stimulus for Wotan to take the Nibelung gold, by whatever means, in order to secure Freia's release and restoration of her precious food.

The mythical wolves of Teutondom, to which Wotan gave his food and which are so much associated with the god Wotan, are not to be found in the *Ring*, at least not in the same manner in which they appear in the myths.

Wagner makes every effort, however, to signal the association of the Supreme God and these animals, this time by means of a unique dramatic arrangement. In the first act of *Die Walküre*, as Siegmund tells Sieglinde the story of his life, the Volsung says that his father, who is really Wotan in the guise of mortal man, was called *Wolfe* ("Wolf"), and that his father was truly a 'wolf' to cowardly foxes, that is, a threat and danger to lesser beings. This association of the Wotan of the *Ring* and the wolf is again prominent later in the music-drama when Fricka, in the course of her verbal denunciation and censure of her husband, exclaims that now that Wotan has taken on new names, he roams the forest as *Wälse* ("Volsa"), the *Wolfish*.

The final physical attribute that the myths associate with the Wotan cult-figure was one of unusual distinction. The Supreme God, in the course of his existence, had lost an eye! This physical impairment, however, did not represent an unusual aspect of early Teutonic thought. As with most other factors in the lives of the gods, physical handicaps reflected some of the reality that was found in human existence, and the Teutonic gods, like humans, knew pain and suffering, and even disablement. Wotan was not the only supernatural figure who had suffered a physical disability: Tyr had lost a hand to the monster-wolf Fenrir, Wotan's son Hod was blind from birth, Sif, Donner's wife, had suffered the loss of her hair at the hands of the demonic Loge, and Loge himself was lame and moved about with a limp. Wotan's loss, however, was unique in that it had been self-inflicted, the result of an intentional act of the god as he sought to gain wisdom and knowledge of the universe. The story of this incident is prominent in Eddic literature in a tale that tells of a water-spirit named Mimir ("Mim") who was the Guardian of the Spring of Wisdom that flowed at the base of the World Ash Tree. Wotan, always desirous to garner wisdom, wished to drink from this spring and thus become a wiser god. Mimir was willing to allow the god to drink of the spring's waters, but he required that Wotan give one of his eyes as payment for that drink. Wotan consented to Mimir's demand. He gave one of his eyes, and then drank from the spring. Mimir prized highly the eye that he had received from the Allfather which he used as a cup from which he himself drank each day and with which he watered the World Ash Tree.

There can be no doubt that Wagner was uniquely attracted to the Eddic story about Wotan's eye. The composer not only caused his god to have but one eye, but he also took much of the mythical tale about Wotan's eye that he found in the *Edda* and wove it into his drama, making no less than three references to this physical defect of Teutondom's primary god. In the *Ring* it is Wotan himself who first draws attention to his condition. In the second scene of *Das Rheingold*, as the god talks with his wife, Wotan tells her that the price he paid to woo and to win her was one of his eyes. Wagner's explanation of how the Supreme God lost an eye, which is projected by means of dialogue in his music-drama, is undeniably incorrect, at least mythically. It is not the manner by which Wotan lost an eye that is the substance of the *Ring's* second reference to the matter, but the missing eye itself. The reference in question is made in the final act of *Siegfried*, as the young and naive Volsung hero follows Forest Bird to the mountain on which Brünnhilde sleeps. On his way, the youth encounters a stranger who, in reality, is Wotan. As the two talk, Siegfried notes that the god is missing an eye. Wotan, who by mortal standards is Siegfried's grandfather, informs him that it is with that missing eye that the youth is now looking at him. Siegfried is totally unable to comprehend the full meaning of the Allfather's words. The third and final reference to the matter of the Supreme God's missing eye, one that again is concerned with the manner in which the god suffered his misfortune, is to be found in the Norn scene of the "Prelude" of *Götterdämmerung*. Now, the explanation of how the god lost an eye essentially duplicates the story that Wagner had found in Eddic literature. As the trio of Norns reviews what has happened in ages past, the First Norn tells her sisters that once, long ago, Wotan took a drink from the spring that flowed at the base of the World Ash Tree, a spring in whose waters rippled the wisdom of the universe. The Norn continues by saying that the price that Wotan paid for a drink of the waters of wisdom was an eye.

The two different versions of how the Supreme God of Teutondom lost an eye that Wagner included in his *Ring* give immediate cause for the inevitable question as to why Wagner had allowed such an error to remain in his drama. The question takes on an immense importance when one realizes that one of the versions is not only incorrect, but is also of the composer's own creation. Additionally, this entire rather conspicuous thematic blunder originates in the mind of a person who was not only intimately immersed in the Teutonic mythology that was his source, but also in a mind that was doubly intent on presenting that mythology in such a way that his nation, its people, and their culture would rejoice, indeed applaud him for his intellectual and emotional projection of what he thought was a national pride.

The question that was posed earlier, that is, why did Wagner do as he had done, really cannot be answered. Only a reasonable assumption can be offered, and even that response is flawed. It is widely known that Wagner did not write the four parts of his *Ring* in the order of their intended presentation, but rather in their reverse order. Therefore, although Wagner included the mythically correct story of Wotan and his eye in the fourth opera of his *Ring*, which in matter of fact was the first written, he did not approach the first of his four works, *Das Rheingold*, which contained the incorrect version, until some four years after he had begun his drama. It is therefore possible, although highly improbable, that Wagner simply forgot what he had written earlier. Such conjecture is meaningless when one realizes the genius as well as the absolute qualities of Wagner's mind that were then coupled with his penchant to be as mythically correct as possible. Then again, it is also fact that over a period of some ten years Wagner often reviewed his work frequently modifying, altering, or otherwise changing much of his text. In that light, it seems most probable that he was well aware of the incorrect version of the matter, and for whatever reason did not change or did not wish to change his text. Regardless of all that occurred, and of all that took place, the two versions remained in the *Ring*, and the question posed remains today still unanswered.

Wotan's exchange of an eye for the waters of wisdom is one of the more prominent incidents in the god's mythical existence. This physical loss depicted, perhaps more than any other single mythical belief, the god's serious as well as persistent intent to gain the wisdom of the world. At the same time, this loss of an eye became the means by which Wotan acquired a physical characteristic that was not only permanent to his figure, but one that also allowed for a unique and vivid physical coloration of his person.

Allusions to Wotan's loss are made frequently in mythical literature, but -- curiously -- there is not to be found in those writings an inference that the god was impeded in any way in the fulfillment of his duties, or hampered in his activities as the supreme deity of the Teutonic peoples.

As the mythical tales unveil specific physical aspects of the Supreme God, so too does that literature make frequent references to his possessions. Again in imitation of the pattern of mortal life, Wotan was the owner of several material items. The Allfather's possessions, if relatively few in number, were functionally proper and appropriate for the realization of his more important godly obligations. Yet, as with other matters pertinent to the gods of Teutondom, Wotan's possessions were generically the kinds of objects that mortals would also possess. The distinction between the two lay in the mythical fact that Wotan's possessions were singular objects, more singular both in function and scope than those counterparts that were possessed by man.

The primary possession of Wotan, that is, the item that belonged to the god and which may be considered as the most significant of all the items that were owned by the god, was his residence. This dwelling was one of magnificent grandeur, and it reflected a majesty and nobility that were appropriate to the god's rank as Teutondom's chief deity. Wotan's home was called *Valaskjolf*, which translates as "Shelf of the Slain" or "Hall of the Slain." (Some mythologists have attempted, unsuccessfully, to relate this structure to another of Wotan's halls, Valhalla, which belonged to the god but which was the home of heroic warriors who had been slain on the field of battle.) Valaskjolf had been constructed for Wotan by the gods, on a site that the Allfather himself had designated. These same gods had thatched the roof with resplendent, gleaming silver. A section of this hall was called *Hlidskjolf*, literally "Door Bench" or "Top Shelf." Hlidskjolf was the celebrated tower from which Wotan could look out over the entire universe to view all that was taking place in its nine worlds*. This 'seat' or 'shelf' was unique in Teutonic thought, and some students of the mythology have likened it to a royal throne. Such a comparison is not entirely appropriate because the magic that Hlidskjolf offered was not available exclusively to the King of the Gods, Wotan. Other gods had access not only to the hall itself, but also to

Hlidskjolf and its powers. The myths tell, for example, that Fricka often joined her husband there as they both looked down into the world. There is also an Eddic poem that relates how Froh once sat on Hlidskjolf and scanned the universe. As he surveyed the worlds, he looked into Jotunheim ("Land of the Giants") and there he saw a most beautiful maiden for whom he immediately felt an intense love.

As indicated above, there was a second structure that Wotan possessed, a hall that was to become the most renown as well as the most revered of all buildings in Teutonic mythical thought. This celebrated structure was Valhalla, a mighty fortress, and the celestial paradise so eagerly sought by mortal warriors as their residence in the afterlife. This structure was so prominent, so important in heathen Teutonic mythical thought that its name still today remains a familiar term in numerous twentieth-century cultures.

Heathen Teutonic concepts held that Wotan's Valhalla was a large and imposing hall. This building boasted 540 doors, through each of which 800 men could walk abreast. Valhalla's rafters were spears, and the roof was made of shields, one laid upon another. Benches stood all about the hall and breastplates lay upon them. A special kettle stood in the center of Valhalla. This was the kettle in which Wotan's cook daily prepared a boar that became the food for Valhalla's residents. (This boar was raised each day in order to be cooked again.)

Valhalla had been erected in Gladsheim ("Place of Joy"). Entrance to the hall was through a sacred gate call Valgrind ("Gate of Death"). A tree grew beside Valhalla, a tree named Laerad, and a hart munched on its leaves. (Some mythologists propose that this tree was the famed World Ash Tree.) A stream flowed from the hart's horns, and this stream was the source for all the rivers of the world. (The rivers are named in *The Poetic Edda*, and one of them is the Rin or Rhine.) A female goat, Heidrun, also ate the leaves of the tree, and it was Heidrun who provided the clear mead that was drunk each day by the inhabitants of Valhalla. This great fortress was surrounded by the river Thund ("The Swollen" or "The Raving") whose tumultuous waters prevented the dead in Hel from crossing in order to gain entrance to this hall of heroes. (Hel was the place in the underworld to which all women, all children, and those men who had not been selected to reside in Valhalla went after death.) Snorri Sturluson wrote in his prose *Edda* that a great forest stretched out in front of Valhalla, a forest that had the name of Glasir, and Sturluson also stated that Glasir was "the fairest woods among gods and men."

Those who resided in Valhalla, like the structure itself, were viewed and measured by the early Teutonic attitudes and concepts that prevailed about war and combat. Those inhabitants, all men, constituted a most select group. In mortal life, these men had been warriors, the bravest of warriors, who had fought most valiantly, and who had died in battle. The bravery and the courage in combat of each man had been the criteria for his selection to enjoy this prized afterlife in Valhalla. After death on the battlefield, each hero was brought to Wotan's hall by Valkyries, who then served as Wish Maidens. Once in Valhalla, each warrior was raised and made a soldier in that army that would defend the gods in The Final Battle*. Each day these warriors fought each other as a means for perfecting their war-skills, and at the end of the day their wounds were healed and they then feasted and reveled together. It was, of course, Wotan who selected the mortal heroes who would become warriors in his army, and as the god once declared, he chose only "the noble who fall in fight." Once, however, the nemesis of the gods -- Loge -- accused the Allfather of awarding "the battle prize" to some who were not worthy of this reward. Wotan studied Loge's harsh words, and then admitted that he had not always been truly discerning in his choice of heroes.

The Valhalla that Wagner brought into his *Ring* reflects the same nobility, the same majesty, the same integrity that was found in the mythical hall that served as its inspiration. Wagner's celestial fortress has the primary function of its counterpart in myth, that is, to house those slain heroes who have been selected to be brought to Valhalla, and once there, to be 'raised' in order that each could serve in Wotan's army. There are, however, certain differences in the two halls, two of which seem to be rather significant, while a third is of less import.

The first of the three differences between the mythical Valhalla and that which becomes so dramatically significant in Wagner's *Ring* is related to the construction of the building. The celestial Valhalla was constructed *by* the gods. Wagner's Valhalla was constructed *for* the gods *by* the last of the Earth-giants, the brothers Fafner and Fasolt. Wagner's arrangement of the matter in this fashion was entirely plausible, at least thematically, because he could now cause his Wotan to renege on the pledge that he had made to the giants regarding the payment for their labors on the castle. And, it would be Wotan's negation of his pledge that would set the entire drama into motion.

The second major difference between the Valhalla of ancient Teutonic beliefs and that which takes its place in Wagner's *Ring* pertains to the inhabitants of the mighty castle. In early Germanic thought, the majestic hall known as Valhalla housed only those mortal men who had met death on the battlefield and who had been selected to serve as a soldier for the Allfather. The fortress was visited daily by Wotan, while other gods, at least major gods, from time to time came to the hall. Wagner had no difficulty in investing his Valhalla with that same major function, that is, causing his Valhalla to become the celestial abode of Teutondom's greatest heroes. But, Wagner's Valhalla also served in another capacity, one that is in no way associated with the Valhalla of myth, and one that was entirely the creation of Wagner himself. The Valhalla of the *Ring*, unlike the fortress of the myths, is not just a place that the gods visited as was their pleasure. The drama's Valhalla is also the *home and abode for the five gods* that are part of Wagner's drama! Certainly, Wagner knew that in the myths each of the major Germanic gods had a personal and private residence and that each of those gods resided in their respective homes. In that light, there was no need, then, to cause Valhalla to serve as a substitute home, to become one home for all the gods. He could easily have resorted to the myths and duplicated the beliefs that he found there. Yet, when one considers the ending that Wagner gave his drama, when one contemplates carefully that final scene of the *Ring*, those last few moments when flames begin to surround the castle, ultimately to consume all that falls within their pathway, ultimately to bring death and destruction to the gods and the corrupt universe that they have created, there is no need to question further Wagner's ideas regarding homes for his gods. With Valhalla as the one home of all his gods, Wagner was able to bring an end to these gods all at one and the same time, which of course was thematically acceptable. But more than just an acceptable ending, with Valhalla as the one home of all the gods, the composer afforded himself a most dramatic ending which, when presented along with the the music that he composed to accompany the scene, would become one of the most monumental moments among all the artistic achievements that have come from the mind and hand of man!

In the myths Wotan presided over Valhalla and all that took place there. Each day the god joined the champions at mealtimes although, as pointed out earlier, the god did not eat, but, rather, gave his food to his two wolves. When the god made his daily visit to the hall, he was always accompanied by his two ravens, Hugin ("Thought") and Munin ("Memory"), that he sent out each day to fly about the universe and then to return with all the news of the world. These are the same two ravens that Wagner placed in his drama. Although the *Ring's* birds are unnamed, and their existence is more inferred than actual, they become a part of the work at least on two occasions. The first mention of the two ravens is found in the first act of *Götterdämmerung*, when Waltraute visits her sister, Brünnhilde. The Valkyrie has traveled to earth from Valhalla to seek Brünnhilde's aid to prevent the doom and death of Wotan and the other gods. Waltraute tells how the dejected and depressed Wotan has set free his pair of ravens, not knowing if they will return with any welcome news. The second instance in the *Ring* of Wotan's two ravens occurs in the final moments of the same drama. Brünnhilde has caused a pyre to be erected, and to have Siegfried's body placed there. The former Valkyrie then takes a firebrand and, as she tosses it on the pyre, which quickly catches fire, Wotan's two ravens fly up from the surrounding rocks and fly into the distance, on their way to Valhalla, to inform their master of what they have seen.

The third factor in the Valhalla of the *Ring* that is at variance with the Valhalla of Teutonic mythology is what might be called a structural change, a physical alteration of the building. This change, which was the work of the composer himself, is really more inferred in the drama than actual, but the incidental evidence of its realization is quite persuasive. If this aspect of the *Ring's* great hall does not carry the same degree of mythological importance as those already mentioned, it is, nevertheless, a modification of the basic substance of the myths, and therefore is worthy of note. In the last scene of *Das Rheingold*, Loge invites the captured and bound Alberich to look down from their spot on the mountain peak upon all the world, to view that universe which the gods wish to rule. Then, later, in the first act of *Götterdämmerung*, as Waltraute pleads with Brünnhilde to come to the aid of the gods, she tells how the saddened Wotan sits in Valhalla, sends out his ravens, and looks forlornly about the world. The inference in both of these incidents is, of course, to Hlidskjolf, the celebrated site from which Wotan and the other gods could look down upon the universe to learn all that was happening. Mythically, Hlidskjolf is not a part of Valhalla, but of Wotan's personal residence, thought by many scholars to be a kind of tower. Wagner's move to bring this feature, or at least the magic that it offered, into Valhalla was probably prompted by the fact that he was not allocating personal residences to any of his gods and Valhalla was to serve as a single structure for all of them. Whatever the reasons, it remains that some of the magic that graced the great god's residence finds its way, if haltingly, into the drama of the *Ring* and Wagner's Valhalla, with Wotan as its lord, reflects the essence of its counterpart in myth.

The god Wotan also had other possessions. These items were not structures but, like his residence and his battlehall, they were objects that could readily be associated with the patterns of human life. Yet, it must be stated that if these objects were common to the society of the day, and if these items functioned much as their counterparts within the culture functioned, each of the god's possessions was unique in the universe and each held special powers that made it appropriate only to the gods. And, in the case at hand, the distinctiveness of each item made it apt and relevant to the figure of the chief god as he ruled over the universe. These rare items that belonged to Wotan were three in number: a ring, a spear, and a horse.

Wotan's celebrated ring had been made of gold by the dwarfs Eitri and Brokk. It was in its making that the ring acquired the first of its supernatural powers, that of reproducing itself. Each ninth night the ring 'dropped' eight gold rings of like weight. (The number *nine* was the special number in this Germanic society, and time was measured in *nights*, rather than in 'days.') Since gold was considered treasure, it was by means of the magic of this ring that the gods had whatever wealth they needed or desired, and it was this same magic that gave the ring its name, Draupnir ("Dropper").

The mythical concept of Draupnir as wealth and treasure is evidenced throughout the ancient mythical tales. One of the Eddic poems features this concept of the ring, and in a most direct manner. According to the verses, Froh decided to win for himself the love of Gerd, a giantess. To gain that end, he directed his servant to present the maiden with two gifts of gold. One of these gifts was eleven apples of gold and the second gift was the ring Draupnir. Gerd refused both gifts, stating that there was wealth enough in her own land. (The myths do not reveal how Wotan's ring came into Froh's possession.)

A second magic that was associated with the ring Draupnir allowed it to become one of the most sacred objects of early Teutonic beliefs. In Wotan's hands, and when the Allfather used it in an act of consecration, Draupnir was capable of bringing life back to the dead. The most prominent and the most notable of such acts is that which involved Wotan's favorite son, Balder. An Eddic tale recounts how Balder had been slain by his brother. The young god's body was about to be cremated when Wotan placed Draupnir on the pyre. Balder returned to life and from his place in Hel he returned the ring to his father. (Despite his godhood, Balder could not be admitted to Valhalla because he had not died a hero's death.) It is this mythical incident that causes some mythologists to refer to Draupnir as "Balder's Ring."

As might be expected, the mythical power of the ring Draupnir to raise the dead was also associated with Valhalla and its inhabitants. The myths do not reveal the specific means by which the dead heroes who had been selected to become warriors in Wotan's army were brought back to life after they had been transported to Valhalla from the battlefield. However, there are those who suggest that Wotan realized the act through his supreme godhood and his use of the ring Draupnir and its magic. This suggestion has been prompted, and indeed supported, by documented evidence of a cultural practice among the early Teutonic peoples that can readily be associated with the ring that belonged to the great god. The early Germanic peoples believed that a ring, any ring, when worn by a warrior who had died in battle, would prompt the Allfather to consider the use of Draupnir to grant the slain combatant the much-desired afterlife in the celestial fortress as a warrior in the army of the gods. It was quite customary, therefore, for the men of that society to adorn themselves with rings when they were about to enter battle. These rings, which usually were quite numerous, were regularly those that were worn about the upper arm, on the wrist, and around the neck. If, by chance, those rings were made of gold, as was Draupnir, the belief held that there was an even greater assurance that if the wearer were slain in battle, the attention of the Supreme God would be gained.

There was yet a third power that was unique to Draupnir, a force that was quite unlike the magic that allowed the ring to reproduce itself, or that of raising the dead. This power was essentially an intangible force, a force that did not achieve either visible material ends or corporeal results. This third magic was really a silent spirit, more a noble but forceful authority that infused in the participants a state of mind that addressed a moral principle that was of the highest order within the society of that day. This principle was that of fidelity to one's promise, the faithful adherence to a vow, a pact, or an agreement. And, Wotan's ring became, in a very real sense, the sacred witness to these oaths. It has been noted already that an oath of any kind was sacrosanct among the ancient Teutonic peoples, and that a violation of one's sworn word was one of the culture's two most serious crimes. Because Wotan once swore an oath on Draupnir, a ring, again any ring, became the object on which an oath should be sworn. According to cultural practices, if a swearer who had taken an oath upon a ring broke that oath, he could be condemned to death. The oath that the Supreme God had taken, and to which Draupnir was witness, was in effect that he had no information concerning the being who had been responsible for the theft of Teutondom's much-coveted Mead of Poetry. As the myths reveal, Wotan's oath proved to be false in that it had been the god himself who had committed the theft. Although these myths do not indicate specifically an immediate punishment for the god, it is generally concluded that Wotan's false oath was one of a series of acts that resulted ultimately in the destruction of the universe and the downfall of its gods. (Some interpretative scholars relate Wotan's act to mankind's instinctive tendency for self-preservation, at whatever cost, while others cite Wotan's theft and his oath that denies any knowledge of that crime as acts that are representative of the corruption that is present in the societies of the world.) Regardless of any possible interpretation or symbolic meaning that is attached to the broken oath of the god, the use of Draupnir as witness to the oath that Wotan gave allowed the ring an added function, an added quality, and an added use that became a vital component of heathen Teutonic thought.

Wagner had no dramatic reason to include a ring as a possession of his god, Wotan. Such was obviously true because it would be a ring that would become the single most significant and consequential feature of his entire four-part drama. As might be expected, however, there were similarities as well as differences between the ring of the music-drama and the mythical ring Draupnir. Wagner's ring, unlike its mythical inspiration, would be unnamed, yet it would be of such meaning that it would become the centerpiece of the drama and would become part of the title that the composer would give to his lengthy work. Like the Draupnir of myth. however, Wagner's ring would be of gold and it too would be forged by a dwarf craftsman of another world. Again, like the Draupnir of old, the ring of Wagner's tale held a special magic, but this would be a magic that would be unique to it and to Wagner's drama. This singular magic was a power that would allow its possessor dominion over the entire world. The ring of Wagner's drama was also unlike the ring of the myths in that it carried a curse that had been placed upon it by its maker, a curse of death for each of those who came into ownership of the ring. And again unique to Wagner's ring, that curse is realized as each of the owners in turn take possession: Fasolt, Fafner, Siegfried, Brünnhilde, Hagen, and finally Wotan and the gods. (Although they only covet the ring, its curse also falls on Gunther the Gibichung and the Nibelung Mime.) Wagner's ring comes full-circle when, at the end of the drama, the composer causes it to be returned to its rightful owners, the maidens of the Rhine.

The second of Wotan's trio of nonstructural possessions was a spear that bore the name Gungnir. This famed weapon, celebrated throughout the myths, had been made for the god by the sons of Ivaldi ("The Mighty"), the craftsmen-dwarfs who also had made the gold hair that grew on the head of

Donner's wife, and the magic ship that belonged to Froh. Wotan's spear, like his ring, held a magic that allowed it to function in a way that was not possible for similar objects that were possessed by even the most powerful and skillful of warriors. Gungnir's magic was that it granted Wotan victory in battle! Wotan's spear, when hurled by the god, struck every target at which it was aimed, and it brought death to everyone over whom it passed while in flight. Indeed, Gungnir held such magic that it was befitting only to a god, and then only to a principal god such as Wotan, whose position as the chief god of Teutondom was greatly strengthened by possession of this spear.

Gungnir assumed an early prominence in ancient Germanic beliefs. It was this spear that had prompted what has been called "The First War" of the universe, also known as "The Great War." Wotan's race of gods, the Aesir, and the Vanir, a clan of gods that was religiously active in the region of the Baltic Sea, were at great odds because the Aesir had murdered Gullveig, a sorcerer who practiced "the black art" and for whom the Aesir had an intense hatred. The two groups tried to arbitrate the matter, but neither side would yield. Finally, in desperation and in great anger, Wotan hurled Gungnir into the group, and the war began. It was Gungnir and its magic that ultimately allowed the Aesir gods to be successful in this struggle, and the spear's role in the combat takes on an unusual significance. As a result of this first war of the universe, the initial gallery of Teutonic gods was reconstituted and the divine hierarchy as it is now presented in the myths emerged.

Gungnir and the magic that it afforded were primary to Wotan's divine supremacy and religious dominance. The spear remained closely associated with the god throughout his godhood, and this association, like other matters that formed the body of this early Germanic religious thought, reached its zenith at *ragnarök**, the fated downfall and destruction of the gods. Snorri Sturluson recounts this facet of Gungnir's existence, telling the tale in the manner of the *volva* or "wise-woman" who served as prophetess to the gods. He writes that when Wotan rides out to do battle in the last war of the universe, he will be robed in military attire worthy of his rank, and he will carry Gungnir in his hand. Sturluson's words indicate that it was Wotan's intent to use Gungnir against the enemies of the gods, but, as the prophetess says, Wotan is slain and his race of gods is defeated as a cataclysmic end comes to all the world, including the great spear of Teutondom.

The Wotan of the *Ring*, like the Wotan of Teutonic beliefs, also possesses an imposing spear which, if not a duplicate of the mythical Gungnir, is, nevertheless, associated with the Allfather and his divine position. If the spear of Germanic myths was forged by a dwarf craftsman and bore a name, Wagner's spear had been fashioned by Wotan himself, from a branch that the god had torn from the World Ash Tree. It is true that Wagner's spear, which is unnamed in the *Ring*, is in and of itself a formidable weapon, but in the drama it has no magic that allows it to function uniquely in combat or war. The magic of the spear of the drama, if magic is the proper word, is what truly must be viewed as a twofold function. As a first function, this spear serves as the symbol of the Allfather's authority, a symbol of Wotan's supreme godhood. Thus, when the Volsung youth Siegfried slashes Wotan's spear into two pieces, in effect, the first god of Teutondom becomes powerless, his divine rule is negated. It is at that moment when Wotan's godhood is rendered impotent, no longer able to function as it had in the past.

If Wagner's spear serves as the symbol of Wotan's divine authority, it is that same spear that also defines the limits of that primary authority, which becomes the second of the two functions. The great spear of Wagner's *Ring* is the article that preserves the sanctity of oaths, the divine property that binds the maker's word, his pledge, to his pacts. This function, which is of major importance to the storyline that Wagner brings to his drama, is dramatically operative through the runes* that Wagner has caused to be carved on the spear's shaft.

The third of the famed items that Wotan possessed was a horse, an animal that was named *Sleipnir*, and the animal that was to become the most celebrated creature in heathen Teutonic beliefs. The appearance and the use of horses in early Teutonic mythical thought was not at all unusual because that animal held a vital role in the routine life of these people, and their mythical thought was merely reflecting that reality. As a result of that reality, the gods of Teutondom frequently rode horses as they journeyed about the world on their divine missions, and most of them rode horses as they came each day to meet at the foot of the World Ash Tree. And, of course, it was horses, ridden by Valkyries, that transported slain heroes to Valhalla. Indeed, several of the horses of ancient Teutonic thought are even named in *The Poetic Edda*. It was, however, Wotan's horse that was not only the most important, but also the most prominent horse in all of Teutondom. This creature was really the finest of horses, or, as the animal is described in mythical poetry, "the best of steeds."

Wotan made frequent use of Sleipnir. He rode the horse each day to the World Ash Tree where he presided over the council of the gods. Wotan once rode Sleipnir to Niflhel, the murky land of mist and fog where Hel, the Guardian of the Dead, resided. The god made this journey through the darkness of the netherworld in order to learn what evil dreams had come to his son, Balder. *The Prose Edda* contains an account of yet another journey that Wotan made on the back of Sleipnir, a journey on which the horse ran swiftly through the air and over the sea to the Land of the Giants. Once there, Wotan wagered that there was no horse that equaled his Sleipnir. A giant, Hrungnir, heard the god's claim, and became quite angry because he too was the owner of a fine horse whose name was Goldmane, a horse that he felt was a much better animal than Sleipnir. Hrungnir quickly accepted Wotan's wager. The giant then leaped on his horse, and chased after the god. Sleipnir was the faster horse and the giant not only lost the chase, but in his attempt to overtake Wotan he ended up in the Land of the Gods where he then suffered a series of confrontations with the foremost enemy of the giants, Donner.

Sleipnir's significance in Germanic mythical thought can be comprehended directly, by his association with the supreme god Wotan, and also indirectly, by the rather thorough account of his origin. This celebrated horse was the offspring of Svadilfari, a stallion that belonged to a giant, and Loge, the demigod of Teutondom who had transformed himself into a mare. The myths tell how the giant made a pact with the gods to build a fortress. The pact stated that the giant would receive the goddess Freia, the sun, and the moon as his wages, but only if he completed the structure within a specified period. In order to meet the terms of the agreement, the giant needed Svadilfari to transport the huge stones with which he worked. The work progressed well, but in time it became amply clear to the gods that the giant would complete his work by the deadline. The deities of Teutondom became quite concerned, fearful that they would have to hand over to the giant the stipulated rewards that had been listed in the pact. The gods wished to have their new fortress, but at the same time they did not wish to relinquish the goddess, the sun, and the moon. Faced with this dilemma, the gods turned to Loge whom they forced, under the threat of torture, to come to their aid. Loge recognized the seriousness of the situation, and he pondered what to do, deciding, finally, to take advantage of the power of natural instincts. The crafty demigod changed himself into a mare and then skillfully lured the giant's stallion deep into the forest. Without his horse, the giant was unable to finish his work by the deadline and thus the gods retained the fortress as well as the goddess Freia, the sun, and the moon. As a result of the union of Svadilfari and Loge in the forest, the stallion Sleipnir was born.

The relative uniqueness of Sleipnir's origin is matched by that of his most prominent physical characteristic. Sleipnir had eight legs, which gave him the mythical swiftness for which he was known throughout the world, as well as the ability to run through the heavens, over land and sea.

There is a second uniqueness about Sleipnir, a matter that is not of great mythical importance, but nevertheless a matter that begs consideration. The matter in question deals with the color of Sleipnir's skin, a topic that offers a most interesting history, at least from a cultural point of view. This animal is either grey or white, depending upon which of two distinct depictions is accepted. In continental Teutondom, this famed animal was grey, while in the Nordic regions of Teutondom, the animal was white. These different concepts of Sleipnir's color do not represent mythical disagreements, or even contradictions; each in its own manner is correct because each is a reflection of cultural beliefs regarding these colors that were prevalent in specific Teutonic regions. In northern Teutondom, that is Scandinavia, the color *white* was recognized as the most visible of all colors. It was because of this acceptance of the color that leaders of groups were usually attired in white clothing and military leaders were especially fond of white war clothing. Further, those same military chiefs regularly rode on white horses! It is therefore most usual for the supreme god's horse to be white, as it regularly is in the accounts found in the Scandinavian sagas. In the southern Teutonic region, which essentially included continental Europe, the color *white* was also a special color, but in these regions its significance had nothing to do with visibility. In southern Teutondom, the color white was synonymous with death! White was the color symbol of death, as it is yet today in several cultures throughout the world, and hardly the color for the great horse of the Allfather. As a consequence of this related but distinct belief, when the color of the great horse Sleipnir is stated in the tales and stories of southern Teutondom, that color is regularly given as *grey*. It is interesting to note that in Sturluson's *Edda*, which contains what are essentially Nordic versions of the myths, the worldly Icelander depicts Wotan's horse as *grey*, rather than the usual northern *white*. Without doubt Sturluson was well aware of the cultural symbolism of these colors in the two regional cultures, but he was also a Christian, as were those of his day who inhabited the southern climes of Teutondom, and it is not unusual to find Christian thought fused into his numerous works. Thus, as Sturluson depicts Sleipnir as a grey horse, he may well have been swayed somewhat by that Christian thought, and it is perhaps accurate to state that in the case at hand, this northern writer probably felt more at ease with the southern Teutonic symbolism as the basis for his determination of the horse's color.

Like the beliefs regarding the color of Sleipnir, there is yet another mythical aspect of Wotan's horse that can be found in two versions. This matter concerns Sleipnir as the father of another famed horse of Teutondom. Throughout all of the early literature, that is, in the myths as well as the sagas of the region, the legendary hero Siegfried was the master of a horse known as Grani. It is in *Saga of the Volsungs* that Grani's ancestral line is discussed, and according to that account this creature was sired by Sleipnir and he was presented to the young Volsung by Wotan himself. *The Poetic Edda* presents a radically different version of this same matter. First, the verses of this *Edda* make no mention at all of a relationship between Sleipnir and Grani! These verses go on to reveal that Grani was sired by a stallion that belonged to King Hjalprek, and it was the hero himself who chose Grani from among all the many horses that were owned by the king. (Wagner had no dramatic interest in the ancestral line of the Eddic Grani, and the horse's history certainly was not a theme that had any significance in his *Ring*. Consequently, the composer merely brought the Grani of the myths over to his drama, converted the name into the German form, *Grane*, and gave him first to the Valkyrie Brünnhilde, who later gives him to Siegfried as the steed that the Volsung hero will ride as he sets out on new adventures.)

Wagner's Supreme God, like the Wotan of ancient Teutonic thought, had his personal horse. This animal is unnamed in the *Ring*, and is very much a secondary figure in the poem, garnering much less attention than Brünnhilde's horse Grane. Wotan's horse is mentioned, nonetheless, three times in the drama, each time in a distinct and separate music-drama. It should be obvious that Wagner is not going to give his Wotan a horse that has eight legs, like Sleipnir, and neither is he going to relate this horse in any way to the Grane of his story. This animal, nevertheless, makes its way into The *Ring*, the first time in *Die Walküre*, in the third act, when the Valkyries tell how they see the infuriated Wotan as he rides his "heavenly steed" at full-run in pursuit of his daughter Brünnhilde who has defied a command that he gave. Wotan's steed is met the second time in the second act of *Siegfried*, at that moment when Alberich sees a bluish light speeding through the forest. Of course, this light is Wotan who races to meet the dwarf astride his famed horse. Later, that same bluish light is seen as the god hurries away from Fafner's cave. The third and final reference in the *Ring* to Wotan's horse is found in *Götterdämmerung*, when Waltraute pleads with her sister Brünnhilde, and informs her that the forlorn King of the Gods, in the moment of his greatest sorrow, slowly mounted his steed and then set off, to wander alone in the universe.

Such were the possessions of the mythical Allfather Wotan and the magic that was associated with each, and the manner in which Wagner's *Ring* treated each matter. That mythical magic, individual and distinct with each object, was critical in one way or another in heathen Teutonic thought. Each of the powers that is a part of myth was significant to Wotan's supreme godhood. Each mythical magic allowed the god to function in specific ways. Each divine force permitted the god to achieve ends that reflected the divine majesty of his figure. Yet, each of these several powers was really tangential to an even greater and more imposing might, a limitless authority that gained undenied omnipotence for the god. The early Teutonic mind was unswerving in its acceptance of Wotan as the true lord of the universe, as the intangible and unseen force that *caused* everything in the world to react to his call and to respond to his command. So intense and so profound was this acceptance of Wotan as Supreme God of the universe that he was mythically capable of doing anything that was within the dominion of any of the other gods of Teutondom, and he could also undo anything that had been accomplished by those same deities, and further, Wotan was capable of realizing any matter that the other gods could not achieve. This absolute belief that the people had in the god Wotan gave them a divine figure to be trusted as well as to be feared, a god who could serve them as supreme benefactor, a god to whom they could turn when their needs were great or their distress was severe. In a word, it was Wotan, and only Wotan, who was the giver of highest blessings, the judge of all activity, the final arbiter in all matters.

Wotan's capabilities, that is, his acts, his feats, his deeds, and other related accomplishments, were possible because of the divine powers that the god possessed. And, these powers were figuratively limitless in number, and endless in scope. The myths of Teutondom abound with accounts of the marvels that came about because of the high god Wotan and his magic. There is even one poem in *The Poetic Edda* that is devoted almost entirely to divine counsels, charms and redes that the supreme god of Teutondom could exercise at will.

This authority, this power that Wotan possessed was such that each single bit of mythical magic transcended the realm and range of human abilities or capabilities, which, of course, represented the pattern of heathen Teutonic thought regarding the gods and their existence. However, despite the magnitude of these forces, each somehow, and in some manner, touched upon some facet of human life, and it was the results of Wotan's magic that allowed a grouping of these powers into two major classes. In one group there were those powers that were concerned with the world that surrounded mankind, the world in which man lived, or in a most generic sense, the world of nature. An example of these powers was Wotan's control of the wind. The god could create a fair and gentle breeze, or he could bring about a violent storm. Such power caused the seafaring people always to invoke his blessings before each voyage on the waters. As if that power were not awesome enough in its own right, the great god could cause a fearsome storm at sea and then, at the height of that storm, walk untouched and unharmed upon the mighty waves. Another example of the authority that Wotan held over the world in which mankind lived was the god's regulation of rain and sunshine. And, depending on the manner and the intensity with which he brought these two facets of nature to the people, there could be an abundance of crops or, to the other extreme, a devastating drought that would prove to be quite ruinous. Wotan was thus a powerful ingredient in the life of that vast majority of the people who worked the earth for their food. But, it was not only wind and rain and sunshine that came under Wotan's control. All of nature responded to his word, and if that were not enough, Wotan's authority allowed him to override whatever forces in nature that were possessed by a lesser god. Wotan's wishes in all aspects of the natural condition of the world were final and absolute!

The Wotanic forces that constituted the second grouping, like those of the first, were concerned with the condition of mankind's life. Now, however, instead of acting upon the world that surrounded man, these forces were directly concerned with mankind's personal existence, with his daily activities, with the routine that dominated the life of that day. Some of these magic powers have been mentioned elsewhere, but as additional examples of the great god's forces were his ability to change hatred into love, and his power to lessen pain, or to cause it. Wotan could also cure illness, or create it. He could bring the dead back to life, and he could also bring wealth and fortune to an individual. To the warriors of this society, Wotan could grant battle helmets and mailcoats. And, to that society that had elevated war to the highest level on the societal scale, to that society that had made war a way of life, the great god could grant life or death in battle, and he could bring about victory or defeat at any time!

Wagner's Wotan uniquely projects an overall image that is quite similar to that of the great god of Teutonic myth. The Wotan of the *Ring*, however, does not exercise the numerous and varied individual magic powers that are part of the mythical figure. Indeed, the god of the *Ring* cannot wield such powers because Wagner wisely did not vest his Wotan with those forces for which there was no thematic or dramatic need. Wagner attempted to convey the idea of Wotan's might and strength, that is, the god's authority, by means of related dialogue as well as the several actions that the god takes as he plays out the numerous aspects of the drama itself. It seems that there can be no doubt that Wagner was quite successful in that regard.

The mythical literature does not reveal specifically how each of Wotan's numerous and varied powers originated, or how each came into the control of the allfather god. In the myths many of the god's powers simply are, and they are subject to Wotan's commands, to the great god's wishes, to his will, a process that without doubt is also at work for the god of Wagner's *Ring*. Despite a seeming inattention to what most properly can be called 'a matter of faith,' that is, an unquestioned belief in the god and his powers, there is throughout the mythical literature an ever-present and pervasive inference that Wotan's divine supremacy in all matters came about through his profound wisdom and his vast knowledge, a wisdom and a knowledge that allowed him a complete perception and a total understanding of every individual and everything that was in the universe. This wisdom and this knowledge were not inherent in Wotan's godhood; they were qualities, or indeed attributes, that he had sought actively and persistently during a peripatetic existence that was dotted with numerable journeys throughout the universe. It is a mythical fact that because of Wotan's continual and extensive travel on many journeys, the god acquired a name that reflected this activity, a name that eventually became almost as wellknown throughout the Teutonic world as his proper name. Wotan's most important byname was *Wanderer*, a name whose significance was immediately apparent to Wagner, a name and a guise that he would give to his Wotan throughout the entirety of the third drama of the *Ring*.

Wotan's continuous search for knowledge and the kinds of knowledge that he was successful in acquiring are most appropriately illustrated in two major mythical tales. One of these accounts tells of the god's journey to the Spring of Wisdom that flowed at the base of the World Ash Tree. The act of the god drinking from the spring and giving one of his eyes to the spring's guardian, Mimir as payment for that drink has already been discussed. What is significant at this point, however, is an understanding that it was from the waters of this famed spring that Wotan gained a worldly wisdom, a sensitive awareness of the universe as well as a means to perceive and to discern all things in that universe and the ways by which he could make judgments concerning the world. (Wotan's evaluation of the vast knowledge that he had acquired from the water and of the mythical spirit with whom that spring was associated is reflected in a mythical tale that recounts the matter of the first war of the universe, the great war between the Aesir and the Vanir which has already been noted. To conclude this conflict a pact was made whereby the two races of gods would exchange hostages. For their part, the Aesir sent Mimir and the lesser god Honir. When the Vanir received these hostages, they promptly cut off Mimir's head and returned it to Wotan. The Allfather was most grieved at the actions of the Vanir, but he acted quickly to recoup for his loss of the wise guardian of the Spring of Wisdom. Wotan applied his magic to the severed head, which then gained the power of speech. Thus it was that the wisdom that was Mimir's through the water of his spring was now ever-available to Wotan.)

The second tale that is mythically important in the matter of Wotan's knowledge and wisdom is an Eddic poem that relates two separate incidents, each specific to a knowledge that granted the god certain magic powers. The poem is titled "Hovamol" ("The Ballad of the High One"), a lengthy poem that is essentially a collection of proverbs and associated counsels that reflect the collective wisdom of the heathen Teutonic society as well as the people's ideas regarding such matters as courage, truth, and loyalty.

The first of these incidents is that in which Wotan came to possess what is regularly called *Mead of Poetry*, and occasionally *Mead of Inspiration*. When drunk, this magic mead allowed one to understand the art of poetry; the drink revealed the secrets of the beauty of poetry, and it gave the drinker the means with which to comprehend the inspiration that had created that poetry. This treasured mead had been brewed by dwarfs who had mixed the blood of the wisest of giants, Kvasir, with honey. In a separate incident, another giant, Suttung, had sought revenge on the brewers of the mead because they had slain his parents. Suttung captured the dwarfs and took them far out to sea, where he left them to their fate. The brewers of the magic drink begged for their lives, and as a last resort they offered to give up the mead if they could be brought to safety. Suttung accepted the offer and when the mead came into his possession, he carried it away and hid the treasured drink deep within a mountain. Wotan had always desired to possess the marvels that the Mead of Poetry granted, and now aware of its location, he set out on a journey to gain the magic of the mead for himself. The Allfather traveled to Suttung's mountain. Once there, he transformed himself into an auger-snake and bored his way through the mountain until he reached the quarters of Suttung's daughter where the mead was stored. Wotan then changed forms again, seduced the giant's daughter, and drank the precious liquid. Wotan then changed himself into an eagle in order to fly back to the Land of the Gods. During his flight, some of the mead spilled from his mouth and fell to earth where it was gathered up by humans who from then on had the wonderful gift of poetry.

The second incident recounted in the poem "Hovamol" that is relative to Wotan's quest for knowledge is one of Teutonic mythology's most celebrated adventures. This is a tale that unveils itself in only four stanzas, but in those few verses the Teutonic peoples conceived the manner in which the supreme god Wotan came to possess the coveted runes* of Teutondom, the associated wisdom that these runes allowed, and the magical powers that were possible through this wisdom.

The account begins when Wotan tells how he gained physical possession of the mighty runes in verses that have become some of the most frequently quoted lines of Teutonic mythical literature. Wotan says:

> I hold that I hung on the windy tree,
> I hung there for nine nights full.
> With my spear I was wounded,
>   and offered I was
> To Wotan, myself to myself,
> On the tree that none will ever know
> What root beneath it lies.

Suffering the wound from his spear, Wotan hung alone and unattended on the tree, which is of course the World Ash Tree. The god says that no one came to give him aid; no one brought him food or drink. Then, he adds:

> I looked below.
> I took up the runes.
> Shrieking, I took them up,
> and, then, back I fell.

The significance of these verses, made possible through the runes of which they speak, cannot be overstated. That 'magical power' that was associated with those runes, that 'secretive' or 'mysterious knowledge' that the runes allowed, cannot be dismissed in the slightest, yet, oddly enough, neither can it be understood fully unless the cultural function and use of runes by the ancient Teutonic society is understood. The early Germanic people held that *everything* that took place in the world that surrounded them, *everything* that occurred in their personal lives, *everything*, was caused by unseen, irresistible forces. The belief in the existence as well as the potency of these forces was so ingrained in the culture, so much a part of daily life that in a very real sense these beliefs, and the forces that they had created, governed, indeed controlled, every aspect of life, thought, and endeavor. These beliefs were so extensive in scope that the forces that came within their purview were essentially limitless in number and kind. The less significant and less mighty of these powers were usually contained in the songs and the charms of the people. The truly powerful forces, those that were often capable of achieving ends that exceeded any capability of mortal man, were -- in the main -- a part of the runes, and the belief in these forces, which automatically meant acceptance of the respective rune or runes, formed much of the ritual and most of the rites that developed within this early society. In quite generic terms, it was believed that runic powers brought some form and some degree of good or evil to a person, a group of people, a tribe, a situation, an incident, an object, and even in some situations, to the powers of another rune.

The power that the runes contained unquestionably was an active, driving force within the early Germanic society, yet other beliefs, equally as strong, held that the runic powers were not readily available to society as a whole. The individual forces of a rune could be activated only when that rune was correctly 'worked' or 'interpreted,' and that process was known only to a select few, often but to a single individual. Only those who had somehow acquired the 'secretive' or 'mysterious knowledge' could effect the action of a rune. Since each rune was known to have numerous different and distinct powers, a separate 'knowledge' was necessary to exercise each of those individual powers. Obviously, then, the greater the number of powers that one being could exercise within a single rune or among several, the greater was the domination of that individual over others of the society. (Among the heathen Teutonic peoples it was regularly women, most often old women, who "worked" the runes. These women, who usually lived alone and in a remote or isolated place, were looked upon either as prophetesses or as witches, both of which were societal positions that were determined by the kind of 'secretive knowledge' that each had acquired and by the powers that each could exercise. Needless to say, these women were either sought constantly by the people, or fearfully avoided. In either case, they were always respected.)

There was only one figure who could possess *all* the runes of Teutondom, and that figure, naturally, was the High One of early beliefs, the Supreme God, Wotan. The god had gained the runes through his experience on the World Ash Tree, when, as he hung head down, he saw them and took them up. Although Wotan had suffered much during that ordeal, both his physical and his mental state were to improve when the magic of the runes passed into his control. The changes were essentially immediate. Health and strength returned to him, and he grew well and began to thrive. Wisdom came to him, and then each of his deeds led him to another deed, and each of his words led to another word. Wotan then learned nine songs, each of which contained a mighty power. Those nine powers were the power of words, the power to reign over spiritual forces as well as natural forces, power in religious acts, in investigations, in practical affairs of life, power in matters of peace and power in matters of war, and power in sacrifice. At long last the Allfather of the universe now had the worldly knowledge that he had sought, and with that knowledge he could rule all the forces of the world!

The Wotan of myth moved quickly to assimilate the wisdom that he now had into his godhood, and to use the magic of the runes in the exercise of his divine rule. There is no doubt that this early culture believed that all things in life, indeed all things in the world, either came from or were dominated by the Supreme God, and Wotan's assimilation of the runes and their forces into himself was a convenient and evidently satisfactory way for the people to account for the reasons or the causes of much that transpired in their lives. At the same time, the matter of Wotan and the runes allowed for an extension and an intensification of the cult of the god, a cult that quite early on became primary among these people.

The extent to which Wotan used these runes is readily seen in the numerous mythical accounts of the god's acts and deeds that came about through his application of powerful runic forces. Indeed, there are even those of Wotan's uses of runes that have caused certain rather unique mythical conclusions to be reached, unique in that they represent character elements that really do not mesh or blend with other elements that one finds in the total mythical depiction of the god. Two such conclusions are to be found in an Eddic poem in which the god appears as Hropt ("Crier" or "Teller"). One bestows a singular recognition on the god and a second distinguishes him in a rather special manner.

The Eddic verses state that once the god had gathered up the runes that lay beneath him on the ground, he *arranged* them, and then he *wrote* them, after which he *made them into thought*! Some students of Teutonic mythology assert that these actions represented an act of conversion, that is, an act of converting the runes into *beliefs*, the act of transforming the runes and their 'secretive knowledge' into tenets of the dogma that the heathen society made integral to its way of life. It was these same students, however, who also proposed that it was because of these actions that there emerged a special recognition of Wotan, a recognition that is both unique as well as spurious to his godhood. The Eddic literature had stated that once Wotan had taken up the runes, he "arranged" them, and then he "wrote" them. Such words, these students suggest, represent the two actions that are fundamental and necessary to the origin of what can be termed mankind's most valued creation, writing! And, as can easily be surmised, these same believers then contended that the verses actually pictured Wotan as the *creator of writing*! This concept of the god did not gain much support over the years, probably because there is no further reference to the subject throughout the vast remainder of Teutonic mythical literature.

It is again language in this Eddic poem that becomes the source for a second interpretation that allows a special honor for the god Wotan. This new glory evolves from those verses that tell of other of Wotan's acts with the runes and their magic. The verses tell, if succinctly, that the god first shaved the runes from the wood on which they had been carved. Once these runes were separated and free, Wotan gathered them in, and then he mixed them with the Mead of Poetry, that precious liquid that was so sacred to the culture. Then, as the verses recount, Wotan "sent them on ways so wide." It is these quoted words that have caused some scholars to view Wotan's actions as a truly magnanimous gesture, as the act by which the runes, and all that they signified in the culture, were made available to mankind, the act that allowed the human race to know the runic magic and to have the 'secretive knowledge' that worked that magic. This interpretation of the few words then spurred these students to conclude that Wotan's sharing of the treasure with mortals, and his revelation to them of runic wisdom, was really an act of edification, an act of enlightenment, an act of instruction. And, since this was the first instruction the world had received, Wotan now had gained the honor of being the *first teacher* of the universe!

The Wotan of Wagner's drama is not a principal in any series of activities and adventures similar to those that the mythical god underwent in order to gain knowledge and wisdom. Yet, this supreme god of the *Ring* roamed the universe and, in his own manner, sought knowledge just as zealously as did his mythical counterpart. The major difference in this aspect of the two gods' existence is simply that Wagner's deity is clothed in his gown of wisdom and knowledge by means of dialogue, that speech in the drama that informs, explains, or otherwise depicts the god and his continuous, ever-present search. It is early in *Das Rheingold* that this facet of the god's being begins to unfold. In one scene, Fasolt addresses the Allfather, telling him that he is more wise than he and his brother Fafner are clever. Then, later, in the same drama, the first indication of Wotan's search for knowledge arises when the god desires to call upon Erda, the earth-mother, in order that he can know all that there is to know. The Supreme God is very much aware that Erda can teach him much because she knows all that there is to know, and she can also foresee what is still yet to be. Yet again, this time in *Die Walküre*, there is additional evidence of the wisdom that the great god has gained as he journeyed throughout the world. In that scene in which Wotan and Fricka are discussing the brother-sister pair, Siegmund and Sieglinde, the god tells his wife that all she knows is that which already has occurred, while he, on the other hand, envisions that which is yet to come. Then once again, now in *Siegfried*, the god has assumed the guise of Wanderer and has come down to earth to continue his travels. In the second scene of the first act Wanderer informs the Nibelung Mime that he has wandered far and wide in the world, that he has sought knowledge, and he has learned a great deal. And again, now in Act III, Wanderer tells Erda that he has roamed at length, always seeking counsel, knowledge, and wisdom, and that he now calls upon her to give him additional knowledge of the universe.

It is in *Siegfried* that another facet of the *Ring* Wotan and his remarkable store of knowledge surfaces. The specific incident is in the first act of this music-drama, when Wanderer confronts Mime in the latter's cave. The god, dressed in his blue mantle and wide-brimmed hat that hides his missing eye, challenges the dwarf to what may be called a "Question Contest." This form of personal confrontation, that is, a wager between two individuals as to which can ask questions that the other cannot answer, apparently was a popular diversion in the ancient Teutonic society. Wagner was not original in the matter of his "Question Contest" between Wotan and the Nibelung dwarf. He drew his stimulus and his model from an Eddic poem in which there is a related activity. There is also a similar contest in *The Prose Edda*, a contest in which Wotan and a giant each wager his head that he can answer the other's questions. Wagner's Mime and his Wotan each wagers his head, betting that he can answer any three questions posed by the other. In its own simple but nevertheless effective way, this mythical activity that Wagner adapted from the Teutonic past served him well in his dramatic determination to convey the idea that his Wotan was indeed a knowledgeable and wise god!

Wagner felt no need to furnish details regarding all the manners by which his Wotan specifically acquired his profound and extensive knowledge and wisdom. It is equally obvious that the composer sensed that there was little if any dramatic need to explore the world of runes* that was so intensely accepted and applicable in the early Germanic culture. Although Wagner would not embellish his drama with particulars, he was aware of and he acknowledged the significance of the runes within the ancient Teutonic culture by causing runes of truth in pacts to be carved upon the shaft of Wotan's spear. (In the myths Gungnir was one of the objects on which runes could be written.) These are the only runes that make their way into the *Ring*. They are, thematically at least, runes that are of fundamental import because they specifically define an area of Wotan's divine authority, and it is the god's violation of that authority that establishes the theme and the basic argument of the drama.

The knowledge and the wisdom, the magic and the powers that came to the Wotan of the myths through the waters of the spring of Wisdom, the Mead of Inspiration, the runes, the charms, the songs, and the counsel that he received from Mimir's head were all important factors in the god's divine supremacy. These several elements gave Wotan control of the universe, and it was these same elements that permitted this god to function in the numerous divine roles in which he was cast, and for which he gained considerable mythical renown. Of all these individual divinities, however, there was one that was of greater import and of more profound significance in the religious beliefs of the heathen Teutonic peoples than all others. This primary godhood, which can readily be interpreted as a reflection of the principal activity of that culture, and indeed perhaps its very purpose for existence, was that of *God of War*.

There was no dramatic need for the Wotan of the *Ring* to be presented as the God of War. The storyline that Wagner brought to his drama focused on a distinct and quite different aspect of Wotan's godhood, a feature to which the matter of war and combat were unimportant, if not alien. Yet, a full mythical picture of the god would be lacking without an understanding of these specific features of this Teutonic divine being.

History has revealed that the people of the ancient Teutonic world viewed physical struggle and combat as a primary routine in their lives. From the earliest of times, as these people sought to sustain themselves, confrontation was a regular pattern of their activity. Physical dominance was necessary for physical survival; physical dominance became necessary for physiological survival. These historic factors, which became uppermost in the Teutonic character, were evident regardless of whether the people remained somewhat stable in a single locale or they moved about. Physical combat was something more than simply physical conflict. Combat was battle, and battle was war, which -- in turn -- was a thought, a posture, an attitude that ingrained itself deeply in the societal mind of the early Germanics. War, in all its forms, was fundamental to the culture, war was a way of life, indeed, a destiny. This same history that depicts a war-oriented attitude by means of the number of armed conflicts also indicates that this cultural conviction toward war reached an intense and frenzied apogee during the tumultuous and violent years that are known today as the Age of the Vikings (800-1100 A.D.). During those active years the culture thrived on exploration, on invasion, on conquest and subjugation, as well as on the occupation of foreign territories.

History records the statistics of the innumerable war-like activities of the early Teutonic people. But if that history records only the material facts concerning these movements, it is the mythical literature that provides ample evidence of the hostile attitude of these people and the incredible role that Wotan had in that way of thought. It can rightfully be said that in the Germanic mind, Wotan presided over every aspect of war! As already has been noted, this god's name meant "fury" or "wrath," and he had been the principal factor in the first war of the universe. Wotan was also possessor of the great spear, Gungnir, that always granted victory in war. In addition, it has been shown that Wotan's favorite structure was Valhalla, where he had gathered an army of raised warriors that one day he would lead into battle against the enemies of the gods. Indeed, if only for these factors, the god merited the name *Heerfather* ("Father of Armies").

There was, however, more, much more to Wotan's divine rank as God of War. Mythical beliefs held that as God of War, Wotan was the absolute determinant in any and all matters of combat. It was through his knowledge and by means of the magic that he could work with that knowledge that this god demonstrated all that he could do in matters of war. As the literature records, Wotan could spur a disheartened warrior by giving him courage, or as the Eddic verses call it "manly heart." Wotan could offer protection to warriors by stopping arrows in their flight, or by making blunt an enemy's sword. The god could reverse the evil and the hatred that a foe exhibited. It was Wotan's magic that gave the god powers to decide matters of even greater importance, that is, those of victory or defeat or conquest in battle, and all of this for a single warrior or for an entire army. And whether victorious or defeated, it was Wotan who determined which of the warriors was to die and which would survive a conflict.

The belief that Wotan had the power to grant life or death to a warrior who was fighting in combat was one of the most prevalent concepts associated with Teutondom's God of War. This belief was a significant segment of that societal attitude that held war to be a way of life, and death in combat to be the only means by which a warrior could avoid a most unwanted afterlife in the darkness of the netherworld, Hel. This unwavering faith in the powers of Wotan was manifested by the use of the god's name as a battle cry, as the cause for invocation of the god prior to an impending battle, and also as the foundation for the rites that often accompanied, and always intensified, that invocation. These religious incantations to Wotan were the means by which the god's blessing and his divine favor could be obtained, the means by which a warrior might be destined to fight bravely in combat and, if slain, to be chosen by the god to serve in the great army that he had raised in Valhalla.

The faith in what the Supreme God could do for warriors, coupled with the beliefs of what could transpire, of what could be their fortune in battle, became so prevalent and so etched in the societal character that it was not unusual for those fighters who sought a "hero's death" to induce upon themselves a unique physical transformation, a process whose name remains a word in modern Germanic languages. There were always warriors who were intent upon joining the God of War in his celestial fortress, and frequently these fighters became so seized, so overcome by that intent that they worked themselves into a state of emotional frenzy, a state in which they no longer thought of mortal life or death, but of a paradisiacal life in the service of the Supreme God. Those who reached this irrational state often became so maddened as to be uncontrollable; their eyes lay back in their heads, they howled like wild animals, they perspired profusely, and they often foamed at the mouth. Each of these physical changes was accepted as a visual sign of Wotan's powers at work, and those warriors so touched by the god went fearlessly into battle and fought in a manner that can only be termed as recklessly fierce and ferocious, if not savage. The people of the day likened the actions of these fighters to those of a wild bear that had been attacked and which was literally fighting for its life. These people saw a similarity in the two kinds of actions, and they began to use the bear to refer to these crazed warriors: They claimed that those who had received these blessings of the Allfather were wearing "bear shirts" (bjorn-serkr), a word that has survived in English as *berserk* and *berserker*.

The cult of Wotan as God of War naturally recognized the god as the greatest of warriors. Wotan was the "fighter of old," the warrior who had waged and won the first war of the world, the warrior who had known combat in Valland ("Land of Slaughter"), in a war for which he had never allowed peace to be made. It was Wotan, the wise warrior of Teutonic thought, who had arranged all the wars of the world and it was Wotan who watched over all combat, the god who spoke of "spears to redden" as he prepared himself and trained his army in Valhalla for the violent battle that was destined to be a prelude to the destruction of the universe.

The Supreme God Wotan was, however, something more than a mere warrior, even more than an arranger of war. Teutondom's God of War was also the infallible counselor in all matters that pertained to war! It was Wotan's knowledge and wisdom that gave his godhood a special awareness of the signs that were best for waging war, signs that he then passed on to mankind. Wotan proclaimed, for example, that victory in combat would be had by the warrior who had encountered a black raven during his journey to the battlefield, and the god also predicted that victory would also come to the warrior who had met two other fighters who were eager to achieve fame. The god also announced that triumph in battle would be had by those who had heard a howling wolf that was standing beneath an ash tree, and he declared that good fortune awaited the warrior who saw the enemy first. Such signs, favorable as they were for the warrior, were not the only pronouncements on combat that were made by the Germanic peoples' God of War. Wotan also spoke of matters that signaled defeat in war. The god had said, for example, that a warrior would never know victory when he fought while facing the sun, and the god warned that misfortune would befall the warrior who stumbled as he was about to engage in combat.

There was yet another facet to Wotan's counselorship in matters of war, an attribute that was more important than all others. The Supreme God of Teutondom, in addition to all else, was also the supreme military strategist of the universe. As in the numerous other divine roles that were a part of Wotan's figure, so too in this capacity as military strategist was it knowledge, wisdom, and magic that accounted for the god's supposed unerring knowledge regarding those military movements and maneuvers that were most advantageous to an army. There is sprinkled throughout the Teutonic mythological lore ample evidence of this segment of Wotan's godhood, yet there is one of Wotan's numerous military counsels that has attracted the attention of students and scholars of Germanic mythology more than any other. As part of a general counsel on war, Wotan advised that combat forces that wished to be strong and invincible during an attack on an enemy should arrange themselves in a tight *wedge* formation, a military movement that guaranteed victory! It is true that throughout the centuries there have been strategists of all cultures who have studied, developed, and refined the art and science of warfare, but it is curious to note that early in the twentieth century there was a movement among the military strategists of several countries to adopt the wedge-formation as the basic military configuration for their respective forces.

Despite Wotan's powers as God of War, and in spite of the extensive range and formidable might of those other powers and forces that were interwoven into the mythical figure of the Allfather of Teutondom, this High One of all the heathen Germanic peoples, this Supreme God was destined to know total defeat and destruction. The god's magic, his knowledge, and his wisdom -- all of which had contributed to his divine power -- would be of no avail to him as he witnessed the defeat of his army and then suffered an inglorious death as the world that he and the other gods had created became engulfed by violent, cataclysmic acts of nature.

The end that came to the world and to all that was in that world was really an expression of the early Germanic societal concept that all things of the universe, and indeed, the universe itself, were finite, each with a beginning and an end. Such thought reflected a concept that overshadowed all others in early Teutonic thought, a concept that was fundamentally as significant as that which gave existence to the gods. This end, this ultimate doom, this final destruction of the gods and the universe is referred to frequently throughout the Germanic myths, and it is also depicted in some detail in at least one of those tales. The turn to numerous particulars about any given topic or theme is not characteristic of Eddic poetry, and therefore when any given matter receives such an unconventional treatment, it must be assumed that the subject so treated is most unique, one of significant value, or perhaps concern, to the people of that culture.

The account of Wotan's end, that of the other gods, as well as that of the world is depicted in the Eddic poem that is generally accorded to be the most famous of all the mythical literature, and indeed the most important. This celebrated poem is titled "Voluspo" ("The Wise-Woman's Prophesy"), and it is in these verses that Wotan hears firsthand about his fated downfall. According to the verses, Wotan was on one of his many journeys about the universe, searching for new knowledge and added wisdom, when he encountered a *volva*, or wise-woman. (Some scholars theorize that Wotan sought out the *volva* and caused her to be awakened from the dead and then to rise from the grave.) When at last the *volva* speaks, she tells Wotan of past ages, of the creation of time, of the creation of the world, of the origin of the dwarfs, of the creation of the first man and the first woman. She then tells the god of the World Ash Tree and of the first war of the universe. There can be no doubt that these Eddic verses that present the visionary words of the *volva* became engraved on Wagner's mind, and that the scene served him as a direct inspiration and primary stimulus for the Norn scene in the "Prelude" of his *Götterdämmerung*. The student of both the Eddic verses and Wagner's scene will encounter a remarkable similarity, a unique resemblance between the two incidents. That Wagner hoped to mirror the *volva* and her words seems obvious, yet that copy would not be so much in what precisely is said, but rather in the general theme, the manner of speech, the ambience, and the total mood and sense that is projected by the three fates of Teutonic thought.

As a way of revealing to the god of myth how extensive is her knowledge, the *volva* then reveals to Wotan some of his most intimate secrets, matters known only to himself. It is at this point that the wise-woman begins to tell of the calamitous events that await the gods and the world over which their divine rule had been supreme.

The downfall of the gods will occur during the violence of war, during the last battle of the universe, that final struggle in which the deities of Teutondom are confronted by their numerous and powerful enemies. Snorri writes in *The Prose Edda* that at the fateful moment Wotan will mount his horse Sleipnir and will lead his army of raised heroes out of Valhalla, to the field of battle. The Supreme God will wear a gold helm on his head and a coat of mail will envelope his body. In his hand the Allfather will carry his spear, Gungnir. In this final struggle Donner will confront the World Serpent, which he will slay but, nevertheless, the god will die quickly from the venom that the monster of the seas has breathed upon him. Froh will face Surt, the leader of an army of fire-giants that has invaded the Land of the Gods, and each will slay the other. Heimdall, the god of the Rainbow Bridge will fight Loge and each shall slay the other. Wotan, the Allfather of the universe, the High One, the Wanderer will perish in the powerful jaws of the wolf Fenrir.

The deaths of the gods initiates the onslaught of the cataclysmic forces that will overwhelm and destroy the universe. As Wotan's son avenges the death of his father by slaying Fenrir, the fire brought by Surt and his fire-giants spreads and consumes the world. When the body of the World Serpent that Donner has slain falls back into the sea, the waters rise, overflow, and then flood the world.

There is an amazing correspondence between the mythical *ragnarök** that is so vividly revealed in the Eddic verses and the end of the gods and their world that Wagner brought down upon his divine ones. The differences between these two interpretations of the end of the universe are really only in detail, not in the truly vast, cosmic scene that each presents. In his drama, Wagner starts the physical end of his gods with the fire that begins to consume the world, flames that will reveal the dejected Wotan and the other gods as they sit in Valhalla expecting, indeed awaiting the end that they know is to be visited upon them. As the smoke and flame reach into all the corners of the world, the Rhine swells, and then overflows its banks. The threads of devastation are rampant, overwhelming.

In the Eddic verses the *volva's* prophesy of the destruction of the world ends with one of the most striking and stark stanzas of Eddic literature, verses that uniquely depict Wagner's singular and epical twilight of the gods as intensely as they do the *ragnarök** of ancient Teutondom. The wise-woman says:

The sun turns black, the earth sinks in the sea.
The fiery stars down from heaven are whirled.
The stream grows fierce from life-feeding flames;
'Till fire leaps high around heaven itself.

The Wotan of myth, the Wotan of the *Ring*, and his world, are no more!

VI

LOGE

The figure that Wagner placed in his *Der Ring des Nibelungen* and which he called *Loge* is, in a very real sense, a dramatic creation of the composer himself. It is possible, indeed quite probable, that there are those followers of the Wagnerian art, and especially those who have given serious thought to the composer's monumental four-part drama, who will believe that the word 'creation' is inappropriate, if not out of place, in any study of this supernatural being. Yet, it is important to note that despite all that may have surfaced about Wagner's Loge and his mythical history, this character does not exist *per se* in the ancient Teutonic myths! The Loge of the *Ring* comes into his existence in Wagner's drama as the product of the composer's genius talent to extract the pertinent and significant attributes of two distinct supernatural beings that are part of the early Teutonic beliefs, and then to fuse and to blend those features in such a way that the result is at once a new and thoroughly individual being as well as one that reflects the major significant attributes of each of his mythical models. (Wagner was to do much the same with his Freia.) Thus, to understand the *Loge* that wanders about in Wagner's Nibelung drama, it is imperative to become familiar with those two supernaturals that serve as stimuli as well as inspiration for the composer's God of Fire.

The first of the two figures that contributes certain of his features to the singular Wagnerian Loge is a rather vague and usually overlooked being called *Logi*. This individual made his way about in the very earliest of Teutonic mythical beliefs, and there is a dearth of substantial data about him. However, this lack of information, coupled with some rather inconsistent myths, presents no real problem to modern day scholars because this Logi was really of little mythical significance, and whatever import he had was quite isolated. He departed the Germanic mythical scene in the prehistoric times of Teutondom.

As already acknowledged, the mythical data pertinent to this figure is quite sparse. The supernatural being called Logi apparently was the second of three sons who were fathered by the giant Fornitor. This trio of offsprings consisted of Hler, who represented *water*, Logi, who represented *fire*, and

Rari, who represented *air*. The name -- Logi -- seems to have been derived from an earlier name, Lothur, which apparently meant *blaze* or *glow*. In the Teutonic beliefs of the far-distant past, it was this Lothur who had given "heat ... and goodly hue" to the newly created mortals Ask ("Ash") and Embla ("Elm"). (The Supreme God, Wotan, gave *soul* to these mortals and the god Honir gave them *sense*.) This Logi of the ancient past was not a god of fire, that is, he was not a true and accepted deity of fire and flame, as many have believed and would cause others to do the same. Rather, this Logi was really the *natural force that is fire itself*. He was once called *light* by Skadi, the daughter of a giant, the same giantess who married Njord, the father of Froh and Freia, and there is a mortal who resides in the pages of *The Prose Edda* who had the name of Logi and who was also known as *Wildfire* because he burned things. Such is the total mythical information, scant and somewhat unrelated as it is, but there was enough there for the basis of the Wagnerian character, at least the basis for that part of the figure that the composer would call God of Fire.

The second supernatural being who figures as a principal facet in the makeup of the Loge of Wagner's *Ring* is one about whom, unlike the earlier Logi, there is a quantity of mythical information. This being figuratively makes his way through all the pages of the two *Eddas*, and he also appears in sundry tales and stories of the early Teutonic era, and it would be this supernatural figure who would furnish Wagner the vast majority of attributes that he would weave into his *Ring* character.

The mythical individual that was to play a most significant role in the makeup of Wagner's *Ring* figure had the name of *Loki*, which is a word that somehow relates to *locks* and *bolts*. At some unknown time in the distant past, the earlier Logi and this later Loki came together, to fuse into a new and distinct supernatural being. Thus it was that at one time, during that period when the mythical individuality of each figure had disappeared, but before the newer figure had definitely emerged, the names of each of these figures meant essentially one and the same thing. However, as this new mythical figure began to make itself known within early Teutonic beliefs, and as the *G* of Logi, became the *K* of Loki, it became apparent that not all of Logi's attributes had shifted automatically to Loki. One feature of the earlier being was fire, at least the sense of fire, and that would be one of those attributes that was not carried over from the older Logi to the newer Loki. Rather, this fire that was the essence of Logi seems to have made its way into the service of the netherworld, a place that was known in its time as Hel, where it essentially remained. Thus it was that Logi, both as a name and as a supernatural figure, was to fade from heathen thought and Loki was to become the name and the figure that would survive and which would become an integral part of the Germanic beliefs. In time, however, even the word Loki, as well as his figure, lost much of its allure, and by the seventeenth century the word had all but disappeared from the German language. The word is in fact extinct in modern day German, except when reference is made to the mythical being who became so prominent in the Eddic literature.

The Loki of myth, the supernatural that was to be ever so prominent in the Teutonic mythical tales and who was to give Wagner the essential attributes for his Loge, was the son of a giantess named Laufey and a giant who bore the name Farbauti. Nothing more is known about Loki's parents, other than their names and the fact that they were giants. While the myths do not infer in any way that the Eddic Loki is a giant, the mythical fact that his parents are of that race would be sufficient mythical reason to exclude this figure from membership in the divine hierarchy of Teutondom. (The gods, like the giants, were a race unto themselves.) And, although this Loki spends his entire existence among the gods, and usually in their company, in the Land of the Gods, and has no contact whatsoever with mortals, he is nowhere recognized as a god and neither does he reflect any of the divine features nor demonstrate any of the divine powers that are so characteristic of the numerous authentic deities of Teutondom. (As will be seen shortly, the mythical Loki does possess certain magic that he works from time to time, an attribute that allows him to be at least a supernatural, if not a god.) This Loki of myth is, rather, a supernatural being who serves as a vigorous and ever-active nemesis of the Germanic deities, a constant source of trouble, confusion, chaos, irritation, misunderstanding, and even embarrassment for the gods of Teutondom.

The Loki that is found in the *Eddas* has a wife, Sigyn. Two sons, Vali and Narfi (sometimes called Nari), were born of this union. These sons become prominent in ancient Germanic thought because of an incident that included their father. Balder, the favorite son of Wotan and Fricka, was slain by his blind brother, by means of a scheme that had been devised by Loki. The gods were greatly incensed by this act and they became furious at its originator. They then seized Loki and bound him to a rock with the intestines of his son Vali, who had been killed and torn to pieces by his brother whom the gods had turned into a wolf! This popular tale is somewhat reversed in *The Prose Edda* in that Vali is the wolf who kills his brother Narfi whose intestines are then used by the gods to bind Loki.

As was customary among the gods of Teutondom, and especially evident in the case of the Allfather, Wotan, this mythical Loki had several names by which he was known. Mythologists usually include as bynames the words *Logi* and *Lothur* that have already been mentioned, and then they add another byname that is frequently found in both *The Poetic Edda* and *The Prose Edda*, *Lopt*. However, the most appropriate name that was attached to this cunning schemer of Teutondom was *Laegjarn*, a name that translates as "Lover of Ill", and a term that uniquely describes this sly and crafty being of the early Teutonic world.

The Loki that wanders through the myths of Teutondom had two brothers. One was called Byleist, about whom nothing is known, other than his name. A second brother is named Helblendi. Curiously, this name is also one of the many names by which Wotan was known. Such curiosity is reduced somewhat when it becomes evident that there is a strong relationship between Loki and the Supreme God, or at least such is what Loki maintains. It is this Loki who says that he and Wotan once swore an oath of blood brotherhood. (In early Germanic thought such an oath bound the participants together and caused them to be treated as if they were in fact full blood relatives.) Unfortunately, there is no serious mythical evidence to support this claim and, furthermore, it would seem that this act to which Loki refers is really one of adoption by Wotan, rather than one of blood brotherhood. The myths seem to indicate that one of the Loki figures (Lothur, Logi, Loki), was in fact adopted by the Allfather of Teutondom. This latter relationship gains credibility when Idun, the goddess of the apples of eternal youth, speaks of Loki as Wotan's "wish-son," a term used on the early Teutonic culture to mean "adopted son."

Regardless of whatever relationship, if any, that existed between the Loki of myth and the Supreme God, this fascinating figure has other familial relationships that assume a significant import in the life of the gods, and which, at the same time, add a quality consideration to Loki himself. This mythical being fathered, with Angrboda, a giantess, three of the most monstrous creatures that ever were to populate heathen Teutonic thought. When the gods learned of this trio, and the harm that each could bring to them, Wotan sent out some of the lesser gods with instructions that Loki's offsprings be captured and brought to Asgard, the Land of the Gods, where Wotan himself would determine what was to be the fate of each. (A second Eddic myth tells that Loki once ate the cooked heart of a woman which caused him to be with child. In due time he gave birth to a monster which, according to some Germanic myths, was the first of the race of monsters in the universe.)

The first of Loki's monster offsprings was Fenrir, the wolf, who was also known as *Hrodvitnir* ("The Mighty Wolf"). The gods consulted with each other and finally decided that they would keep Fenrir among themselves, to raise and to bring up. This was a decision that the gods would one day seriously regret! Fenrir lived among the gods and he became the creature that consistently pursued the moon, threatening to swallow it once he caught up to it. Fenrir fared quite well living among the gods. However, he grew and grew until he was so large that when he opened his mouth his lower jaw touched the soil of earth and his upper jaw touched the stars in the heavens! Fenrir's strength also increased to match his growth and, finally, the wolf was so large and so strong that all of the gods feared him, and none would go near this creature. Indeed, none of the gods would approach Fenrir except Tyr. (The name of this god, *Tyr*, became *Tiw* in the English of the Anglo-Saxons, which then became the basis for the name of a day of the week, *Tiwesdag*, or in modern English, *Tuesday*.) Finally, the gods decided that Fenrir was so dangerous that he must somehow be chained. A dwarf then made the chain Gleipnir, which consisted of six kinds of material: the spittle of a bird, the nerves of a bear, the beard of a woman, the root of a mountain, the breath of a fish, and the noise of a cat's step. However, as Tyr approached Fenrir, to hold him while the gods chained the animal, the wolf bit off Tyr's hand. In his adulthood, Fenrir formed a union with a giantess and the pair had two children. One of these offsprings was Skoll, who stole the sun, and the other was Hati, who stole the moon. It was the wolf Fenrir that would confront Wotan at the time of The Final Battle*, and who would then devour the god. (Wotan's son, Vidar, would avenge his father's death by slaying Fenrir.)

The second of Loki's three children with the giantess was a serpent, Jormungandr. When the gods held Loki's offsprings in captivity, they decided that Jormungandr should be thrown into the sea. Wotan himself assumed this responsibility, which he carried out as the council of the gods had determined. Jormungandr fared well in the waters of the seas where he grew so large that, in time, his body circled the world and he could bite his tail. It was because of this great size, and the fact that the serpent's body circled the earth, that this child of Loki soon became known as *Midgardsorm*, or "World Serpent." When the destruction of the gods and their world (*ragnarök**) commences, and the gods of Teutondom march out to meet their enemies, it is Donner who will do battle with this monster serpent. The great god will slay this creature with his mighty hammer, but he will die also, killed by the venom that the World Serpent had breathed upon him.

Loki's third child by Angrboda was Hel. According to the myths, Wotan decided that this offspring of Loki should live out her life in the underworld. The Supreme God thus sent Hel into Niflheim (Nebelheim) where, according to *The Prose Edda*, she was given authority to rule over nine worlds provided that she share all that she had with those who were sent into her world. This netherworld was called Hel, and those who were sent there were the dead, that is, women, children, and men who died of disease or who had died ignobly in battle and therefore could not enjoy an afterlife in Valhalla. At *ragnarök**, Hel will captain a ship that comes from the north and which is loaded with the dead of her world who are intent on invading the Land of the Gods and doing battle with the gods who live there.

Loki, the prototype for Wagner's Loge, had no cult, that is, he was not invoked or worshipped in any way. In spite of Loki's non-divine status, this unique being spent his entire existence among the gods, in the Land of the Gods, where he gained a less than enviable reputation. Despite the mythical fact that Loki was a handsome figure and "fair of face," as the myths describe him, he was well known because of his evil disposition. This supernatural being becomes, essentially, what can be termed a most maleficent mischief-maker among the gods, a treacherous but ingenious figure who seems to run rampant throughout the Land of the Gods. Gefjun, who is a goddess according to Sturluson, says that this Loki is famed for his foul mockery, and that deep within himself, he loathes the gods among whom he dwells. There can be no doubt that the Loki of myths is a sly, truly hateful character, a being who devises most of the ill or harmful incidents that occur in the Land of the Gods or which involve in one way or another one or more of the deities. Loki is a liar, a cheat, and an injurious figure who is continually promoting matters for himself regardless of the effect or results that others must suffer because of his activities. At those times when Loki volunteers to help or to assist the gods, it is usually an assistance that he offers with some guile because he excelled all others in the art of cunning. At times, however, this same Loki is capable of making the gods laugh, but even in their laughter these same gods did not trust him, and, with few exceptions, they had some negative remark to say to or about him.

This Loki, this mythical master of trickery and treachery, was, nevertheless, somewhat like the gods in that he had certain personal possessions, each of which held some special magic. One such possession was a unique sword that was named *Laevatein* ("Wounding Wand"), a weapon that Loki himself had forged out of runes*, as he worked beside the doors that opened into Hel. Loki was quite careful with this weapon which he kept in a chest that was fastened with nine locks! The special magic that lay within Laevatein's powers was such that it was the only weapon that could kill the cock Vidofnir ("Tree Snake"). There seems to be some mythical confusion about this Vidofnir because the Eddic verses that tell about this animal give no added information, and further, these verses also infer that this creature is identical either to the cock Gollinkambi ("Gold Comb") or to the cock Fjalar. The former is to waken the gods at the time of their predicted downfall, and the latter animal is to awaken Surt and the fire-giants who will cross Bifrost, the rainbow bridge, at the time of *ragnarök**.

The master of cunning in the supernatural world also had some rather unusual shoes. These shoes permitted Loki to run through the air and over the vast expanses of the oceans and seas. Although the myths tell of these special shoes, they never give Loki the opportunity to run about in them, possibly because he was constantly travelling about in the company of the gods, or possibly because this supernatural was lame in one of his legs and therefore walked with a noticeable limp.

(There is both a curious as well as a rather odd possession that was Loki's, one whose setting will be of special interest to followers of Wagner's *Ring*. It is by means of 'false mythology' that this matter comes to our attention, false mythology being a tale, a story or other incident that is purposely fabricated in the style and form of the ancient myths but which is really only the product of someone's creative and imaginative mind and pen. This mythically undocumented possession is a hall or an abode that purportedly belonged to Loki, a residence that he and nine dwarfs had constructed. This hall was called *Lyr* ("Heat Holding"), and it rested balanced on the point of a spear and was completely surrounded by magical, flickering flames!)

It was stated earlier that Loki travelled a great deal, mostly in the company of one or more of the gods. One of these journeys, this time with Donner, was to Utgard, where the great strength of the God of Thunder was put to test. Another journey, again with Donner, was to Geirrodargardar, the land of the giant Geirrod. This trip was made at a time when the god did not have his famed hammer or the iron gloves that he usually wore when he threw the hammer. On yet another trip with Donner the two will attempt to retrieve the god's hammer which was stolen by Thrym, a giant. To aid them in their mission, Donner is dressed as the goddess Freia and Loge accompanies as a maidservant.

This supernatural being, who is sometimes called the thirteenth god, is often involved in incidents in which the gods, in one way or another, suffer the brunt of his actions. At times, Loki's actions can be of some embarrassment for the gods, while at other times the gods will suffer some physical or mental injury. Occasionally, Loki will even attempt to supersede, by whatever means possible, the divine powers of the gods. There is the popular tale in which the mythical Loki cuts off the hair of Sif, Donner's wife, and a second tale in which he is the cause of the abduction of the goddess Idun and her magic apples of eternal youth. In this latter story, the gods demand that Loki help them. To reply to their order, Loki changes himself into a bird, flies to where the goddess is, causes her to be transformed into a nut which he then grasps in his talons and soars to freedom. Another celebrated tale tells of Loki's adventures when he accompanied Wotan and the god Honir on one of their journeys. While on this trip, Loki kills an otter that is really the son of a farmer who then demands a large payment for the loss of his son. There is yet another tale in which, in order to help the gods, Loki changes himself into a mare and attracts a giant's stallion into the forest. The result of this union was the birth of Sleipnir, the horse with eight legs that becomes the famed horse of the Allfather Wotan and, at least according to some of the myths, the father of Grane, the horse that belonged to the Volsung hero Siegfried. (Wagner brings the mythical Grane into his drama and gives him somewhat of a prominent role, but he does not relate this animal and Loge in any way whatsoever. The Loge and the Grane of the *Ring* are two separate and individual entities.)

Loki also becomes very much involved in a matter that surfaces at a great feast that is offered by Aegir, a sea god, and at which many of the deities are present. Loki kills one of Aegir's servants, for which the gods then force him to leave Aegir's hall. The wily Loki is greatly angered at what the gods have done to him. In his anger, he returns to the feast, intent on having his revenge on the gods. Once inside the hall, Loki begins to insult each of the gods present. He accuses Bragi, the God of Poetry, of cowardice and effeminacy. He accuses Idun, Bragi's wife, of having an affair with the slayer of her brother. He points the finger of blame at Wotan, stating that the great god has awarded prizes to men who are less than deserving heroes. (These prizes are, of course, an afterlife in Valhalla.) He accuses Fricka of having slept with Wotan's brothers, Vili and Ve. He denounces Freia for having slept with all the gods who are in attendance, and for having slept with her own brother, Froh. Loki then tells Tyr that the god's wife once became the mother of his (Loki's) son. Loki then informs the group that he once slept with Skadi, the wife of Njord, whom he then accuses of fathering Froh and Freia with his own sister.

Such was the essential nature of the mythical character known as Loki. Indeed he lived among the gods, but he was not a deity himself. If this life with the gods allowed him a plentiful existence, and caused him to be a factor -- quite often a major factor -- in their functions, this hyperactive mythical being was really their scourge, the source of much irritation, the cause of much affliction. Loki was a being that could not be trusted, and the gods placed no faith in him whatsoever. Yet, this wily supernatural being, this master of cunning is something more than a mere irritant, something more than simply a mischievous figure. Indeed, this Loki who wanders at length through the myths of the early Teutonic peoples is, in fact, the primary and principal enemy of the gods of Teutondom, the one being of all the Teutonic mythical beliefs who early on should have been somehow restricted or limited in his movements. Of course, no such action was taken by the gods, and Loki proves to be the one most serious and most harmful mythical poisons in Germanic beliefs.

Loki shows himself to be a figure that really has a hatred of the gods. At *ragnarok**, that fateful time when the gods must ride out to battle with their enemies, a struggle that they are doomed to lose, each of the deities confronts a single foe. Loki, who has sailed out of Hel headed for the Land of the Gods as captain of a ship loaded with the dead, is destined to fight the god Heimdall, the Guardian of the Rainbow Bridge. The two combat each other, one on one, but in the end each slays the other. Loki has met his end, as have the gods of Teutondom.

The *Loge* that Wagner brought into his *Ring* is very much a blend of a small quantity of the early *Logi* and a generous portion of the later *Loki* of Teutonic myths. It is from the first of this pair of mythical figures that Wagner extracted the idea for a Guardian of Fire, sometimes called a God of Fire, which, if it is but a fraction of the makeup of Wagner's character, it is, nevertheless, a most important aspect of the *Ring* figure. There are several incidents in Wagner's story that serve as dramatic evidence of this side of the character Loge, a figure who actually appears in only one of the four dramas,

Das Rheingold. The first of such happenings comes not too long after Loge has made his initial appearance, when the angered Donner rushes at the wily figure who has spoken so haughtily, and so evasively. The God of Thunder is quite angry, and he threatens Loge with his mighty hammer, calling him "fire" which he is about to extinguish! Then, later, when Loge and Wotan are in Nibelheim, to attempt to secure the gold that Alberich has amassed, Loge speaks to the Nibelung dwarf in a most consolatory manner. He reminds the dwarf how once in the distant past he was warmed by Loge's fire, and how the dwarf found comfort in his light and flame. Loge continues much in the same vein, this time asking Alberich what he would have done if he had not heated the dwarf's forge, thus allowing him to make so many valuable items of gold. Later, in the last scene and during the final moments of this drama, as the gods prepare to enter Valhalla for the first time, Loge lingers behind the gods, and thinking aloud, he says that he senses a burning feeling within him to flare into flame, to burn those who have subdued and conquered him. Loge is referring, of course to the very gods that he is watching enter the most celebrated structure in the Teutonic myths.

Even when Loge is not a physical part of the scene, his role as flame and fire is made dramatically apparent. A fine example of this aspect of the fire-god's role is made amply clear in the final moments of *Die Walküre*, at that point when the Supreme God has just put his favorite daughter, Brünnhilde, to sleep. The god looks long and lovingly at the sleeping figure, and then he loudly voices Loge's name, not once but twice. Wotan has called out to the rogue of Teutondom to come to where he is, to surround the rock on which Brünnhilde sleeps with his hot fire. It is at Wotan's command that the entire final scene becomes engulfed in a great swath of fire, flames that are translated into sound, into that music that represents the flickering flames that are Loge.

There is yet another incident, again without the presence of the Guardian of Fire, in which reference is made to the role that Loge has in the Wagner drama. The scene develops in the Norn scene of *Götterdämmerung*, and begins when the First Norn sees a light in the distance and asks her sisters what it is. The Third Norn replies that it is "Loge's Host" (army) that is dancing around Brünnhilde's Rock, that it is each of the many flames that

Loge has become that burns so brightly. Then, it is again the First Norn who speaks, desiring to know what happened to Loge? She says that she remembers another day, another time when he "broke out in brilliant flame."

There can be no doubt that Wagner wished to bring to his Loge the quality of heat and flame and fire that were once the collective characteristic of the far-distant Logi. Yet, it was to be the single segment of that early mythical figure that was to reside in the Loge of his *Ring*, and it would be to the chronologically closer Loki that Wagner would turn to round out the figure of his drama's Guardian of Fire. And, it was in the myths that he found all that was needed to accomplish his self-appointed task.

Wagner displayed no dramatic interest in many of the external matters that were associated with his mythical model. The Loge of the *Ring*, for example, has no possessions like the shoes, the sword, and the residence of the supernatural being of the myths. In fact, at one point in *Das Rheingold* Loge shows what might be called a disdain for material possessions, stating that he wanders at large, and likes what he does. Loge infers that possession of things would place too great a burden on his whims.

Loge also says that he has no desire for 'hearth and home.' It would be this aspect of Loge that would support Wagner's development of a fire-god without the family or familial relationships that the mythical figure displayed. In the *Ring* Loge has no wife, and neither does he father children, monster or otherwise, as he does in the myths. (In the myths, the supernatural called Loki is responsible for the birth of Wotan's horse, Sleipnir which, as has been stated earlier, may have fathered Siegfried's steed, Grane.)

It is true, of course, that Wagner created a kind of relationship for the Loge of his drama when he makes his figure a "cousin" to Donner, Freia, Fricka, and Froh. (These four gods also have a familial relationship, that of brothers and sisters, which is another relationship that is original with the composer.) It would seem, however, that the relationship that Wagner creates between his Loge and the four gods is not meant to signify a true blood relationship, a familial tie that is secure and binding. Rather, the kinship between Loge and the gods serves more to indicate that Loge is related to the gods because he is a supernatural, as are the gods, but he is not a deity as they are, and therefore he must remain on a lower level of the mythical scale and be related to them in a manner less familial than that of brother and sister. The bond of 'cousin' seems to serve the situation quite well!

As with most other mythical familial relationships, Wagner also dismisses that bond that related the Loki of myth and the Allfather god as blood brothers, or as the god's adopted son, whichever is the true mythical case. As elsewhere in his drama, the composer felt that there was no need for such a relationship, neither because of thematic considerations nor because of some dramatic sequence. Yet, if the actual ties between the two do not appear openly in the *Ring*, either in the dialogue or by means of some action on the part of the players, there is an inferred strong intimacy between these two unique beings, a connection that is sensed almost from the first moment that Loge and Wotan come together. It is in the second scene of *Das Rheingold* that the Supreme God seeks to hasten the arrival of Loge in order that he can apply his skills to resolve the matter of the payment to Fafner and Fasolt for their labors on Valhalla. There is an urgency in the god's words and his tone of voice, an urgency that would seem to indicate a sincere basic trust that Wotan has for the fire-god.

If Wotan exhibits the signs of confidence in Loge, that show of trust is somewhat deflated when the god hears his wife ask why he has such faith in this being when he has done them so much harm in the past? Fricka adds that she can see no end to the mockery, no end to the derision and the ridicule that Loge has brought upon them. Wotan realizes the truth of his wife's words, but tries to temper the impact of what she says by stating that good advice comes from this Loge, that he knows how to turn the hatred of an enemy to profit, that such action requires skill and cunning, and that Loge has that necessary cunning and skill.

It is quite evident early on that Fricka has no feeling at all for the figure that Wagner called Loge. A short time after this attitude is clearly established, when Loge asserts that he is driven by whim and he denies that he ever made a promise to Wotan to resolve the matter of the god's difficulty with the giants, she snidely asks her husband if he really knows the kind of rascal is this Loge in whom he has put his trust? Donner and Froh have witnessed the scene, and for a short time they stand aside to absorb all that is taking place. Finally, they too, become enraged at Loge. Donner says that he will confront the rogue and implies that he will use his hammer on him. When Froh hears Loge state that he had made no real promise to Wotan other than to think on the matter of the giants and their payment, the god bristles with anger and he spurts that a better name for Loge is Luge ("Liar")!

It is now evident that Loge does not have the confidence of any of the gods. He is aware that they consider him to be a most untrustworthy figure, sly and crafty, and not to be believed, much like the way the gods of myth felt about the Loki of their time. This belief is made even stronger and more apparent when Wotan himself finally tells Loge that he brought him as a friend, but that all the others have no trust whatsoever in him!

Loge is not too disheartened because the gods hesitate to accept him at his word. He seems to toss aside their verbal attacks, and in fact, he soon learns that the gods are more concerned about the fate of the goddess Freia than they are about him. Soon, he and the gods of the *Ring* become involved in the development of a plan that will obtain the release of Freia from the giants. Loge adroitly turns the ideas of the gods to the gold that the dwarf Alberich took from the Rhinemaidens, and what the Nibelung has done with the magic that the gold offered. Loge uses his well-developed skill to entice Wotan to seek out Alberich's ring which gives the possessor the powers needed to rule the world. Wotan begins to show more interest.

Loge continues to employ his skill in the art of flattery. He convinces Fricka that she should prod her husband to seek Alberich's gold because it would make fine jewelry for her, the kind of finery she has always valued. Fricka is most pleased to hear those words, but when Loge informs her that the gold will also help her to keep her wandering husband at home, to keep him true to her, she is won over! Almost immediately she turns to Wotan and urges him to lay claim to the treasure. Wotan admits that the control of the gold is tempting, but he wonders how it can come into his hands. Loge's beguilement continues as Donner and Froh also become convinced that the treasure should somehow come into their hands. At last the gods are of one mind, of one mind in their desire to gain the gold. When Wotan then inquires how he can win Alberich's hoard for himself, Loge pertly and openly replies that it can be stolen! The wily fire-god then quickly reveals yet another facet of his true nature when he states that it is very much in order for one thief to steal from another thief!

The gods then begin to become weak and pale. When Wotan learns that the condition has been brought on because they have been deprived of Freia's golden apples of eternal youth, he is firmly convinced that he must win the gold to secure Freia's release from the giants. Abruptly, he calls out to Loge to travel with him to Nibelheim. Once again, as in the myths, the god and the fire-spirit are on a journey together.

Once in Nibelheim, Loge sets his skills to work as he coaxes the whimpering Mime to reveal the manner in which Loge treats him. Then, when the resolute Alberich comes into the scene, Wagner's fire-god effuses at length about the wonderful things he has heard about the Nibelung. Alberich is wary of Loge, telling him that it is envy that has brought the pair to the bowels of the earth. It is at this point that Loge reveals himself as fire and flame as he reminds the dwarf how much he has warmed him in the past, comforting him as he shivered, and gave him light, and made it possible for him to do his work at the forge.

Alberich is not taken in by Loge's words. He calls Loge a rogue, and then spurts that Loge is really a false friend, that the only thing about him that he can trust are Loge's lies! Loge is unabashed by these negative remarks as he continues to extol the dwarf, laying on praise for what the Nibelung has done with the powers he now has. Then, in time, he begins to question the dwarf, indicating that all the treasure that Alberich shows him does not prove that he has worked any magic. Alberich is taken in by Loge's cunning and at his verbal thrusts, he vows to assume whatever form Loge wishes. Of course, it is Loge once again coaxing, tempting, challenging in order to obtain whatever end he desires. And, in this situation it is Alberich himself that he wishes to harness. The dwarf transforms himself into a giant snake to reveal the power of the magic of the Tarnhelm. Alberich, ever gullible, or is it naive, again falls victim to Loge's constant but false praise. In the end, Wotan and Loge seize the dwarf and the god soon becomes owner of the Nibelung hoard. As Loge and the Allfather later talk about this adventure, it is Loge who freely admits that it was both cunning and force that humbled Alberich and won his treasures.

Wagner's Loge has worked his skills with keen finesse, ever aware of the answers that his questions will get, ever aware of what action his requests will receive. The fire-god has performed his assignment well, he has achieved for the gods that which they believe will be the resolution to their problem. Now, as these gods prepare to enter Valhalla, the ingenious Loge stands aside, knowing that the gods have committed a great error and that they really have given approval for their own doom. He is seized with an instant desire to break into fire, to burn those who had subdued him, but he restrains himself, leaving to another time to do whatever he reasons to do. It is at this point, as the first drama of the *Ring* ends, that the supernatural being known as Loge fades from the story. Except for those times when reference is made to Loge as fire and flame, he makes no further appearance in the *Ring* story, not even in the ultimate doom and destruction that is his fate in the myths.

There can be no doubt that the composite Loge of Wagner's music-drama is very much the *Logi* as well as the *Loki* of early Teutonic beliefs. While Wagner's figure is the physical aspect of Logi, that is fire and heat and light, he is much more the substance, the nature, the character if you will, of Teutondom's Loki. The mythical figure that the composer placed in his poem is, essentially, a balanced blend of the concrete of Logi and the abstract of Loki. The Loge of the *Ring* is artful, he is astute, he is shrewd, he is almost an identical duplication of the figure that roamed the mythical past. Like the prototype, Wagner's Loge is an endless source of troubles, a font of problems of all kinds. He instigates confusion, a confusion that often borders on chaos. He is disliked by the gods, but they seem to be well aware of his abilities, and so they tolerate him. Wagner's Loge is cultless, that is he is not invoked or addressed in prayer, a duplication of the religious status of the mythical figure. Wagner's Loge is again a reflection of his mythical counterpart, but yet in other ways. The figure in the *Ring* is a mischief-maker, a treacherous but ingenious, devious being. In the drama as in myths, this Loge is a liar, and he is not above cheating if the matter will then be to his benefit. The Loge of the *Ring* also excels in cunning. Wagner's Loge is the epitome of immorality, in all its various meanings. Indeed, of all that Wagner found in the ancient thought of the Germanic peoples, of all that he brought into his landmark drama from the mythology of his native soil, it seems that his Loge is probably the most mirror-like of all his characters, the one figure that more than any other resembles the model from which he was drawn. In many ways, Loge is an exact depiction of the wily figure that is found in the myths. Yet, despite the almost immaculate resemblance of the Loge of the *Ring* and the Logi-Loki inspiration, Wagner skillfully and most aptly gave his Loge, not the problems and situations of the myths, but rather those of the story that he had created. Thus, Wagner's Loge moves about as does his counterpart, but he applies himself to the composer's created situation. And, he does all that without the slightest tinge of affectation or artificiality, without the slightest show of stumbling, bumbling mannerisms. It is almost as if Wagner had seen the dramatic need in the drama, and then went about the business of creating a figure that met each and every one of those needs. Wagner's Loge remains today one of the best drawn characters of nineteenth-century operatic literature.

Supplement A
WOTAN'S OTHER NAMES

The religious dominance that Wotan exercised throughout ancient Teutondom was given added color and additional luster by a myriad of secondary names by which the Supreme God of the Teutonic peoples was known. The original and principal name, *Voden*, early on underwent several linguistic changes, all of which ultimately resulted mainly in *Odin* (*Othin*) in Scandinavia, and *Wotan* (*Wodan*) in the southern region of the Germanic lands. These were the names that became primary in their respective geographical areas, and these are the names by which the god is still generally known today. However, the Allfather of early Teutondom was not to be denied his multiplicity of character, of being, and of divine purpose, most of which eventually became translated into distinct and individual terms that became names for this first god of the heathen Teutonic peoples. It was the god himself who freely admitted in the myths that as he wandered about the world, he was never known by only one name!

Wotan's secondary names, all of which are found in Eddic literature, are more accurately *bynames*, or as Sturluson terms them, *eke* names. Each such name is essentially a descriptive term, a word whose meaning relates in some way to the god's many activities, his physical appearance, his divine functions, his magic powers, or even his attitude. A few of the god's bynames have come about as the result of an incident, an event, or some special occasion in which the god acts or performs in some special manner. Some of Wotan's bynames are used repeatedly in numerous mythical tales, such frequency and use serving as an unquestionable indication of the extensive cultural acceptance of those names. Other of the words have had less usage but nevertheless have been accepted as names for the great god. Collectively, these bynames become a composite of the numerous and varied segments of this god's complex figure as well as a mythical example of the multifaceted view that the early Teutonic people had of their god of gods.

The names that are presented here serve only as a record. There has been no attempt or desire to make any of them a part of some story or tale, and there is no suggestion of the relative importance or significance of any of the names within Teutonic beliefs.

Wotan's bynames have been listed in alphabetical order according to the usual and accepted orthography in English. At times, these spellings are distinct from the originals because of differences of alphabets (e.g. *Astriʒ - Astriʒ*) or because mythologists have attempted to accommodate the foreign letters to the equivalent or near-equivalent English letter-sounds (e.g. *Pund - Thund*). Now and then a name has accepted variants which are enclosed in parenthesis. An attempt has been made to offer a translation into English of these names. Some bynames, however, do not lend themselves to a succinct translation and, therefore, in some cases only an interpretation is possible. On occasion, it is not possible to translate a given name or even to offer a brief interpretation because the meanings of some originals have no meaningful equivalent in English.

Notes on Pronunciation

g	Always hard (*gate, gear, girl*); Never soft (*general, ginger, gyrate*).
hl ⌐ hn hr hv ⌐	No equivalent. Can be approximated by an exaggerated initial breath.
j	As the *y* in *yes*.
s	Always hard (*those*); never soft (*as*);
ᚦ	Used in initial position. Pronounced as a hard *th* (*thick*). When in the initial position in the names that are presented here, this letter always becomes *th*.

ð The original pronunciation of this medial or final letter was a soft *th*. (e.g. wither). English has preserved the in two forms: As *th* (fadr / father), and as *d* (Odin / Odin). This letter, as a medial or final consonant, in the names that are presented here is retained as *d*.

The Bynames

1.	Alfader	"Allfather"
2.	Astrid	"The Raider" or "The Rider"
3.	Baleyg	"The Fiery Eyed" or "The Flaming Eyed"
4.	Biflindi	"Spear-Shaker"
5.	Bileyg	"The Shifty Eyed"
6.	Bolverk	"The Evil Doer" or "The Doer of Ill"
7.	Farmagud	"God of Cargoes"
8.	Farmatyr	"Helper of Cargoes" meaning "God of Sailors"
9.	Feng	"The Seizer"

10.	Fimbuldul	"Chief Poet", "Great Counselor", perhaps "Fountain of Knowledge"
11.	Fjolnir	"The Many Shaped" or "The Much Knowing"
12.	Fjolsvid	"Wide of Wisdom"
13.	Fjorgyn	In its feminine form, this name is that of lord (Earth)
14.	Gagnrad	"The Gain-Counselor"
15.	Gangleri	"Wanderer" or "Way Weary"
16.	Gaut	"Father"
17.	Glapsvid	"Fast (Wide) in Deceit"
18.	Gondlir	"Wand Bearer"
19.	Grim	"Hooded"
20.	Grimnir	"The Hooded One"
21.	Hangagud	"God of the Hanged"
22.	Haptagud	"God of the Gods"
23.	Har	"High" or "High One"

24. Harbard	"Greybeard"
25. Helblindi	"Hell Shaker"
26. Herfader	"Father of Armies," "Father of the Hosts," "Heerfather"
27. Herjan	"Ruler of Armies" or "Ruler of the Hosts" or "Leader of the Hosts"
28. Herteit	"Glad of Armies" or "Glad of the Hosts"
29. Hjalmberi	"The Helmet Bearer"
30. Hnikar (Nikar)	"The Overthrower" or "The Overthruster"
31. Hnikud (Nikud)	See: Hnikar
32. Hor	"The High One"
33. Hropt	"Crier" or "Teller"
34. Hroptatyr	"Teller for the Gods"
35. Jafnhor (Jafnhar)	"Equally High"
36. Jalk (Jalg, Jalgar)	"Gelding" (?)

37.	Kjalar	"Lord of Keels"
38.	Nikar	See: Hnikar
39.	Nikud	See: Hnikud
40.	Ofnir	"The Bewilderer"
41.	Omi	"The Shouter"
42.	Oski	"God of Desires"
43.	Rani	(?)
44.	Sanngetal	"The Truth Teller"
45.	Sath	"The Truthful"

(The original of this name should have developed as "Sad" in English, but that was a term that already existed in that language, but with quite different meanings. The conflict of these two identical words was avoided by retention of the original pronunciation with a letter-equivalent spelling.)

46.	Sidgrani	"Long Beard"
47.	Sidhott	"Broad Hat"
48.	Sidskegg	"Long Bearded"

49.	Sigfader	"Father of Victory"
50.	Sigmetod	"Creator of Victory"
51.	Sigtyr	"God of Victory"
52.	Skilfing	"The Shaker"
53.	Svafnir	"The Sleep Bringer"
54.	Svidar	(?)
55.	Svidrir	(?)
56.	Svidur	(?)
57.	Svipal	"The Changing" (?)
58.	Thekk	"The Much-Loved"
59.	Thridi	"The Third [One]"
60.	Thror	(?)
61.	Thrud	Possibly "The Thin One"
62.	Thund	"The Thunderer" or "The Roaring"
63.	Tveggi	"The Twofold"

64. Ud	(?)
65. Vafud	"Wanderer"
66. Vak	"The Wakeful"
67. Valfader	"Father of the Slain"
68. Vegtam	"The Wanderer"
69. Veratyr	"Lord of Men" or "God of Men"
70. Vidrir	"Ruler of Weather"
71. Vidur	(?)
72. Vigsigor	"Victor in Battle"
73. Ygg	"The Terrible"

The Eddic literature contains other words that are equally descriptive as those in the preceding list. Although these words function as adjectives rather than as nouns, it is possible that any or all were also bynames of the god Wotan. Translations of some of these terms are:

a. Ruler of the Gods
b. Father of Men
c. God of the Ravens
d. Terror of the Gods
e. The Old Wise One
f. The Celebrated Fighter of Old
g. The Weapon-Clothed God
h. King of Singers
i. The Man of the Mountain
j. God of the Runes
k. Father of All Things

INDEX

B

BALDER,
Cremated, 108;
Fairest of the gods, 124;
His death, 172
His evil dreams, 147;
Resurrected, 142;
Son of Wotan and Fricka, 40;
Volva sees his death, 65

BALEYG,
Wotan, 189

BALLAD OF GRIMNIR, THE,
Eddic poem, 130

BALLAD OF THE HIGH ONE,
THE,
Eddic poem, 154

BALMUNG,
Siegfried's sword, 76

BALTIC SEA,
Home of Vanir gods, 2

BATTLE CRY,
Wotan's name, 163

BATTLE, THE FINAL,
At *ragnarök*, 9, 112,
113, 138, 174;
Froh, 65, 95, 105

BEAR SHIRT,
Berserker, 60, 163-164

BEAUTY,
Freia's, 18

BELI,
A giant, 105

BEOWULF,
Froh in, 94

BERSERKER,
Fight Donner, 60;
Warriors, 163-164

BESTLA,
Wife of Bor, 121

BEWILDERER, THE,
Wotan, 192

BIFLINDI,
Wotan, 189

BIFROST,
At *ragnarök*, 65, 176;
Froh-Guardian, 113;
Rainbow Bridge, 58, 63,
111-112, 113

BILEYG,
Wotan, 189

BILROST,
Variation of Bifrost, 111

BILSKIRNIR,
Donner's residence, 58, 70,
101

BLESSED VIRGIN, THE,
Freia's name, 5

BLOOD,
Altar stone, 87-88;
Blood brotherhood, 128-129;
Mead of Poetry, 154

BLOOD BROTHERHOOD,
In the *Ring*, 129
Wotan-Loge, 128-129

BLUE,
Wotan's cloak, 130-131

BOAR,
Freia's 6, 14, 16-17;
Froh and boar meat, 109-110;
Froh's, 6, 14, 16-17, 50, 60,
61, 106, 107-108;
In Germanic culture, 108-110;
In Valhalla, 137
Sacrifice to Froh, 12, 88, 110

BOLVERK,
Wotan, 189

GODS AND GODDESSES,
Children of Wotan, 123;
Dwellings, 101-102;
How viewed by Teutonic
peoples, 122-123;
Human in concept, 39;
Human in form, 34, 38-39;
Loge, an enemy, 178;
Pact with a giant, 20, 147;
Physical disabilities, 133;
Prepare to enter Valhalla, 184
Relationship in *Ring*,
5, 101, 180-181;
Their wealth, 141-142;

GOLD,
Alberich's ring, 45; 7;
Alberich's, 68, 132,
Cup of gold, 125; 144, 182;
Eleven apples, 103;
Freia as a measurement, 17
Froh's boar, 108;
Rings, 143;
Sif's hair, 58, 133, 144-145, 177;
Wotan's gold helmet, 167, 52;
Wotan, giver of wealth, 152

GOLD COMB,
A cock, 175

GOLDMANE,
Hrungnir's horse, 147

GOLLINKAMBI,
A cock, 175

GONDLIR,
Wotan, 190

GÖTTERDÄMMERUNG,
Act of blood brotherhood, 29;
Altar stones, 48-49, 88;
Composition, 113;
Donner invoked, 83;
Final scene, 140;
Norn scene, 134, 179;
Sacrifice, 12, 110;
Stimulus for Norn scene, 166;
Twilight of the gods, 90-91;
Wotan's horse, 150;

GÖTTERDÄMMERUNG, (Cont)
Wotan's missing eye, 134, 135;
Wotan's ravens, 140

GRAM,
Siegfried's sword, 76, 105

GRANE,
Brünnhilde's horse, 90;
Mythical Grani, 150;

GRANE, (Cont'd)
Sired by Sleipnir, 149-150, 177,
180

GRANI,
Becomes Grane in *Ring*, 150
Sired by Sleipnir, 149-150;

GREAT COUNSELOR,
Wotan, 190

GREAT WAR, THE,
See: THE FIRST WAR

GREEDY, THE
Wotan's wolf, 131

GREY,
Color of Sleipnir, 148-149

GREY BEARD,
Wotan, 129, 191

GRID,
Mother of Vidar, 124

GRIM,
Wotan, 190

GRIMM, JAKOB,
On Freia, 11;
On Vili and Ve, 121;
On Wotan's physical qualities,
129;
On Wotan, 121

GRIMNIR,
Wotan, 130, 190

WISE-WOMAN'S
PROPHESY, THE,
Eddic poem, 166

WISH MAIDENS,
Valkyries, 131

WITCHES,
Travel at night, 126;
Women, 157

WODAN,
Wotan, 118

WODEN,
Wotan, 118

WOLF,
A howling wolf, 164;
Fenrir, 65, 124, 167, 173-174;
Hati, 174;
In the *Ring*, 132-133;
Loki's sons, 172;
Skoll, 174;
Witches ride, 126;
Wotan's 15; 131;
Wotan, 15

WOLFE,
Wotan, 132

WOLFING,
Siegmund, 15

WOMEN,
Witches, 157;
Work runes, 157

WOODBIRD,
See: FOREST BIRD

WORLD ASH TREE,
At *ragnarök*, 65;
Conceals a warning horn, 112;
Council spot of gods, 22, 31, 59, 64, 68, 96, 112;
Laerad, 137;
Spring of Wisdom, 3, 133, 134, 153;
Wotan hangs from, 155-156,

157;
Wotan's spear, 146

WORLD SERPENT,
See: MIDGARDSORM

WOTAN,
A trinity in himself, 121;
Accused of selecting unworthy warriors, 138, 177;
Aesir god, 2; 101;
Allfather, 9, 15, 31, 40, 41, 44, 55, 64,
Animal sacrifice, 11, 13-14, 15, 49, 51, 88-89, 68, 73, 85, 93, 101, 102, 106, 112, 117, 123, 124, 125, 129, 130, 131, 132, 133, 134, 136, 139, 143, 146, 150, 154, 157, 159, 164, 165, 167, 172, 177, 181, 187, 189
Argues with Fricka, 44, 127-128;
As wolf, 15, 132; 123;
Banishes Brünnhilde, 78, 134, 139;
Blood brotherhood, 128-129; 110, 117;
Bynames, 187-194, 159, 160, 166;
Calls on Erda for her knowledge, 160;
Chapter V, 117-168;
Confidence in Loge, 181;
Confrontation with Donner, 129;
Counselor in war, 164-165;
Creator of writing, 158;
Fated to die, 165-166;
Father of all things, 123, 194;
Father of Armies, 162;
Father of Donner, 57-58, 68, 98, 125;
Father of Heimdall, 112;
Father of Meili, 57, 125;
Father of the Gods, 29, 124;
First teacher, 159; 187;
Fjorgyn, 29;
God of War, 95, 161;
Greatest of warriors, 164;
Helblindi, 172, 191; 144-146, 161;

STUDIES IN THE HISTORY AND INTERPRETATION OF MUSIC